BREAKING FREE, STARTING OVER

Parenting in the Aftermath of Family Violence

Christina M. Dalpiaz

 PRAEGER

Westport, Connecticut
London

Library of Congress Cataloging-in-Publication Data

Dalpiaz, Christina M.
   Breaking free, starting over : parenting in the aftermath of family violence/
Christina M. Dalpiaz.
      p.   cm.
   Includes bibliographical references and index.
   ISBN 0–275–98167–3 (alk. paper)
   1. Family violence. 2. Victims of family violence. 3. Children of abused wives.
4. Parenting. I. Title.
HV6626.D35 2004
362.82'924—dc22   2003062436

British Library Cataloguing in Publication Data is available.

Library of Congress Catalog Card Number: 2003062436
ISBN: 0–275–98167–3

First published in 2004

Praeger Publishers, 88 Post Road West, Westport, CT 06881
An imprint of Greenwood Publishing Group, Inc.
www.praeger.com

Printed in the United States of America

The paper used in this book complies with the
Permanent Paper Standard issued by the National
Information Standards Organization (Z39.48–1984).

10 9 8 7 6 5 4 3 2 1

In Loving Memory
To my brother, Daryl Wayne, who taught me strength and perseverance,
thank you. You were larger than life and the biggest man I will ever know.
It was a privilege to be your sister.

And

To my Grandmother, Bertie, who was my rock and my teacher,
I am forever grateful for the opportunity and honor to learn about
life through your eyes. When I grow up, I want to be just like you.

Contents

Contents

Foreword

I have been fortunate these last dozen years to know Christina Dalpiaz as a colleague and friend. I have seen her in action, working with people on all levels, displaying an incomprehensibly bottomless capacity to help. She is a "24/7" source of inspiration and comfort, spilling over with practical ideas and plain, level-headed wisdom about coping with family violence, understanding family dynamics, and applying healthy approaches to family problems.

In this, her second book, she focuses her considerable energies on one of her most intense causes. Her aim is to help people create better environments for their children—specifically, children who have witnessed or been victims of family violence. Contrary to what many assume, Ms. Dalpiaz believes that the answer for such kids is not necessarily in how they behave as it is in how adults respond to them. Professional counseling, treatment, mentoring, and effective parenting need to be where adults focus their efforts. She believes that adults need to be patient with these wounded children. Her philosophy is, *You can take your children out of the abusive environment, but it may take years to take the abusive environment out of your children.*

The author recognizes that creating healthy settings for children of family violence requires that parents understand that they are able to change negative family dynamics. Parents can break free from ineffective parenting approaches, learned perhaps from their own childhood experiences, and "change toolboxes" for tools better adapted to their children's needs.

Thus, Ms. Dalpiaz has two overarching goals in this book. The first is to show the bad behavior of these children for what it often is: *a reaction to severe trauma*. Understanding the effects trauma often has on children can help us find better ways to handle specific behavioral problems and, ultimately, help children modify their behavior in appropriate ways. The second main goal of this book is to equip parents mentally for this kind of approach—to help them get ready to act on their new understanding of their children's problems and to help them realize it lies within their power to change the negative dynamics.

It might seem at first that a single person with no child of her own would have little to offer families who have experienced violence or parents struggling with children's behavioral problems. But that impression would be wrong. Wrong first because of the author's own family past, which she has had to overcome. She is, in a way, her own case study and proof that a positive life is possible after abuse. It takes patience, learning, and determination, but she is living proof. The impression that she has little to offer would be wrong also because, in her professional work, as in her own personal life (Ms. Dalpiaz has had custody of her teenaged nephew since he was five), her experience of putting the ideas in this book into practice has won her accolades from other professionals and heartfelt gratitude from many families. She has used her insight to teach other families how to cope more effectively with the violence.

Ms. Dalpiaz has the welcome gift of being able to remind us of things we've known all along (if only we took the time to listen to ourselves). This book mixes common-sense reminders and original ideas to bring home her important points. *Breaking Free* also has things to say to people other than families who have experienced violence. In addition to being a collection of valuable suggestions to help people in that situation, this book is packed with common-sense advice that can help *all* parents in their quest to find the right approaches to bringing up their kids.

Parenting is the hardest—but *best*—job around, as Ms. Dalpiaz would say. And, she would add, it is also the most important one. It is worth doing the job as well as we can. I expect you will agree that this book can make it a little easier.

Yash Holbrook

Preface

In 1983, I became a newlywed. Like most young brides, I was excited about starting out my new life with my handsome and charming husband. And my dream was to live happily ever after. Within six months, there were shotgun holes covering my kitchen, knives placed to my throat, and then finally a full-fledged fist to the face. Luckily, I had the strength and courage to get out. This is when I began my quest to find out how this happened to me. As I educated myself, I realized that witnessing my parents fight had made their behavior seem normal. At this point, I decided to dedicate my life to kids of family violence. I wanted to help parents learn how their behavior impacted their children.

Ironically, in 1993, I gained custody of my five-year-old nephew, Katlin, because he was also living in a violent home. I felt confident that I could find the resources he needed. After all, I had been an advocate for ten years at this point. What I soon realized was that there weren't any "real" resources for kids back then—only brochures and endless phone numbers that led me in circles. I felt frustrated and defeated by the lack of support for children of family violence. I began to wonder, "If I, a victims' advocate with knowledge and financial resources, cannot find help for a kid, how does an average battered woman running for her life find what she needs to help her children?" What I found was a system that simply did not meet the needs of these kids. Needless to say, I found my purpose. That's when I started CHANCE (Changing How Adults Nurture Children's Egos), a non-profit agency that provides support to parents who are breaking free and starting over.

Although it takes an organization like CHANCE to raise awareness, it also takes a community to respond and make the necessary changes. My challenge to all of you is to ask what you can do to change the lives of these children. Let's join forces to help them see their lives differently and teach them that nonviolence is a choice.

Acknowledgments

I want to take the time to thank a few professional people who made this book come to fruition. First and foremost is the man who made it possible for me to work with battered families, Mr. Robert Agard, Director of Health and Human Services in Gilpin County, Colorado. Bob, thank you not only for employing me, but also for the technical assistance in writing this book. You encouraged me not to overgeneralize and you corrected me when I was being blatantly overemotional. Thank you. Next is my dear friend, Dr. Kimberly Laird, who took the time to read my book for major mistakes. "Kimmy" has supported me since the dawn of time and has helped me through many dark periods of my life. Thank you for your undying support. Yash Holbrook, yet another great person, has always been there for me. He has helped on many occasions with writing articles, reviewing chapters, and editing my first book to ensure its highest quality. Yash, you will always be my buddy. Last, but certainly not least, is Jo Blum. Jo works for an incredible organization called Families First. She was there for me through the entire editing process. Jo, you have been great, thanks.

I want to also say thank you to all the incredible parents and children who allowed me to work with them. Without you, this book would not have been possible. Your courage and strength are overwhelming and you have impacted my life more than you will ever know.

On a personal level, I would like to thank my nephew, Katlin, for being my inspiration. We have had a hard road to travel and the journey is not quite over, but I am praying for a happy ending. Katlin, I've said it before and I'll say it again, "You are the bravest guy I know. Someday, I hope that you can find the peace and love that you deserve."

Introduction

For the purposes of reading this book, the first item on the agenda is to stress the need to redefine domestic violence as family violence so that we can expand its reach to all of its victims. Society has been able to lessen the atrocity of battered women and their children by defining and minimizing their experiences as tiffs between two partners. The violent episodes are much broader than that, they involve psychological terrorism and emotional deprivation, which impacts everyone who knows the victim. Because society often looks at two adults fighting as a "private" issue, it unwittingly perpetuates the cycle of violence and plays a significant role in re-victimizing battered families. For the remainder of this book, I will refer to these abusive experiences as *family violence* so that we may get a broader picture of how the violence impacts society as a whole. It not only affects the victims, it touches the lives of their parents, children, co-workers, and friends. It emotionally and physically influences so much more than we ever thought.

The goal of this book is to help anyone who has experienced family violence, whether directly or indirectly, to recognize and understand the dynamics involved and to move in a healthier direction. For the parents of children who have witnessed the abuse, this book serves to enhance your abilities for *parenting in the aftermath of family violence*.

Introduction

In 1983, I was a battered woman. As I would learn, I was luckier than most. I got out of the relationship while I still had my self-esteem. Batterers usually do not hit their victims until they know they can. They wait until their victims are psychologically and emotionally beaten-down. The reason I am so lucky is that my ex-husband miscalculated and hit me too soon. Still, the violence greatly impacted my life, and my quest to understand how this happened to me has forever changed me. I was a very strong and independent woman and I could not understand how something like this could possibly have happened to me. This only happens to other people, right?

Wrong. What I have learned is that this can happen to anyone and that victims of family violence are groomed for their position. They are often unaware that they are enmeshed in an abusive relationship until it is, unfortunately, too late. Their situation can be equated to the following example: An experimenter once placed a frog into boiling water and it immediately jumped out. The frog recognized the danger and leaped to safety. Later, however, the experimenter took the same frog and placed it in a pan of cold water on the stove, gradually turning up the heat until eventually the frog boiled to death. The frog adapted to the temperature and could not recognize the danger. This example parallels how victims become entangled in violence. Next, it is important to learn what to do to recover from the devastating impact of family violence.

My journey toward discovery began when I was trained as a volunteer at a local battered women's shelter in 1986. Not only did I learn that the violence was not my fault and that I wasn't alone, I also learned that my childhood played a significant role in how I was groomed to become a victim. This is also where my passion for understanding and helping children who witness family violence began. I have come to understand so much about their experiences and I am grateful for the opportunity to share my insights. As mentioned, after ten years of working in the field of family violence, I was given custody of my five-year-old nephew, who was also a product of family violence. Now, I had the opportunity to take the information that I had learned and apply it to my own life. Little did I know how much more there was to learn and how hard the journey is for families recovering from abuse. I will share some of my personal stories along with some from my professional experiences. Through this sharing, it is my hope that we will all have a better understanding of how our children are affected by family violence and what we can do to guide them through the stages of healing.

Introduction

For each of you, this book may represent different periods in your life. Many experiences and insights shared here will be profoundly similar whereas others will be variants of what you have experienced, and some may be beyond your range of experience. What I want you to know more than anything is that you are not alone. My hope is that you will gain the knowledge and power to take back your lives for the sake of your children.

There are many victims who suffer every day from emotional, psychological, and physical abuse. Society-produced myths about battered women would have us believe that they are mostly minorities who are uneducated and poor. The fact is that family violence has no socioeconomic or cultural boundaries. It could affect the people sitting next to you, me, you yourself or one of your family members. It is time to shatter the myths, break the cycle of violence, and live healthier lives.

Protective factors are usually among the reasons why most victims finally escape their abusive relationships. Many explain that they stayed in the abusive relationship because of the kids, but when you ask battered women why they left, many will also say because of the kids. Most often victims feel overwhelmingly ineffectual for not protecting their children and at some point their protective factors kick in and make it possible for them to leave. I hope this book will serve to minimize or eliminate the guilt caused by these inadequate feelings and help anyone experiencing this pain to build a stronger sense of power.

But first, acknowledgment that the abuse happened must occur before the healing process can begin. Next comes the painful realization that the children were gravely impacted. As a result, children who are exposed to family violence react differently to the world around them. Discipline, to them, has an entirely different meaning than it might have on unexposed children. Exposed children most often internalize the adults' anger by either withdrawing or fighting back. Neither reaction is healthy. Therefore, it will be important to recognize these differences and to change interactive styles to meet these children's individual needs. Most parents want to make life better for their children, but many just do not have the skills to do so. If this is the case, this book will serve as an excellent reference.

In the aftermath of family violence there is often an inconsistency with rules and expectations, which confuses children. The primary objective of this book is to promote healing through developing safe and consistent boundaries for these children. Kids need adults to show them that they are special and important. When children survive severe deprivation and abuse, they often remark, "There was one person who cared about me." It is my intention to make you that one person, whether you are the victim or someone who loves the victim and her children.

Although this book focuses primarily of women's abuse, it is important to note that men are also victims of violence. But because they do not speak up as often, little information is available regarding their victimization. There are also lesbian and gay couples who suffer from violence. The point here is that though this text focuses on women, violence should not be tolerated by anyone.

Another note worth mentioning is that I have had the opportunity to work with some batterers themselves regarding their parenting, and I have witnessed some incredible changes. The bottom line is that violence is a choice—if people want to change, they can. But, it takes commitment and self-reflection.

I will stress throughout this book that you, as the victim, didn't get here overnight, and your problems cannot be solved overnight either. Be patient. The biggest obstacle that you will face is society's judgment. Others will not truly understand the violations that you have endured. Many professionals are trained to operate with little emotion, and they often do not see the abuse for what it really is—an atrocity. People who employ this type of attitude remind me of the emperor who isn't wearing any pants. Although everyone can see that he isn't, the kingdom still doesn't acknowledge it. We need a dramatic social shift in order to support battered parents and their children. I hope this book will give you the tools needed to make this possible. Good luck and good parenting!

CHAPTER 1

The Grooming Process: How Abuse Begins and Ends

Sticks and stones may break my bones, but words will forever hurt me.

Understanding How You Got Here

"How did I get here? How did this happen to me?" These questions are familiar to all of us who have experienced family violence. I began asking myself these questions soon after the collapse of my marriage. How could I, a strong woman with definite opinions and clear ideas of right and wrong, have been so blind? Though I considered myself tough and resilient, I somehow found myself in an abusive relationship. I left my marriage feeling baffled. Then, ten years later, I gained custody of my nephew, Katlin. He too was a product of family violence. What was the common denominator between us? What made us targets for abuse? This began my quest to learn why and how family violence happens. Now, I would like to share the insights learned from my quest to help you start your journey toward healing and to help you become a better parent.

The first step of your journey begins with understanding how a batterer psychologically breaks down a victim, thus making abuse possible. This dynamic is best described as a grooming process. The most important aspect of family violence begins here. Grooming can be longer or shorter according to the situation, but the grooming behavior itself is nonetheless distinct and predictable.

This chapter is broken down into three sections. The first presents the characteristics and stages of the grooming process that culminate in physical violence. The second shows how it is possible to fight the process, to put an end to it, and to recover a sense of security. The third discusses the lasting effects that the process has on you and your children. My objective is to help you recognize how you got to this point. This will make change easier and enhance your parenting styles so that you can begin a new life with your children. Let's begin.

First and foremost, batterers generally only hurt those they know they can. Contrary to what society thinks, batterers are in tune to their partner's needs and use it for their gain. They recognize and exploit their family's weaknesses. This adeptness guides them to carefully choose their victims. They know how to target the strengths and weaknesses of their prey. Once they collect their data, they can work their partners. A gradual breakdown occurs—victims' identities are stripped from them, making them putty in their batterers' hands. The batterers sabotage and destroy their victims' most precious thoughts (the ones that make them who they are). This includes hobbies, religious beliefs, or the victims' relationships with others.

The grooming process is a very calculated and careful progression. Take time to think about the ways your batterer broke you down. Then calculate how long it took before he physically hurt you. Undoubtedly, had he hit you on the first date, you would not have tolerated it—and he knew that. He had to get to you on an unhealthy emotional level first. Batterers want silent victims, ones who are powerless to speak out. The best way to accomplish this objective is by psychologically tearing down their victims.

The Grooming Process

The grooming process that precedes physical violence has several recognizable characteristics, including:

- Emotional violence (confusion, terror, and guilt)
- Isolation from others (no support group, physical relocation)
- Financial control
- Children as a weapon

The Grooming Process: How Abuse Begins and Ends

Often, victims do not comprehend that they are enmeshed in the violence until it is too late. To make matters worse, children are usually involved, making leaving difficult. Batterers will use their children against their victims—especially when other tools have failed. Because children are likely to be the weakest spot in their partners' defenses, batterers exploit their children to keep the victims in line.

It is important to note that physical violence is never used until the batterer knows it is safe to do so. To accomplish this, the victim must be isolated emotionally from her entire support group. Contact with friends and family are expressly forbidden. She may not be permitted to work, and money is no longer easily available. Initially, to groom her properly, the batterer has to manipulate through guilt. He finds ways to let her take the responsibility for the conflict. Once guilt no longer works, emotional abuse begins. He will attack anything that makes her believe in herself. Gradually, she finds herself with nowhere to turn and no outside influences to discount what he is saying. Eventually, she begins to believe that what he says is true. She slowly begins to feel as though she were crazy. If you are a victim, you understand how she feels. The exposure to the abuse eventually penetrates every aspect of her life. Then one day the realization that she has become an emotional hostage to a hostile captor seems so overwhelming and unimaginable. The victim had been brainwashed and she didn't even know it.

Stages of the Grooming Process

Family violence begins with a grooming process which progresses through definite stages. A batterer often starts his ploy with guilt intertwined with gifts and attention. He confuses his victim to the point where she doubts herself. She begins taking responsibility for his issues and insecurities. He allows her to believe that she is insensitive or thoughtless. Next, gradual isolation begins; first with friends who he deems "unacceptable," and then culminating in the elimination of everyone else close to her, including her family. He is compelled to take away all outside influences so that she is forced to hear only his perceptions. When psychological maneuvers to achieve his objectives no longer work, the batterer may actually induce a physical move away from the victim's support group. Some moves, like relocating for a job, are subtle, whereas others are blatant attempts to force the family into seclusion. Isolation becomes a critical stage in the progression of family violence.

To assist in the isolation process, the victim must be controlled financially so that she believes she is unable to leave. Her batterer checks receipts and the mileage on the car. He micro-manages her life. He may not permit her to work, or if he does he will take her paycheck and monitor the bills. He restricts her financially to keep her imprisoned. Unfortunately, the control doesn't stop there. Financial control is not enough to make a batterer feel secure. He must have total control and he will go to any length to achieve it.

A batterer will punish a victim who tries to flee or disobey her "master." He threatens to take the children; he says he can prove she is a bad mother; he turns the children against her or withholds child support. For these reasons, she believes she is trapped. And for the victim who has fled, she is often forced to go back.

One victim shared that her ex-husband would send a check for $13.00 through the child-support system to teach her that he was in control and that there was nothing she could do about it. He, like most batterers, has learned from previously abusive behavior that there are no consequences for his deviant actions. Society turns its head, explaining its indifference as not wanting involvement in a private matter. The battering behavior escalates and reaches a point where an abuser feels infallible. Each successful assault allows him to rationalize his behavior further. When a batterer has been permitted to avoid punishment, he can reach a point where he becomes lethal. When you read about a family that has been annihilated through murder/suicide, the common response from outsiders is: "We didn't see it coming." The reality is, "Nobody was looking." There are distinct actions that can be identified if one recognizes this process. The problem is that most people do not understand the precursors to physical abuse. Many victims who die saw it coming. Some prepared wills; some placed letters and pictures of their injuries in lock boxes; and some even planned their own funerals.

The stories that battered women tell are remarkably similar. A cinematographer, taping a training video on victims and their experiences with their abusers, remarked, "This is the same woman, she just has a different face." He was amazed at how outrageously similar the batterers' behaviors were in all of the stories. It would stand to reason, then, that batterers seemingly fit a definite profile. Consequently, efforts should be made to identify these traits and label them. We have profiled serial rapists and killers; these batterers are no different. They have distinct characteristics that every battered woman can identify with. Yet, we continue to blame the victim by diagnosing her with illnesses such as borderline personality disorder, self-defeating personality disorder, dissociative disorder, and quite a few more. To date, the only guideline that remotely indicates what the batterer suffers from is a diagnosis called Intermittent Explosive Disorder.[1] Yet, their behavior is quite methodical and predictable. It appears that the onus is again placed upon victims to *fix* the problem. Somehow they are still made responsible for the abuse. My hope is to change this distorted concept and help others place the blame where it really belongs.

Mr. Brighten, a convicted batterer, has repeatedly threatened his family with bodily harm. Until recently, the authorities did not take his threats seriously. His abuse has increasingly escalated. He now justifies his actions and considers his behavior normal. His explosions are due to losing control over his victims. Unless intervention occurs, the next stage may be serious injury or death for his family.

Although he has been caught twice for his assaults, there have been many times when he wasn't caught. His choices can be compared to drunk drivers. You know it's not their first or second time to drink and drive. They just finally got caught. But, the courts punish them as though this was their first offense. As one district attorney stated, "It's not like he's been caught six or seven times, this is only his second offense." Six or seven times are just too many if we want to save the lives of battered families. Unfortunately, batterers continue abusing because society doesn't see their behavior as serious until it is often too late.

Mr. Brighten has learned the system and knows that he must temporarily keep his distance from his family in order to prevent suspicion. His earlier assault charges, more than likely, taught him to be careful for the time being. He will have to lay low until after his second court appearance. If his punishment is jail, he will have time to regain his perspective. But if not, he will make sure his family understands that they cannot get away from his power. This will further perpetuate the violence, power, and control he currently holds on them. Unfortunately, many courts recommend probation for first and second offenses. This is where the system must re-evaluate its response to family violence.

Now that you understand the grooming process, the next lesson concerns the relationship of these dynamics to the cycle of violence. Once you recognize where you are in the process and take care of yourself, your focus can be shifted to supporting your family. The concept is very much like the flight attendant who announces, "In case of an emergency, place your oxygen mask on first before assisting small children." When your needs are met, your children will live in an environment that is more conducive to healthy change.

Groomee versus Groomer

In the grooming process there are at least two participants: a groomee and a groomer. The groomee is the person on the receiving end of the abuse and is usually the loser, whereas the groomer is usually in total control and calling all the shots. Society doesn't fully comprehend the plight of the groomee. Often victims are asked why they stayed with their abusive partner. Most people don't understand the dynamics that make leaving virtually impossible. Outsiders cannot grasp how someone can tolerate the abuse. Equally important is that victims are also not sure how or if they can tolerate the abuse.

The aim of this chapter is to educate victims and show that psychological, sexual, and emotional abuses are not separate from physical abuse; they are precursors. The batterer exhausts all other precursors before he resorts to physical violence. He needs to be sure his victim is primed first.

The grooming process is orchestrated very slowly and carefully. The calculated timeline is different for each victim. All is contingent upon prior experiences of abuse and how the victim views herself. If a victim was exposed to family violence as a child, she is already partially groomed for the attack, so her timeline may occur more quickly than another adult. Others may take longer depending upon their level of self-esteem and self-worth.

It is important to understand that anyone can be a victim; it is just a matter of when and under what circumstances. I volunteered at a local battered women's shelter to learn about abuse and how it affected my life. I needed to know how a strong-willed, smart, and independent person could get herself into such a predicament. How could this happen to someone like me? Easily. Batterers understand what their potential victims need, where their vulnerabilities lie, and how to use these vulnerabilities to get control over the victim. In my particular case, I grew up craving affection. My childhood left me feeling invisible: unnoticed and uncared for. My ex-husband read me like a book. He understood my need for recognition and tenderness. In the initial stages of our relationship, he pampered and doted on me. He painted my nails and brushed my hair. He bragged to others about how smart and funny I was. He showed outward signs of adoring me, and I ate it up. Little did I know that his real motives were to lure me in. Can you see how I was groomed? This is not to say that a man who pampers his partner will become a batterer. Rather, it is to stress that the batterer will understand your desires and needs. In my case, I needed pampering.

Without intervention, the grooming process convinces victims to believe their batterers' input. The following example shows just how self-critical a victim can become after years of emotional and physical abuse.

> Sherry was in a thirty-year marriage that was incredibly abusive, and her grooming was extensive. During one session, she expressed how inadequate she felt because she did such a bad job at work. After a series of questions, we were able to break down her job performance and determine why she felt so inept. Her conclusion resulted from her boss needing to have the cheese in a designated place in the refrigerator. She kept forgetting and placing the food on another shelf. I followed up by saying, "So you are a lousy worker because you misplaced the cheese?" She began to laugh and saw how silly it felt to be upset with herself.

Although this may seem extreme, it is a fine example of how verbal assaults can debilitate someone. Take a moment to evaluate a time when you felt bad about yourself. Find the root of the negative input and make a choice to either believe what you were told or denounce it. My recommendation is the latter. If you believe the information, you maintain the status quo and remain victimized. But if you denounce it, you move toward a new ideology: one that frees you from your batterer's grip. To accomplish this task, you must start by changing the input into a more positive one. This will not be easy because these negative messages become ingrained into your belief system. You will have to practice encoding new messages to get the old ones out!

So let's begin. Think about all the good things that you do, then look at yourself in the mirror and say with a smile, "I am a wonderful and capable person." As uncomfortable as it might feel, this exercise is essential to the process of breaking the debilitating barriers. Practice this exercise until you really believe what you are saying. It has been said that it takes an average of six hours of concentration to change a behavior or thought. Whether you practice this five minutes each day or thirty, you need the whole six hours, and maybe more. Do the math and decide how long you want to work on this new self-image. Personally, I recommend diving in and giving it your all. You decide.

Groomer

Many experts believe that there are different types of batterers. I disagree. Each batterer appears to start very much the same way. Their behavior is a progression. With each successful assault, whether emotional, financial or physical, batterers graduate to a higher level of grooming. My experience has shown that when they are encouraged to adjust their behavior in the earlier stages, they rarely graduate to the next abusive level. This is done, however, through social intolerance, which means taking their behavior more seriously. Batterers need new interactive skills to break the grooming process. I don't believe anyone *consciously* starts out wanting to be an abuser or to be abused. This is learned behavior that can be unlearned. But intervention must start long before they graduate to a level where they can rationalize their dysfunctional behavior.

Groomee

Experts in family violence sometimes describe victims as suffering from Stockholm Syndrome. This was a phenomenon that occurred during a hostage situation. The victims became emotionally connected to their captors and pleaded with the authorities not to punish their aggressors. The detainees began to empathize with how their captors felt and they forgave the behavior. Everyone else was befuddled. The use of the grooming process, therefore, becomes very critical for the groomer to maintain control. He gets his victim to side with him so outsiders will not intervene.

Guilt may be introduced to make the victim feel bad or unsure of herself. The batterer may resort to shame or pity to regain any loss in position. The grooming creates a situation that makes the victim empathetic to his needs. For example, "Honey, I really miss the kids, how can you keep them away from me? You know how much they love me," or "What will the kids do for a home if you have me locked up? Who's gonna pay the mortgage?" The groomee gets sucked in. She wants to believe that her groomer really means his words, but they are just that: words. An outsider can see the insidiousness of the situation but the insider usually cannot.

Emotional Terrorism: The Batterer's Mental Tricks

Emotional terrorism is a threat of violence toward others for the sole purpose of maintaining control over the victim. Emotional terrorism can be as damaging as an actual event because your mind can run wild with the potential danger. The mere thought that someone can "psych" you out by playing mind games can drive you insane. One victim describes it as, "When he does things like that, I feel I am going crazy." For example, her keys disappeared for an entire day then they mysteriously reappeared. The following day, the key to her mailbox no longer worked. The disappearance of the keys combined with her mailbox malfunction made her paranoid and suspicious. She found herself preoccupied and nervous. A simple act like changing a lock without permission can generate a fear beyond compare.

Another classic example of emotional terrorism, this time affecting a child, is the story of Judy's family camping trip.

> Judy's family was on a camping trip. Her youngest son tried unsuccessfully to open a can of beans with a knife. After beating his son, the father took the knife and repeatedly ran the blade across his own wrist to demonstrate that the dull knife was dangerous. To the young boy, all he saw was a sharp object running across his father's wrist.
>
> This father's behavior had a terror effect. The boy learned that simple mistakes could get him beaten—a lesson that would hang over his head into the future. He also learned to associate his own mistakes with a threat to a loved one, in this case to his father. Both lessons have lasting effects, creating an emotionally terrorizing situation that keeps the victim(s) vulnerable.

Children from family violence are often critical of themselves for making mistakes. In this example the father's actions are emotional terrorism at its finest. What do you think will have the greatest impact on this boy: the beating or watching the knife slide against his father's wrist? This particular scenario is not as unusual as you might think. When a batterer has progressed to this stage of grooming, he is well on his way to losing his ability to rationalize his actions, and his children pay the consequences. Evaluate your circumstance and determine whether your family is being subjected to emotional terrorism. If so, how does it impact them?

The Cycle of Violence and the Grooming Process

In the cycle of violence there are three primary phases. The first phase is tension, where the victim is constantly walking on eggshells. She adjusts her behavior to appease her batterer so he doesn't get upset. Unfortunately, she cannot be successful because he always finds something wrong with her or her actions. The tension phase becomes incredibly overpowering and nerve-wracking. Next is the explosive phase, where the batterer actually strikes out. Sometimes you hear outsiders say, "She asked for it." or "What did she do to piss him off?" More times than not, victims are blamed for their abuse. As strange as this sounds, though, some victims admit at times that they provoked fights to relieve the pressure. They say that the tension phase is so unbearable that they just want it over with. They are willing to take the physical blows simply to get to the next phase, which is a period of calm. This phase is referred to as the honeymoon phase, because the batterer can be temporarily remorseful and attentive and the victim is relieved. But, the beatings intertwined with tenderness get confusing. These intense emotions are attributed as love, because they are so strong. To avoid compounding emotions, the victim should never accept gifts, flowers, or sex from a batterer after a beating. The two emotions get entangled and begin to feel like they are one and the same. Accept gifts only during good times or when they are genuine, never as an apology.

A victim might not be consciously aware of this phase. She may only know that she likes the way he is now treating her, perhaps the way he did when they first met. All she wants is to have the battering stop. She wants to believe that the assault was an accident. Because of the honeymoon phase and his tenderness, the victim minimizes and thinks she can handle the episodes. The victim, unfortunately, does not see through the manipulation and interprets the peace as a reprieve. She hopes that he has had a revelation. He appears sincere and that is what the victim wants to believe. Unfortunately, as the cycle progresses, the tension and explosive phases are more predominant and the honeymoon stage gradually becomes nonexistent.

The grooming process cannot take place without the cycle of violence. This cycle makes it possible for the batterer to psychologically break down his victim and keep her off guard. She will doubt her judgment and her thoughts. The process can be gradual, and a victim often won't know that she is in a violent relationship until it is too late. If you are a victim, learn how to recognize the precursors to grooming so you can change your circumstance. If you care about a victim, approach her indirectly about this sensitive issue. A direct and offensive position will force her to defend her batterer. You must use an approach that is more palatable and easier for the victim to digest. She just wants the abusive behavior to stop. Making her defensive will only serve to keep her in the relationship longer. She can justify her reasons by saying, "You just don't know him the way I do . . . you don't understand what he has been through . . . he needs me."

The Healing Process

Healing has four primary stages: (1) denial, (2) hurt, (3) anger, and (4) acceptance. Each stage must be addressed before healing can occur. To survive the grooming process, victims must move through each stage and anticipate what is in store for them. My goal is to illustrate the extent to which batterers' capabilities reach and to show how breaking free and starting over will change the lives of these families. This book's content references victims who have fled their batterer relationships and are moving forward. For those still living in violence, it is my hope that this information will provide strength and knowledge to get you and your kids to safety.

It is essential to understand that you may waver between the stages. You may feel hurt for a while, then anger, and then hurt again. But as you progress, you will stay in the next stage longer. To move through the stages, find ways to empower yourself and don't allow roadblocks to overcome your desire to succeed.

Denial

One reason victims stay in their abusive relationships for so long is because they have learned to minimize, ignore, and/or take responsibility for the abuse. This is commonly known as *denial* and it is the first stage of the healing process. The victim sees the abuse as an accident or her fault because she should have known that he was tired or having a bad day. Because she has been carefully groomed through brainwashing and isolation, she now relies upon her batterer's input. He convinces her that she is the problem so she downplays the violence. With each episode, she becomes more convinced that she is at fault. She begins to see his distorted perception as her own. To break free and start over, she will need a support system to discount the information that has been mentally inflicted upon her. Breaking the mental isolation is the first step toward progressing past the denial stage.

Denial is a defense mechanism. It permits a victim to rationalize her circumstances because knowing the truth can be too emotionally overwhelming. Once a victim has fled the relationship and is reflecting on what she experienced, the realization that she is a survivor can become consuming. This new reality is frightening to say the least and can cause a gamut of feelings.

Hurt

The next stage in the healing process is hurt. Understand that they call this *hurt* for a reason. You are going to feel pain. But if you don't permit yourself to move into this stage, you will never heal. And as hard as you fight to avoid it, some day the pain will catch up with you. I remember, two years after my divorce, bragging one day to a fellow student, "I go to school full-time; I work full time; I take special classes for my job; I'm in the Navy reserves; I work a part-time job and I workout two days a week." To which the student replied, "What the hell are you trying to forget?" Talk about a slap in the face. Her comment was a major blow to my ego because I thought I was doing great. To prove her wrong, I started eliminating some of my tasks. Guess what? I completely fell apart. I was in therapy within two weeks. I had made myself so busy that I never thought about what my ex-husband had done to me. Consequently, I stayed in denial for two years. It did not make the hurt stage any less painful; it only prolonged my agony. Everyone has to go through their grief when their body and mind are ready to handle it. No one has a right to tell someone else when that time is. I would only caution that procrastinating too long could set you up for other dysfunctional and abusive relationships. You cannot change your life unless you recognize where the problems lie.

In the hurt stage you may be asking yourself why this happened. You have personalized the abuse and embraced the pain. As a result, the emotions become too overpowering. The tendency might be to revert back to denial to feel safe again. After some time away from your batterer, it is easy to forget what he did and let doubt set in— "Was it really that bad?" or "Maybe I overreacted." You may regret leaving because now you remember the good times or you miss the comfort of being with someone. You may have minor setbacks where you start experiencing guilt or remorse for the loss of this relationship and you might want it back. But if you really think it through, you know that you were the only one contributing to that relationship; he was just a warm body, and a mean one at that.

Don't get down on yourself if you yearn for your mate. Your feelings are completely normal. It is natural to work through some of the pain and long for your partner. This thought process is very typical for battered women. You may reconsider your relationship for the sake of the children, and you may lean toward forgiveness. But realistically and logically, reconciliation during the hurt stage is a bad move. Be very careful not to use your children as an excuse to continue this volatile relationship. Your children don't want to be there. If you stay, do so because you need to and not because of them. Your kids are the silent victims and they cannot make their own decisions. They depend on you to keep them safe. Don't use them as a scapegoat for your own dysfunction.

In the case of one victim who considered reconciliation for the sake of the children, I asked her to think back two years and write down everything her husband did to contribute to the well-being of their family. She could only think of one camping trip. I asked for simple examples like bathing the children, reading them stories, or making them smile. There wasn't anything else. Next, I asked her to write down the things he had done to hurt the children over the last two years. She suggested that she only go back six months because the list would be too long. This statement speaks for itself. She realized without hesitation that there were many more bad things than good. She then tried to justify his behavior and remarked that the kids needed their father. I asked if she would want her daughter to have a relationship with her father if she knew her husband was a child molester. She said, "Absolutely not! That is horrific and he doesn't deserve to ever see her." In this victim's case, her batterer choked her and threatened to kill her in front of the children. I asked her to tell me whether she felt that what he did was devastating to her children. Although he didn't kill her, the children watched in horror, believing that she was going to die. By the end of the session, she recognized that she was just lonely, hurt, and feeling scared. Because he had verbally apologized, he momentarily confused her and she thought she wanted the relationship back. Victims desperately want to believe their batterers, but without early intervention, statistically they do not change.

Anger

The anger stage follows next. This stage is probably the most intense of all. It can be scary for everyone involved. Victims have learned the hard way that anger is just one letter away from danger. Spilling a glass of milk can literally mean a black eye or a busted lip. Therefore, victims going through the healing process try to avoid anger as much as possible because they realize how frightening it can be. To heal from anger, however, you must deal with it. Anger does not just go away, it eats you up alive. Eventually, the buildup of anger can cause an implosion.

What you have to understand is that anger doesn't always mean rage. Learning how to moderate your reaction makes healing come sooner. This stage is a necessary one, but anger must be channeled correctly. This is probably the most frightening stage for you and your children. When you lived in violence, there was really only one person permitted to express himself. The rest of the family was expected to "stuff it." In this stage, thus, the floodgates may open and everyone may be simultaneously angry. You are definitely going to need a support system to help you through this stage because staying angry too long will destroy you emotionally. Yet, your family must experience anger to some degree in order to heal.

It is important to note that boys may be stuck in this stage longer because they have been conditioned to hide their "weak" emotions. Unfortunately for boys, anger is the socially acceptable way of dealing with pain. As a consequence, what appears as anger really involves other disguised emotions. As far as girls are concerned, this stage might need to be encouraged because girls have been taught that it is "not polite" to get mad. Do not be resistant to expressing anger. It is too important. Just make sure your anger is expressed effectively and channeled properly.

With the anger stage comes the ability to understand that your batterer really didn't care about what or who you were. In this stage, you begin to blame your partner for his behavior, which allows you to stop taking responsibility for his actions.

Acceptance

You must reach all the stages of healing to meet the final stage of acceptance. It will be harder to have a healthy relationship with someone new until you have embraced this stage. For your kids' sake, don't expose them to any further dysfunction. Make sure you understand how you got trapped in the cycle of violence so you do not repeat your mistakes. What your children witness will forever transform their lives. My motto is, "Children are creating their future past. Take today and ask yourself, 'What will my children remember?'"

Participating in a support group will reinforce that others have experienced the same abuse. You will hear stories much like your own and recognize that your abuser's traits are similar to other batterers. With support, you can identify and completely understand that the abuse was wrong, but more specifically that it *was not your fault.*

The Aftermath of an Abusive Relationship

Victims often believe that once they have left their partner or the divorce is over, they can completely sever the relationship with their batterer. They may believe that the restraining order will protect them. But *au contraire,* this is just the beginning and is usually when the violence escalates the most. This statement is not meant to frighten you but rather to warn you not to minimize the capabilities of your abuser. The fact is women are more likely to be victims of homicide when they are estranged from their husbands than when they live with their husbands. The risk of homicide is higher in the first two months after separation.[2] So, when a batterer says he is going to kill his partner, he may mean it. This is a very critical period and safety precautions should be taken. Leaving has disrupted his power and control. He will do whatever it takes to regain the advantage.

To reclaim control, your batterer might make comments to the children, knowing they will repeat them to you. These words serve to keep you in check. An example would be, "Dad said he was going to buy the land next to us and build a house so he can watch us." This statement can frighten a victim; yet, the batterer has not "legally" violated his restraining order—he's simply concerned about his children. Society may not see this comment as a threat, but the victim certainly does. It is a mental chess game where the batterer is working toward a checkmate.

During a separation, the batterer wants the restraining order dropped. Therefore, the grooming process takes on a new form. The batterer resorts to unfamiliar methods of coercion and tricks to confuse a victim's sense of reality. For example, he may now appear to have genuine concerns for his children. His gestures confuse the victim. He has finally expressed an interest in his kids and this is what she always wanted. He convinces her to drop the restraining order so he can see them. In one case, the victim bought into her batterer's ploy when he said he wanted to be a part of the children's lives. He asked that the restraining order be dropped. During the proceeding, her ex-husband lied to the judge about the details of the assault. The frightened victim recognized that she had just been tricked. She later remarked how glad she felt that the judge didn't listen to her request. Otherwise, this man would have had a license to harass. She realized that he was only using the kids to have the restraining order lifted. She was shaken when she recognized how far he would go to get to her.

Batterers understand that their victims are more receptive to forgiving them if they appear hurt and remorseful about losing their children. The batterers' goal is to invoke pity so their victims will not abandon them. After all, grooming takes time—why start over with a new victim when the one they have is so ripe.

One victim shared that her ex-husband threatened to kill her animals. Months later, several of her animals mysteriously vanished without a trace. She underestimated her batterer's capability to perform such a dastardly deed. Her mistake was that she projected how she felt onto her batterer. Abusers do not think like victims do. To understand this more clearly, compare batterers' emotions to a wall. You would never try to rationalize with a wall. It is an inanimate object that cannot think or feel. Without treatment, batterers are much the same way. They are shut down emotionally and are unwilling to empathize. If in doubt about a batterer's capability, err on the side of caution. When I warned the previously mentioned victim to protect her animals, she regrettably responded, "I didn't believe you." Batterers cannot afford to let their victims regroup and regain composure. All attempts to use psychological tactics keep the victims in a constant state of turmoil. Each time the victims relax somewhat, the batterers must create new forms of terrorism. They use any method possible to maintain the status quo. The following story illustrates what lengths a batterer can go to control his family.

> April, a mother of three, wanted to go to the movies with her sister. Her husband expressed his dissatisfaction. But she went anyway, leaving him with the children. When she returned, she noticed a noose hanging in the garage. She ran into the house to find her husband passed out with a hunting knife in his hands. Frantic, she raced upstairs to check on her children. She was relieved to find them safe. The message he sent was loud and clear: This time you were lucky . . . don't ever mess with me again.

When batterers fail in their attempts to confuse their victims, they get amazingly creative in their tactics to regain the control. Imaginative and resourceful, abusers know which buttons to push. In this case, the batterer achieved his objective: April never went out again, and she lived with the terror of knowing he might easily harm her children if she did not "behave."

Another batterer's tactic is to describe to his estranged partner that he has found someone special who makes him very happy. The victim feels she is at fault. The children get the same message and believe that their mother could have tried harder. Now, the grooming process starts with the kids. If they are convinced that she was the problem, the batterer can continue to manipulate and control her through the loss of her children's affections. He can disrupt and destroy her new family dynamics.

The exposure to violence may lend itself to allowing the children to adopt the batterer's attitude. They may act out and blame the victim for the abuse. They have learned from years of watching who wins. They see that his violence works and his needs are met. If dad is removed from the family structure, the children might lash out because they are uncomfortable with the new dynamics (i.e., mom's in charge and the rules are different). The victim might feel confused and guilty, thinking she made a mistake. Misunderstanding her children's emotions might cause her to minimize what happened. After all, the bruises are gone and perhaps no physical scars were left. The victim may begin taking some responsibility for the abuse, forgive the abuser, and want to make amends. However, returning to the relationship *is not the answer*.

To handle this turmoil, recognize how difficult it is for the children to be stuck in the middle. Your kids may react harshly to you but they are not really angry with you. In Chapter 2, some of these issues will be addressed. But for now, do not, I repeat, do not personalize your children's behavior. Step away from it and understand that their father has learned to manipulate them like he did you.

Helping Children Through the Grooming Process

Children also personalize their batterer's behavior and need help understanding how deviant these acts were. Next, they need to recognize that they did not deserve to be mistreated. As many victims know, the emotional, verbal, and physical treatment is beyond normal comprehension. For example, a seven-year-old girl had to be told by family members that the Easter Bunny was not real. In a rage, her father declared to her that he had killed the Easter Bunny and now she had to eat him for dinner. Imagine a child sitting down to a chicken dinner and believing that she was eating someone who represents good, talks, and brings candy.

This same man held his daughter's head underwater until she could not breathe any longer; he would let her catch her breath then begin the process again. She truly believed he was trying to drown her. Yet, he convinced her mother that he was just playing and that she was just being a baby. What he did was not funny, but when you have been groomed to view things through your batterer's eyes, you can minimize a great deal.

Behavior to this magnitude can have life-altering effects, penetrating every aspect of life. These children become perfect targets and fair game for their peers, teachers, or others who prey upon their vulnerabilities. No longer is the abuse restricted to their batterers. Now, the world becomes a fearful and dangerous place.

I know firsthand how family violence can make a full circle. I was taunted relentlessly. Kids beat me up, dragged me down sidewalks leaving me covered with road rashes; they tortured and beheaded my animals then left them for me to discover. My home, the place where I should have been able to seek refuge, only subjected me to further abuse. There was nowhere for me to hide; I felt alone and frightened. The whole world seemed out to get me. As a result, kids, like I did, lose their willingness to trust others. They meet everyone with suspicion and apprehension, even when people genuinely want to help. They develop the idea, "Why should I trust this teacher when I can't even trust the people who brought me into this world?" Trust is probably the number one obstacle to recovery. You will learn how to guide them through this process of regaining trust in Chapter 7.

As victims themselves, children can be in different stages of healing and may interpret the violence differently. Therefore every child must be treated in a manner that is specific to his or her needs. A passionate child may linger in the hurt stage, whereas a willful child may have already progressed to the angry stage. If your family has suffered abuse, your children may all be processing differently and your approach should be based on where they are emotionally. There are a lot of adults, including teachers, who use an authoritarian approach to keep kids in line. I guarantee that this approach will only serve to exacerbate the children's problems even further. A supportive and understanding approach works more appropriately to motivate kids.

To help your children move in a more positive direction, be aware of their triggers (automatic responses). What makes them react negatively? For example, if your child feels stupid, that will be his trigger. Therefore, focusing positively on educational needs will build his self-esteem. When a child believes he will fail, he won't try. The consequence is that he gives up, which reinforces his belief that he is stupid.

A trigger for some children might be that they compare their self-worth to others. Although this is a natural reaction for most kids, a child from family violence takes it one step further. She will look for other children who are less adequate so she can belittle them. She has learned that the best way to feel good is to make someone else feel badly. Because her perpetrator has taught her to be critical, she will fight others to better herself and she will do this through abusive behavior.

One of the most damaging triggers for children is their search for perfection. Kids from family violence often strive for flawlessness so that others can't criticize them. They may never try tasks that they do not feel they can accomplish because they don't want to be corrected. Not being perfect equates to inadequacy.

One trigger for my nephew, Katlin, was his need to win, no matter what the cost. The thought of losing made him explosive. How do you, as a parent, help your children become more accepting of failure? First, you must *desensitize* them to being wrong. The best example I have is when Katlin came home bragging that he had beat another student in chess.

Katlin: "I won in chess today."

Me: "So, did you play a good game?"

Katlin: "I don't know."

Me: "Well tell me when you know."

(Frustrated and deflated, he walked away.)

The next day

Katlin: "I won in chess today and I played a good game."

Me: "Did your opponent play a good game?"

Katlin: "I don't know."

Me: "Well tell me when you know."

(Flustered and agitated, he walked away again.)

The following day

Katlin: "I won in chess today; and I played a good game and my opponent played a good game."

Me: "I am so glad the two of you played a good game."

(Katlin appeared puzzled.)

Days later

Katlin: "I played a good game in chess today; and my opponent played a good game; but I lost."

Me: "That's great that you both played a good game."

This exercise may seem cumbersome, but it really works. Katlin is a top athlete today; but he will quit a sport when he thinks *others* are taking the game too seriously. What this and many other similar exercises did was teach him how to do his best without having to win. We set our kids up for disappointment when we reward them for winning, because someday someone will be better than them at something. If their value is based only upon being the victor, they will eventually feel badly because they cannot always win. How they regard themselves should never be contingent upon someone else's ability to do better or worse.

When you teach kids to strive for their best, then they will be their best. Another example is a little boy who became frustrated because he was learning to roller skate and he kept falling down. He snorted, "I hate skating, I suck!" I explained that the reason he was falling down was because he was trying harder than the other kids. I told him that if he was not falling down, he wasn't getting any better. I assured him that anyone can skate safely; but to skate for skill he must fall down. Within one week, his mother reported that he was skating like crazy. I had showed him that failure was part of learning.

If you want to change children's triggers, you must continuously remind them that it is all right to make mistakes. Once their perceptions change, they can accomplish great things. Do your best to alter the outcome. It won't be easy to undo the damage, but with persistence all things are possible.

When I speak to adults who were exposed to family violence as children, they often describe similar feelings of failure. One woman shared a childhood issue she had carried into adulthood. She was fearful of cooking because her father always criticized the meals she prepared. Those feelings interfered with her ability to cook for her children. To help her see that this belief system was wrong, we began cooking classes. During one class, she criticized herself out loud for dirtying too many dishes. Something so insignificant as dirty pans should not have merited such criticism. What happened was that she was retrieving imprinted old messages that her father gave her. She was beating herself up emotionally for essentially nothing. Without help, she would have remained paralyzed because failure felt bad.

If you have memories such as these, ask yourself if you are being too critical. Hating or berating yourself serves no purpose. Think logically. Do you feel better after you have put yourself down? Absolutely not! So start today—stop repeating the hateful words that were given to you as a child. Remember that your children are learning how to treat themselves by watching how you treat yourself. If you can't be kind to yourself for your sake, do it for theirs.

Everyone carries hurtful memories that can trigger inappropriate reactions. Usually when someone experiences emotional pain, the perception of what was being said can be ten times more hurtful than the actual comments themselves. For example, I know a young man whose father told him that he was stupid. Consequently, whenever someone teases him or makes a comment suggesting that he is less than smart, he personalizes it to the "nth" degree. Years later, his father's comment still haunts him. He still struggles with this trigger.

The sad part is that the batterer probably doesn't even remember saying it, yet the boy is left with the everlasting effects.

I challenge you to generate a list of issues that trigger your children's behavior, then find ways to deal with those issues. Every perception and action builds on the next and you will want to change these triggers so your children's insight can be different.

How Did You Participate in the Abusive Relationship?

There is no excuse for family violence, and you, the victim, should never be blamed for being hit. It is imperative, however, that you understand how you participated in the violence. Many experts say that there is a certain "dance" that partners do around the cycle of violence. There are behaviors that are displayed, which help perpetrators choose their victims. It could be that you suffer from low self-worth or low self-esteem. Perhaps you learned as a child that this is the way couples interact. Whatever the case may be, you must look within yourself and search for answers as to how you may have contributed to the dysfunction. Then you must change that behavior so the cycle of violence will be broken. Learning how you were groomed and how to change the behavior will help you avoid future abuse.

Now that you understand the grooming process, realize the early warning signs, and see how you were sucked into this relationship, you can move forward. This knowledge can help you recognize those grooming traits, get out of other abusive relationships sooner, or establish boundaries that will not permit the abusive behavior to go any further. Because batterers have a need for control, they will not stay in a relationship if his partner does not permit inappropriate boundary-breaking. But this must happen in the earlier stages before physical violence starts. Remember, batterers only hurt the people that they can hurt, so be strong and alert.

CHAPTER 2

The Mask of Anger

Boys who can't shed tears shoot guns.

—*William Pollack*, Real Boys

Understanding the Mask of Anger

Children who must cope with family violence often use a mask to cover their true emotions. This mask serves as a defense mechanism to protect them from the pain that is inflicted upon them. This mask is referred to as the *mask of anger*. The problem here is twofold: (1) children are masking their emotions, and (2) adults are not looking behind the mask and adequately responding to the real issues. In this chapter, we will discuss the mask of anger and how it plays a critical role in the emotional process that your children might be experiencing. The goal is to look beyond this mask and help identify what they truly feel and how to move beyond this point. Some children who witness family violence are described as defiant and oppositional. Most often, they cannot express themselves in a manner that is positive. As a result, they react using negative emotions that are generally expressed and recognized as anger. Depending upon each child's disposition and length of exposure to the violence, reactions can vary. Some children might become aggressive whereas others withdraw. In either case, these kids mask their emotions, which makes healing more difficult. This chapter will focus on lifting the mask and giving kids new coping strategies to deal with their experiences. They cannot do this alone. They need help learning how to identity their true feelings and how to express themselves more appropriately.

My belief is that anger is not a true emotion at all, but rather a reaction to other bad feelings. The best personal example that comes to mind is the time I was preparing my nephew for disappointment when he wanted to go to his friend's house. I warned him that his friend might not be home and that he could be disappointed, but not angry. His response was, "What's the difference?" For a moment I stood perplexed, then I realized that he really did not understand that anger and disappointment were not one and the same. Upon further examination of other children's reactions, I discovered that a lot of the "ticked-off kids" were really feeling other things. This revelation helped me to develop better skills to teach children and their parents how to cope.

As you learn new techniques that help your kids cope perhaps you could apply them to your own life as well. If you have fled your violent relationship, there's a good chance that you also have some issues with anger that need to be addressed. You were forced to leave familiar surroundings and are now the sole support financially, emotionally, and physically for your children. You not only have to deal with what you experienced, but now there are bills, school activities, housework, and so much more to do. How does one sort it all out and still be a loving and caring parent? Commonly, what occurs is that the children are blamed for the chaos because they "just won't listen and settle down."

We often assume that they are the problem when, in fact, it may be us adults. Perhaps children are not *hyper*active so much as we are *hypo*active. I call this phenomenon Hypo-Activity Disorder (HAD). We have HAD it! We are exhausted, confused, and hurt. Now our kids are acting out and we too are wearing the mask. In order to remove it and deal with the underlying true emotions, we have to regain the control that was lost in the abusive relationship. But first, we too have to figure out what we are really feeling so we can be more effective parents. The mask of anger often involves the following feelings:

• abandoned	• betrayed	• confused
• annoyed	• blamed	• defeated
• anxious	• bored	• degraded
• ashamed	• bothered	• despair
• berated	• burden	• difficult

- disappointed
- discouraged
- disrespected
- embarrassed
- excluded
- failure
- fear
- frustrated
- guilt
- hate
- imperfect

- inadequate
- inferior
- insecure
- lonely
- misplaced
- pressured
- rejected
- sadness
- scared
- stressed
- stupid

- unfaired upon
- unloved
- unsure
- untrusting
- unwanted
- unworthy
- vengeful
- withdrawn
- worried

Review the mask of anger and use it to understand the following two examples:

1. If a noncustodial parent tells the children that their family was split up because "mommy made up stories that weren't true about daddy," the kids might come back from their visit with their father and lash out at the nonviolent parent. Think very carefully and determine what the conflicting feelings are. A wide gamut of emotions is present: betrayed, sad, and guilt. To help them, put yourself in their position. Stop seeing them as angry because they are not. From this point forward, do not entertain the concept of angry children. Go one step further and identify the real issues, and verbalize what they need to hear.

2. When the custodial parent is forced to move because she cannot afford their home any longer, the children lose their friends, their school, and the familiarity of their home. The changes are stressful. But does that mean the children are mad? Or are they feeling lonely, misplaced, or unsure of their future? Everything they understood as real is now gone. That's a lot to handle. They probably noticed that their mother cries continuously; she's exhausted, preoccupied, and emotionally unavailable due to her own grief. They aren't confident that she can make good decisions because she doesn't seem "together." When you look deep enough, you can understand exactly what these kids feel. Recognizing that the emotion isn't anger will make coping with their reaction easier.

Now that you have had an opportunity to review and apply the mask of anger to these examples, were you able to recognize the emotions differently? Children will heal more quickly when you take the words *mad* and *angry* out of your vocabulary. Once you think beyond their anger, you can determine their actual feelings, respond more effectively to their reactions, and then teach them to take responsibility for their behavior.

Every child has the potential to react differently to the same situation. Therefore, understanding children's dispositions is crucial to finding appropriate solutions. Do not resort to general responses or blanket statements that aren't conducive to your individual child. If your child is unconventional then conventional reactions won't work. Take the following story as a good example.

> Courtney, a willful child, struggles socially because she impulsively lashes out at others. Her mother understands that Courtney is doing so because she is anxious, but others see her as defiant and mean. Courtney always had to stand up to her father to protect her mother. Now, in the aftermath of family violence, Courtney still reacts by keeping her emotional guard up at all times. The consequence is that she has problems in school. She will not allow anyone to tell her what to do. If others use intimidation or punishment to gain compliance, it only serves to exacerbate the situation further. She is literally walking around with her fists raised, ready to fight. She doesn't trust that she can keep herself safe unless she is alert and prepared. That may mean challenging the whole world, including those who want to help her. Others can only see an angry child, and not what she really is, a kid just trying to stay safe.
>
> Courtney's mother needs to develop a plan and present it to her teachers. The plan should include positive reinforcement and reward rather than punishment. The fact is that wounded children do not care about punishment or themselves. Therefore, punishment simply does not work! They need encouragement and understanding along with positive ways to cope with their situation.

Teachers often struggle with these children because they feel that the kids are disrespectful and obnoxious. With all the academic demands placed upon teachers, they are not equipped to deal with the dynamics of family violence. They have an incredible responsibility to many children and time is limited. They need your help. Question and guide the teachers to make the interaction positive. Otherwise, the reaction toward your kids' behaviors will be less than favorable.

With children who are willful and not easily intimidated, the general approach to discipline used in the schools will not be conducive to meeting their emotional needs. Children will respond better when the adults learn to communicate more positively. Coming from family violence, these kids have seen and survived a lot. There is nothing a teacher or other adult on the periphery can do to scare them. School is the one place where these kids know they can control their lives. They question authority and are more prone to negative behavior because they need to know *why* they are being asked to perform. The bottom line is that these kids want control because they have learned from their violent environment that the only way to prevent chaos is to control everything and everyone around them. Another reason for being less aggressive with these kids is that when they are threatened, the chances are great that they will retaliate. Remember this: cornered dogs bite. If these children feel there is no option but to lash back, they will; I guarantee it. We will learn more about this subject in Chapter 9.

Unmasking Children

Children who have experienced family violence may have low self-regard. They often do not care about themselves and they exhibit depressive symptoms. Therefore, punishment is not appropriate. You can take away as much as you want, but they will not respond in an effective manner. Children, in general, are much more successful with positive praise. Understand that they are more apt to make a good thing better rather than make a bad thing good. This will promote a more positive self-image, help them internalize more easily, and allow them to take off the mask.

To help your children succeed, establish time each day to practice new behavior skills, which will replace their old sets. They may have learned that acting out gets your attention. And for whatever reason, they need that attention right now. Consequently, negative attention is better than no attention. Turning the negative attention around and making it more positive is the place to start. Use the mask of anger concept to determine how your children might be feeling about the changes in their lives. Change is stressful and can cause reactions that appear as anger. Families who leave their abusers have an assortment of emotions. Your children could feel abandoned, rejected, or lonely. They have lost the only life they ever knew. Understanding the real feelings will give you a little more empathy toward your aching children and your attitude can soften. Embrace those feelings and work toward comforting them rather than reacting to the explosions. What they have lived through is not a natural part of childhood, therefore you might need to lower your expectation for normal behavior and build your children in a healthier direction.

Once you understand where your children are coming from, establish a plan to stop the behavior. Say, for example, your child becomes frustrated because he cannot get his shoes tied. His response is to whine, cry, or throw a tantrum. How you respond will make all the difference to how the situation ends. The correct action in this case is to help him feel secure and work with him to complete this simple task. Ask him to bring the shoes to you; have him sit facing away from you on your lap; put your arms around him and enclose him. Next, demonstrate how to tie his shoes; use your imagination to help him visualize how to accomplish this task: "Here are two bunny rabbit ears, wrap them around each other and pull, now you try." If he still appears frustrated, tell him you will do one shoe, and then he can do the other. Have him take a deep breath and let it out before he starts. Then verbalize that you are there to help and that you believe in him. The issue here is not that he cannot tie his shoes; it is that he is feeling inadequate, unloved, and unsure (i.e. due to the loss of his father). Address these issues and the simple tasks will improve.

Children from family violence may revert to an age where they felt safe. Parents often say, "He's acting like a two year old;" or, as in the previous example, "He's big enough to tie his own shoes." Chronologically, kids may seem capable of accomplishing minor tasks; but they are retarded emotionally by the penetrating negative input their batterer inflicted upon them. They may need you to prove to them through nurturing that they are loved and cared for. No matter how ridiculous it may seem to you, these kids require their basic needs for love and belonging to be met before they can become competent. Seeing the situation through their eyes will promote a quicker recovery. Positive growth will occur when you understand that their perception is the only one that counts, and that their behavior is based on their reality, not yours. They will alter their behavior when each can understand the changes in his or her own mind's eye. Sometimes that means taking a step back and viewing your children's needs at a much lower level. Adults can either destroy children or build them. Think in these terms: "It is always easier to build a child than to repair an adult" and, "What emotional outcome will my child have if she understands and trusts herself?"

I remember my six-year-old nephew not wanting to sleep alone. Many people criticized me for permitting him to lay with me. My philosophy, however, is that sleeping with someone feels good and makes one feel safe. My job, as a parent, was to protect him and create security. For us, that meant allowing him to stay in my room. I believe there is a time in every child's life when sleeping with his parent will not be cool. I decided that I would get concerned if he still wanted to sleep with me as an adolescent. As I had predicted, at the age of twelve, he moved into his own room. So what do you think he gained from this experience? Now that he is sleeping alone, do you think any harm was done? Ask yourself what the worst possible outcome can be if you nurture your child a little longer than society thinks you should. Everyone has an opinion and they are free to give it. Trust your own instincts and do what feels right for you and your family. You must support them the best way you know how. Trust your judgment.

It is important, however, to differentiate between enabling and supporting your children. Enabling is when you make excuses and overcompensate to adjust for the abuse. Frequently, the non-offending parent will interact in an overly protective manner with her children. She will make her decisions based on guilt and pity. This is absolutely damaging to children. It will give the children an excuse to fail or give up. Supporting happens when you understand the reasons for your children's behavior, yet make them take responsibility for their actions. You do not want to treat your children like victims; but, you do not want to leave them to their own demise, either. A co-worker once confronted me when Katlin had gotten into trouble, again, and I was helping him find a way out. She snapped, "So when are you going to stop treating him like a victim?" I was dumbfounded and retorted, "What are you talking about?" Her response was, "You are always bailing him out. He's not a victim anymore. Stop treating him like one, he's got a great life and he needs to take responsibility for his behavior." Let me tell you, her comment felt like a hard slap in the face. I was forced to look at how I had been *rescuing* him. It was really hard; but at that point, I decided to help him learn to cope with adversity. Bailing children out or running away is not always an option. Speaking from experience, this exercise in supporting is much more difficult for the adult than the child; but it must be done. The longer you wait, the more difficult it is to undo the damage.

As children get older, if the mask of anger is not handled properly, they may revert to masking their emotions with substances such as alcohol or drugs. It will be important to look for signs such as withdrawal, defensive body stances, lack of eye contact, failing grades, and lack of interest in areas where they were once participatory. At this point, I would recommend using a technique I refer to as *in-your-face* parenting to get your kids on track. This is a very firm and direct approach that conveys, "I love you and I refuse to allow you to fail." This technique requires that you query other adults who are exposed to your children; you restrict their involvement with kids that are high risk; and you require your children to do drug testing if necessary. Whatever it takes, you send the message that you love them and you will not allow them to self-destruct. Your children hear, "I care, I'm listening, and I am paying attention." Some adults feel that teenagers deserve their privacy; I strongly disagree. If your child displays inappropriate behavior your duty is to find out what they are up to. Imagine what might have happened if the young men from Columbine High School would have had a room search.

Often children turn to drugs in a desperate attempt to mask their trauma, or they may simply be looking for acceptance. I strongly suggest that if the signs are there, you search their room to make sure there isn't any paraphernalia or drugs. Children need guidance and boundaries, and these must come from parental expectations. When the pattern is to not confront problems and hope that they will just disappear, you are sending the message that you do not care. To unmask your children, they need to feel safe and know that you are there.

Adults' Impact on Children

In abusive homes, the batterer is rarely happy. No matter how hard a family tries to please the abuser, the victims fail. Children seek approval from their parents and when they cannot obtain that positive feedback, their self-esteem and self-worth are gradually broken down. Some children give up and feel like failures, whereas others strive for perfection. In either case, the children suffer. Children internalize and learn that being wrong is bad. Making mistakes becomes debilitating to the point where the children stop trying. They shut down and are unable to solve problems. Whether silently or aggressively, the mask of anger builds and slowly tears them down.

> Kathy has a sixteen-year-old angry son, Billy. She says that she has absolutely no control over his behavior. He hates just about everything and he doesn't seem to care about anything. He consistently makes derogatory comments about himself and others. He stays out late, and lashes out when confronted about his whereabouts. Billy

remarks that he feels stupid. His current behavior indicates that he may be suffering from low self-esteem and possibly depression.

During subsequent sessions with this family, it was brought out that Billy's teacher verbalized that Billy was a loser. These comments were addressed in Billy's presence during parent/teacher conferences. This teacher obviously does not recognize the trauma this young man is living with. Adults have so much power and children are programmed to believe that the adult is always right. What message did Billy get from his teacher? How does a parent ensure that other negative adults do not influence their children in this manner? And what can they do to help their children recover from this type of emotional damage?

Obviously, this young man is going to need support to feel better about himself. As a parent, Kathy can confront the school staff and make sure they understand that this type of communication will not be tolerated. She has to become his strongest advocate. She may have to consider talking to the school board; writing to the state board of education; or lastly, moving Billy to another school if she meets with resistance. If Billy continues to receive the input that he is currently getting, he will quickly plummet. Another avenue Kathy can take is to help her son understand that he has two choices: (1) he can believe the teacher, or, (2) he can prove the teacher wrong.

You have to teach your children how to handle negativism. They need to know how to cope and respond to cruel and self-serving people. This takes a great deal of practice and continual reinforcement. They will be impulsive and reactive so be available for them when they need you. This may require you to campaign for your children and go beyond what you think you are capable of doing. They may need you to defend them from other adults. Katlin had a teacher who was emotionally abusing her students, including him. I volunteered in the classroom, worked with the principal, and set up strategies with the school psychologist. None of my efforts worked because the teacher didn't recognize that she had the problem. Finally, I initiated a campaign to remove her. The result: we were asked to leave the school. The administration said *we caused* too many problems. A year and a half later, the teacher was fired. The reason? Child abuse. It seems another mother launched a similar crusade. This time, the school decided that something had to be done. Meanwhile, children were damaged in the process. Katlin, luckily, had me to discount the teacher's attacks. But what happened to the kids whose parents blamed them for the problems they had with her? More troubling is how did the kids who never told anyone process the comments she made? If input is not given that contradicts these messages, how will the exposure affect them? Will they be able to rid themselves of the mask?

If you are coming from family violence, you automatically have strikes against you in the "real" world. Society cannot fully comprehend your circumstances. Therefore, you must take a stand for your children, because no one else will. The best way to help them is to have an open line of communication with everyone involved. Volunteer in the classrooms, keep a journal between you and the teacher, and talk to your children daily. This is time consuming, but necessary. You need to invest more time now so you have more time later. Right now, your days are spent putting out little fires, which makes life chaotic. For example:

- Your son was sent to the principal's office again.
- Your daughter struggles daily with her peers.
- Both kids are at each other's throats from the minute they come home.

Exhaustion will set in if too much energy is spent focusing on the negative. Your reaction as the adult will profoundly affect them. Therefore, give them something to strive for rather than correct. Help them find their goodness when other adults can't. The answer to motivating them to do well begins with how they feel: When they feel good, they are good.

When parenting in the aftermath of family violence, you are also dealing with your own grief. And although it is important to understand why your relationship with your partner did not work, your focus right now should be on how to get your kids back on track. Once your life is more orderly and you can handle their crises more effectively, then you can deal with your pain. Concentrating on your children helps you focus less on the trauma you experienced. You do not want to avoid your past, but you don't want to keep reliving it either.

Angry children grow up needing to control everything around them, including their partners and children. Unfortunately, without intervention, they will use aggression and intimidation to control their environments. As we discussed in Chapter 1, we carry our behaviors with us throughout our lives. If your children do not learn how to cope with their real emotions, they will see anger as their only means of getting their needs met. Think about your batterer for a moment. Was his childhood a happy one, or was it filled with the same rage he has now?

Abuse and Its Association

In family violence, there are many associations made that contribute to how children relate to the world. For example, Katlin was exposed to an extremely abusive man who drank heavily. Katlin learned quickly to correlate alcohol with violence. The more his abuser drank, the more violent the man became. Consequently, Katlin's reaction to drinking was over-exaggerated. One night he panicked when he saw me with a glass of wine, and bellowed out, "Why are you drinking that stuff?" Katlin's association made him fearful of alcohol and he absolutely did not want me to drink. I had two choices. I could stop drinking so he could think he was safe, or I could show him that drinking doesn't cause violence, people do. For the next several months, I would warn him when I was pouring a glass of wine and I would ask him to observe my behavior. Then we would discuss whether he thought my behavior was any different. Soon Katlin recognized that, in my case, there was no difference between a glass of wine and a glass of water. Walking him through this process is known as *desensitization*. This is a critical aspect of dealing with traumatized children. They need to see that the association is not real. Once they are desensitized, they will be able to drop their masks more easily.

Abuse and its associations can make life feel dangerous and scary. The emotional tactics that batterers use to control their victims can be so incomprehensible that dealing with the aftermath can feel overwhelming. Another example was a young boy who feared car engines. At the age of four, his abuser threatened to throw him out of a moving car. He developed a fear of car engines because he believed that his abuser's threat was real and an association was made. Consequently, this boy refused to ever get out of a car while the engine was still running. To help him overcome his fears, we started a desensitization process wherein we sat inside the garage with the door shut so he knew that we were contained in the building. I had him roll down his window and look out while the car was on. As he felt comfortable in the garage, we practiced opening the car door with the engine running. Next, we opened the garage door and started the process again. Once he felt safe, we inched down the driveway with the window rolled down. Eventually, he could open the car door with the engine running without being afraid.

Children develop reactions to the violence they experience. If you are victims of family violence who are starting over, your kids might need to be desensitized to those horrific events. Look for issues in their lives that might make them sensitive and help break down these vulnerabilities. Help them recognize that they are safe and that life is different from the past. Eventually, your children can build trust again; but be prepared, because this is not a quick fix. Katlin and I had to work together for over ten years. We saw progress, then setbacks; we experienced joy, then pain. That's the reality of parenting—even more so when you have lived through family violence. The best advice to get through this period is to start each day over, let go of yesterday, focus on today, and hope for the best for tomorrow. There will be a lot of tears and disappointments, but time and tenacity will win out. There were so many days when I found myself in awe over Katlin's progress, only to be discouraged the next day. The key is that we never gave up! But that is not to say that it came easily.

Understanding the Differences in Associations

The manner in which an injury occurs is significant to how children cope with their pain. When they associate injury with intent, the perception is amazingly different. One societal misconception is that physical assault is the more damaging to children's well-being, when in reality, the perception of the attack is more poignant. One example that comes to mind was the time Katlin got a black eye from playing baseball. It was the worst bruise he had ever had, and it looked painful. But, Katlin was proud of his shiner because of how it happened. Imagine, though, if I had given him the black eye in a fit of rage. Would his emotional perception still be the same? Of course, the answer is absolutely not. He would have felt shame and embarrassment, not to mention betrayal. Instead, he held his head high and proudly displayed his injury because of its association. He was excited about the attention. For this reason alone, society needs to stop looking at the physical aspect of abuse and start recognizing the emotional impact it has on children. We have minimized the perceptions and have done a great disservice to them. For example, victims often say, "Well, he never really hit my son, he only threatened him." The threat was always as real as the actual event and was enough to scare this child, so he never had to hit him. Get my point? If someone can be paralyzed and controlled through fear, then consider that person battered.

How to Get Back on Track

Being abused can create a sense of powerlessness that generates anger toward everything and everyone, including your children. Finding peace with this inner turmoil will promote more appropriate interaction, which will help your family get back on track. In Chapter 6, you will learn how to incorporate new parenting skills into your repertoire. As a result, your negative reactions will dissipate, and your kids' will too. Anger is natural; but how you respond to it is more important. Your children have witnessed anger as a terror tactic. Now, to be more effective, anger must be administered in a way that is appropriate, safe, predictable, and shows good intent.

In the parenting class I teach, I ask how many of the parents use time-out as a punishment. Many parents will invariably raise their hands. Then I tell them that time-out was never intended as a punishment, but instead, a positive experience—one where a lesson is learned, rather than an ego is bruised. Zig Ziglar, a motivational speaker, once said, "Discipline is *for* children and punishment is *to* children." Ask yourself which one you are teaching your children. Some parents feel that consequences have to hurt in order for the kids to learn a lesson. This is so untrue. You will want to re-evaluate your method of time-out and make it more positive. The following are the rules I use when applying this technique:

Attitude—should be good, not a punishment, time to reflect

Duration—one minute per every year of age, no more than five minutes

Application—upon completion of time-out, talk about choices and options, use eye contact, and be loving

Ownership—determine who really needs the time-out (it may be you), know your limitations and misgivings

Time-out and other forms of behavior modification are necessary to get your family back on track. This takes time and energy. Learning how to parent differently can seem overwhelming, but if you give it the attention it needs now, your family can learn how to participate more appropriately. Although inappropriate behavior is not acceptable, understand and correct your children accordingly. For example, when they scream at you, it is most likely because they don't feel heard any other way. It doesn't mean that they are trying to be disrespectful. Children have a right to get their needs met. As recoverers from family violence, your job is to help them find acceptable ways to accomplish that without them using intimidation, guilt, or other negative means. Use the following examples to deal with your children's yelling.

> *"Jimmy, I would really like to listen to you, but I can only listen to soft voices. When you say it softer, I will talk to you about it."* (Now walk into another room and don't react to him.)

> *"Jenny, its okay to scream into a pillow, but not at me. Let's try it. Now that you got that out of your system. Let's talk."* (Talk about anger and how natural it is.)

Children exposed to family violence learn patterns of communication and behavior that may take years to undo. They didn't get this way overnight, and they will not heal that quickly either. Remember, they didn't have a choice to be brought into these circumstances. Therefore, parents need to give them the patience and direction they need to heal from this devastating experience. This is a lot to ask, but kids need adults to show them the way. The family must unite as one to overcome this experience together.

When victims initially leave their relationships, the stress can be insurmountable. Ending the relationship may require them to move to another city and leave their belongings, friends, and job behind. To compound matters further, the violence and terror may cause additional emotional problems. It would be easy to lash out at the children and create explosive interaction within the family structure. The stress affects the kids as well. They may lash out and blame the victim for all the changes they have had to endure.

If you find yourself in this situation, just know that your kids will love you later for leaving, but your payoff won't be now. Parenting is a long-term investment, and immediate gratification is rare. When they lash out they are saying, "I hate that I am not in control of my life!" Do not personalize these outbursts. As hard as this sounds, walk away from verbal attacks as much as possible. Eventually, your kids will run out of ammunition. Their outbursts may temporarily detour your objective, but stay consistent and keep moving forward. When an episode is finally over and everyone is calm, discuss how each of you could have handled the situation differently. Your children are on an emotional roller coaster and they will need your help getting off.

Adolescence, especially, is a time for natural rebellion. But compound that with abusive role models and the dynamic can be overpowering. The goal here is for your family to learn what behaviors work and which ones do not. Children from family violence may experience developmental setbacks, which contributes to their problems. Maslow, a psychologist, explained the developmental processes as a hierarchy of needs. He said that growth and development could not occur until the basic needs for safety and love were met. Therefore, you may have to treat your teenagers like eight-year-olds because the abuse has literally stopped their emotional growth. You must meet those deficient needs first before they can move on. So forget chronological age. They may be physically old enough, but emotionally, they are incapable of handling what life throws at them. Lowering your expectations for your children can reduce everyone's frustration and create an environment that is more conducive to being successful.

Automatic Thought

Children with explosive personalities are more likely stuck in a mindset where they have automatic thoughts regarding outcomes. For example, in one family, a teenage daughter would become enraged when she would pour a bowl of cereal and realize that there wasn't any milk. To assist this teenager with her anger, we practiced self-talk. We warned her that obstacles occur and that "losing it" when things go wrong was not an option. So she practiced saying to herself, "Look in the refrigerator before you pour the cereal to make sure there is some milk." Next, she could tell herself in advance, "If there isn't any milk, there are other options for breakfast." As simple as this self-talk appears, impulsive/explosive personalities have an extremely difficult time with negative outcomes.

Many automatic thoughts come from a defensive stance that children learn because of the serious violence at home. Their current self-talk says, "Everyone is against me; and I never get my way." In any case, you must act rather than react to these situations. Find positive ways for your children to express their anger. They can go for a run, hit a punching bag or their bed, or they can write a letter and say what they want. It is important however, for them to recognize that lashing out only causes problems. Your job is to prepare them for the world. They must learn what society expects from them.

If you know what sets your kids off, start thinking about other options and work on supplying them with self-talk sentences that provide better choices. They need to learn how to give themselves new alternatives. Those role modeled to them in the past are not useful, and now you must retrain them. It always takes longer to undo what's been done. So don't be too discouraged when things do not work the first time. Practice, fail, practice, fail, and then practice some more. Eventually, they will get it. Reinforce their behavior by also self-talking. Be the best role model you can be. And when you do self-talk and it works, share your successes with your kids. The more everyone talks out loud, the faster this process takes place. This will improve their automatic thoughts.

Why Children Lie

In lives impacted by family violence, there is a certain belief developed by the victims. They have learned that the batterer will become violent when things do not go right. And as we know, this is a constant state of turmoil because the batterer is never happy. So if a child spills a glass of milk, and the batterer bellows out, "Did you spill the milk?" The natural reply will be, "No!" Why? Because, the batterer's anger made the truth too scary. Consequently, the child is too afraid to tell the truth. You may be saying to yourself right now, "Well they should not be afraid anymore, we left the relationship." Although true, know that you can take your children out of the abusive environment, but it may take years to take the abusive environment out of your children. You will have to encourage and show them that it is safe to tell the truth, but that comes with time. When dealing with your kids, it is so important (and I cannot stress this enough) that you communicate with them *from their perception base and not your own*. If they think the truth is scary, then the truth is scary. You have to approach them from a perspective that says, "I understand your fears and I will help you learn how to overcome them." Never discount or minimize what they feel. You can help your children by making the truth safe. The philosophy should be: If you want the truth, then reward the truth. For example, when you ask a child if she hit her sister, make sure you are ready for the truth. Do not say, "HOW MANY TIMES HAVE I TOLD YOU NOT TO HIT YOUR SISTER!!!" This approach will reinforce that the truth is scary and your effort will be moot. There are other means of correcting children other than punishment. You could say, "Thanks for being honest," then pick up the hurt child, take her to the other room and comfort her. The message will be clear that you do not like the behavior your child displayed without damaging her self-image any further. Correction must be done more constructively if you want to see results.

Why Does Anger Happen?

Through years of experience, I have realized that anger happens when we have no sense of control over a situation. It is when we lose this control that we lose our tempers. We feel helpless and are at a loss for what our alternatives are. As parents there are going to be times when we get mad. However, we can start working toward regaining the lost control and developing a healthier approach to parenting. For instance, as a victim in an abusive relationship, you may have cultivated unhealthy ways of dealing with your children by following the abusive examples set by your batterer. You don't like the way you are treating them, because it feels bad. What you are doing is a habit that must be broken. Now that you are out of the situation, you need to educate yourself and learn more positive ways to deal with your children's misbehavior. An example that comes to mind for me was the time I was volunteering at the battered women's shelter. I walked in on a victim feeding her infant daughter horseradish. Alarmed, I asked, "What are you doing?" She replied with a quiver and a whisper, "I have to make her stop crying, or we are going to get hurt." Is this a bad mother or one that is looking for ways to keep her family safe? Sounds incredible, but you would be amazed at what some people will do to stay alive. Look back on your own life and ask yourself, "What outrageous things did I do to survive?" Decide how much anger you may be harboring as a result of your abusive relationship. Then recognize how to regain your sense of control so your children have a better life. As you learn how to manage your life, you will also be able to manage your anger.

Managing Anger

Parenting is a hard enough job in itself, but your particular situation is compounded by the violence. The emotions your family faces are so much greater than anyone could possibly imagine. Words cannot describe the intensity of emotions that are running rampant through your life. Although these emotions seem insurmountable, you must choose how you react to them. Do not fall into the trap that your abuser used on you. Your batterer probably blamed his anger on what others did. Blaming others allowed him to not take responsibility for his actions. To teach your children that this distorted thinking is destructive, you must role model a more appropriate response. People who choose to allow the environment to control them are considered to possess what is referred to as an *external locus of control*. The bottom line in this perspective is that it is always someone else's fault that they are angry. Those who take responsibility for their anger have what is called an *internal locus of control*. This is where the individuals accept the responsibility for what they do. In order to lead a healthy and productive life, you must take charge of your own behavior and stop blaming others for your choices. To blame is lame, so stop doing it.

To become a person with an internal locus of control, you must first understand what causes you to react and why. Ask yourself if you allow the attitudes of others to get you down or if you can walk away from them unscathed. I'll give you an example. A woman trying to make an illegal left-hand turn in front of me was blocking the entrance to the bank, where I was going. I backed up as far as I could, but she still could not get around me. She wanted me to pass the bank and go around the block so she could make this turn. I refused because she was in the wrong. She finally pulled out and yelled, "Bitch!" My nephew in the passenger seat queried, "Why didn't you get mad and yell back?" I replied, "Because I didn't do anything wrong, and I am not going to let her ruin my day." I could have responded and raised my blood pressure, my heart rate, and my anxiety level, but I chose to let it go. I took away that woman's power. Her day however, was probably messed up because of her anger. Which of us had the internal locus of control? Who made the better choice?

Excessive anger eats away at our bodies and can cause many physical ailments. Some experts even believe there is a correlation between angry people and a higher rate of cancer. When we are angry and stressed, we actually produce chemicals that run through our body for an extended amount of time, creating havoc on our mental well-being. The release of these chemicals places our bodies in a high state of arousal. Being a parent is stressful enough, without allowing anger to consume us.

If you are a victim of family violence attempting to manage your children's anger, you must generate scenarios and options that will allow them to anticipate situations before they arise. For example, if you know your children get upset when they don't get their way, start preparing them in advance for the disappointment. Children do not think much further than the immediate moment. If you can prepare them for possible outcomes, then the surprise is not so great. In life, everything has a consequence, and your job is to teach your children how to use foresight. Give your children several different conclusions so they understand that every action has results: some good, some not so good.

Healthy Anger

As mentioned in Chapter 1, anger is one of the stages of healing, and children need to understand that anger is natural, but it must be channeled and expressed properly. Healthy anger allows for the release of the hurt that has been built up inside. Because most children who witness family violence see anger as dangerous and scary, they may overreact to others who express themselves in an aggressive manner. I will never forget the time I raised my voice in a group and one boy cowered down. I immediately responded, "It must be really scary when grownups yell." His reply was, "Yeah, sometimes they put guns to your head." That statement speaks for itself. The message here is that no matter how safe we think we are, battered children have learned that anger is terrifying. They have learned that when someone gets angry, the consequences are devastating. Understand that dealing with wounded children is different than dealing with those who are not. Utilize other means of communicating your anger so children can feel safe.

Another case in which a young boy reported spilling his glass of milk serves as an incredible and outrageous example. His father called him "Bitch," then he beat and raped his young son. Imagine the rage this young man has, and his only male role model taught him how to express that anger. This young man will need assistance learning healthy ways to vent the anger pent up inside him.

Disrespectful Children

Behind the mask of anger, children often display blatant disrespect toward the nonviolent parent. There could be a number of reasons for this. One is that now that the environment is safe, the kids are acting out the emotions that were locked up inside. Visualize the geysers at Yellowstone National Park. The pressure builds within them to a point where they explode. In the case of children who have been victims of family violence, this release was not possible in the past because the ramifications for acting out around the batterer could have severe consequences. These children need help channeling their anger. They need options so they can release their aggression without hurting others. More importantly, if your family is rebuilding after family violence, you must role model the same behavior you would like from your kids. We expect children to be respectful, but rarely is respect reciprocated to them.

If you are parenting in the aftermath of family violence, your children may be disrespectful toward you because they have learned from their batterer that "diss-ing" (the modern term) you gets them what they want. Or maybe, they yell at you because they feel it is the only way they can be heard. Think about it. When you yell, isn't it so people will listen? Usually, we don't yell because we feel like being mean. It is because we want to get our point across and we want some sort of compliance. I suggest that if your children are diss-ing you, say something like, "I *want* to listen to you because you are important to me (pause). Relax and tell me what's going on without screaming." When you tell them that you want to hear them and that you care how they feel, they are often more willing to use the more appropriate methods of communication. One way to help build better communication skills is to be more aware of your attitude. Kids feed off of the adult's emotions. It will be crucial at this point to not react in anger, but rather act with understanding. These kids have learned negative behavior, and they may test you. So resist the impulse to lash back. Utilizing a time-out for both of you will serve you better, and will be much more effective. Allow your children fifteen minutes to walk away from your conflicts, but then come back and discuss the situation. This break gives you time to re-evaluate your actions. As you practice more effective anger there may be times when they lash out, but they are able to recover immediately. If their attitudes improve, give them a break. The object is to get them to feel successful and view their situation differently.

Children exposed and trapped in family violence did not have the opportunity to view life in a positive way. Now freed, they must relearn how to interact with the world in a manner that will serve them well. If you are victims of family violence, you are virtually starting over with your kids, and the life they once knew no longer works for them. It has to become a part of their past. This process really starts with taking off the mask and letting the world see them for what they really are: great kids hoping for a happy childhood.

The fact that you had the courage and the strength to leave your batterer for the sake of your children shows your commitment to them. The best advice that I can give is to start each day over, believe in yourself, and never give up. Once you understand the mask of anger, your ability to parent will improve and so will the lives of your children.

CHAPTER 3

Breaking the Communication Barriers

Lack of communication gives others the opportunity to draw their own conclusions.

Children who experience family violence struggle with their emotions and how to express them effectively. In this chapter, we will address how to enhance communication and interaction with these kids. Teaching children to communicate is probably the most important part of parenting. When everyone communicates effectively, the rest falls into place.

The key to communication is listening intently. Adults sometimes forget to do that with children. You can get so wrapped up in your own emotional garbage that you fail to recognize what your kids need. In this chapter, you will learn how to view emotions through their eyes. Adults must realize that the children's perception is their reality, whether it is real or not. Fighting that only compounds the problems. It's like saying that there's no such thing as monsters. If they believe in monsters, telling them not to worry doesn't change that fear. If you ever want to see results, focus on the issues from their level of understanding.

As we learned in Chapter 1, there are emotional stages of healing to move through. Emotions, when left unattended, are magnified to a point where communication is misunderstood. Consequently, the relationship between the children and adults can become strained. The only way to recover from family problems is for the adult to initiate the changes. Children are incapable of seeing past their grief; but with your support, all things are possible.

What would appear as normal problems for average children can wreak havoc on these very special children. They struggle with how to effectively express themselves and deal with the intensity of their feelings. This inability to communicate appropriately is often due to being forced to hide their emotions. When there is an abusive parent in the household, verbalizing freely is often not an option for the rest of the family. Consequently, when victims finally flee their batterers, their children may allow the floodgates to open and the emotions often become uncontrollable. Dealing with their emotions can be taxing for a parent who is also struggling with the gamut of emotions she is experiencing.

To assist in this process, four verbal communication techniques will be discussed in this chapter: re-recording, RAVE (recognize, acknowledge, validate, and elicit a response), the sandwich effect, and indirect communication. With the combination of these four styles, your children should be capable of sharing their feelings more easily. Nonverbal communication methods will also be addressed to enhance your understanding of what your children are silently saying.

Re-recording

Children who have been berated, insulted, and humiliated have everlasting viewpoints regarding their self-image. Your job will be to change these viewpoints. Re-recording is a technique in which your children's old imprinted messages are taken and recorded over. You want to dub a new, more positive message.

In family violence, children are often criticized and verbally assaulted daily. They process the information and accept it as true. "I must be a stupid person because I can't do anything right." Children begin establishing behavioral patterns that fit the expectations that they are given. Thus begins a vicious cycle that creates problems that send these children into a downward spiral.

To combat these negative messages they must be given new input that states otherwise. For example, two sisters were constantly fighting. Their mother wasn't sure how much more she could take. Her task was to change her children's interaction with one another by re-recording. She was instructed to notice each time the sisters were not fighting and to tell them how great it was to have peace in the house and that she appreciated their new attitude. She was skeptical and said, "And that's all I have to do?" I said, "At this point, what do you have to lose?" Within one week, she reported with amazement that the kids had stopped fighting. As we talked about their success, I asked if she had ever used statements like, "Why can't you kids ever get along?" or "Why do you girls always have to fight?" She indeed admitted using this form of communication. What message do kids get with statements such as these? What expectations are being set for them?

It's never too late to turn communication around. Think about the negative ways you speak to your children. Write them down and turn these statements into positive ones. It takes work, but you will see some great results. Your kids want your validation and they will *want* to change if you believe in them.

Communicating is a skill and must be practiced as such. Starting today, schedule five times a day where you verbalize and re-record your new expectations to your children. Parents repeatedly say, "How can I tell them something that I know isn't true?" The answer is simple. Your batterer poisoned them with negative expectations that weren't true at the time and now they need you to undo the damage by countering that input.

At the age of five, Katlin was a compulsive liar. His lies were so insignificant that they didn't make sense. I decided to use re-recording on him. Everyday, I commented about his honesty and I'd watch his face contort and jerk. He didn't understand why I was saying this, he thought, "Doesn't she know that I am a bad boy?" I was relentless in my effort to change how Katlin felt about himself. Gradually, his lying stopped. Several years later, he professed, "I used to lie all the time when I first got here." I said, "Yes, I know." Bewildered he said, "But you always told me I was honest." To which I replied, "And you are." The idea behind re-recording is to retrain children to think of themselves differently. The only way to do that is to dub over what they have already accepted as true. The following are examples of constructing positive responses to behavior:

> "I've noticed that you didn't hit your brother all morning, I love that you have learned to keep your hands to yourself."

> "That kid at the mall was screaming at his parents. He must really feel bad about his relationship with them. I am grateful you and I can talk about our frustrations."

"Another kid died from a drug overdose. It must be awful to think that drugs make you feel better. I appreciate the choices you make to be drug-free."

"Wow, that kid brought a knife to school. I am glad you are smarter than that."

"That kid is a sore loser. It's a shame he can't see that winning isn't what is important, but rather, doing his best. You do a great job of that."

Statements such as these move your children in a more positive direction as they recover from family violence. They learn to understand expectation and how to really behave. To make re-recording more successful, announce your children's achievements to others. Make it a goal to talk about your children (a minimum of three times a day) with others when the kids don't think you know they are listening. Set it up so the person you are talking to responds in a positive manner. If you can't talk face-to-face with someone about your children, talk to them on the telephone. You can even pretend to be talking on the telephone if no one is around to listen. This reinforces what they have heard directly from you and promotes a new self-image. For example, the following types of comments are effective:

"Honey, you should have seen Jimmy today, this kid took his toy and instead of hitting him, Jimmy walked away. I was so impressed."

"Mom, Chad is doing so great. He is trying hard not to hit other kids. Last year he hit kids all the time and now he doesn't."

"Sally, Becky made really good choices today. What should I do for her?"

"Last week Julie was constantly hitting her sister, but now she is trying harder; she must be really proud of herself."

There are two other ways of conveying positive messages through re-recording. One is using *I* statements and the other is using *you* statements. Professionals have said for years that using *I* statements works best when confronting problems because using *you* statements creates defensiveness. People personalize *you* messages, their guard goes up, and these barriers shut down the listener. Therefore, *I* statements are essential when concerns need to be addressed.

Use the following as examples for applying *I* statements:

"I really struggle with seeing the dishes in the living room. Let's do something about that."

"I noticed that my feelings get hurt when I am ignored."

"I get a little upset when there is constant fighting. Could I get a break, just for tonight?"

"I had a hard day and I would like some quiet."

Can you hear what the concerns are? Taking *you* out of the conversation can diffuse a lot of the personalization. Review the example sentences and determine whether they are more effective than the following:

"*You've* left *your* dishes in the living room again. *You* need to get them picked up right now."

"*You* are ignoring me again. I hate it when *you* do that."

"Can't *you* two ever stop fighting? *You'd* think *you* would want to give me a break."

"Could *you* just be quiet for five seconds?"

Can you see how *you* statements are much more personal? With that knowledge, consider how utilizing *you* statements works in the positive—those who hear *you* through praise also personalize the comments. Therefore, use *you* rather than *I* statements when addressing good things. Use the following examples to get started:

"*You* must be proud of *yourself* for doing such a great job."

"I bet *you* feel good about *yourself* when you can brighten someone else's day like you did today."

"*You* must know how great *you* are because you never gave up."

"*You* have to know how special *you* are because you shine and people notice."

The message your children re-record subliminally is, "I must feel good about myself." Each time they get this message, it allows the old messages to be dubbed over. When they can personalize good behavior, they build a stronger self-image. When they are responsible for their good feelings, then external validation isn't so critical. They can determine their value and no one else can take that from them. What a wonderful gift to give to your children: the gift of self-actualization. Although everyone enjoys external validation, internal validation is better. When children feel good about themselves, they are less likely to be impacted by unwarranted criticism. They focus on how they feel rather than trying to please others. My youngest sister was much like this. People called her names and she would say, "Who cares?" Today, she is a beautiful and intelligent woman with endless possibilities. She recognized that what others said was simply not true.

When you re-record new positive messages, make sure to use plenty of eye contact. The more you connect with your children emotionally the more quickly they will respond to your communication. If you want the information to sink in, a physical connection is necessary. It's a form of bonding that allows your children to feel good. In the past, they probably dreaded eye contact because your batterer screamed, "LOOK AT ME WHEN I AM TALKING TO YOU!" They learned to fear the connection. Now you must help them gain the sense of security they need to make good choices. Avoid using your batterer's methods when correcting. Your kids need to feel safe when they are looking at you.

Re-recording takes many different shapes. In essence, you must reformat children's minds with new ideas about who they are. Therefore, changing your communication requires rewording your thoughts. Children, particularly those from family violence, often hate the word *no*. They have consistently heard, *No, can't, don't, shouldn't, couldn't, wouldn't.* They are resistant to these negative words and sensitized to them. Therefore, you must change how you speak to them. To begin this process, take as many negative words out of your vocabulary as possible. Only use *no* when it really counts. This is a difficult task, but one that must be conquered if you want to see results.

The following are a few ways you can change how you address your children: "Play over here" rather than "Don't play over there," "Walk" rather than "Don't run" and "Always remember" rather than "Don't forget." It takes a great deal of energy and consciousness to change sentence structure, but practice makes perfect. The effort is worth it when your kids start responding more positively. Initially, there may be some hesitation because they will hear your new communication styles and say, "Okay, who are you and what did you do with my mother?" Relax. They'll come around once they embrace your new ideas.

Cindy's son, Billy, suffers from low self-worth. In the past, his father referred to him as a, *"dumb shit"* or *"stupid ass"* to express his disappointment with Billy's bad grades. Descriptives such as these damage children's self-image and make it difficult for them to do better.

Children only live up to the expectation the adults give them. If a significant adult says that the child is a *"dumb shit,"* then there is not much motivation to be anything otherwise. Cindy needs help finding new adjectives to describe her son. The tough part is getting Billy to buy into the new messages because the other messages were so ingrained into his belief system.

I once heard that it takes forty positive statements to undo one negative statement. The number of times the young man in this example was told that he was stupid will determine the amount of work Cindy has ahead of her. The fact that he was fourteen before she left her abusive marriage will mean that she has a lot of work to do. This may sound discouraging, but kids are resilient. If you dedicate time to changing the way children have learned to interpret the communication, your efforts will pay off. There are no instant gratifications. It takes years to see the fruits of your labor.

One reason why children are so good at accepting negative input is the delivery of its message. How adults choose to express their dissatisfaction is much greater than how they choose to praise. Do we ever yell, "DID I TELL YOU WHAT A GREAT JOB YOU DID TODAY?" or "HOW MANY TIMES HAVE I TOLD YOU HOW GREAT YOU ARE?" Rarely do we acknowledge praise with the same level of energy that we recognize problems. Consequently, children "get it" when we are upset. They know what we dislike about their behavior simply by the way we communicate to them. Now, it's time to show them what we like. Change your delivery and make the message a good one. Recognize good behavior and start focusing on the positives. Raise your children with praise; re-record, change the message, and give them a new outlook on life.

Children need to view the world they once knew as a thing of the past, and they need reassurance that life from this point forward can be different. But this happens one day, one hour, even one minute at a time; that is all you can do. Each time you start to lose your ability to communicate properly, stop; take several deep slow breaths, then look for anything good to talk about.

Non-Critical Time

When you are learning to re-record you have to setup time that is positive. I hear that the first half an hour you greet your kids in the morning and after school is the most important time for setting the stage for good interaction. Therefore, this time needs to be positive.

A mother and her son fought from the minute they saw each other. The boy remarked that he would be nervous because his mother *always* came home complaining that the house was dirty. The mother agreed that she was upset because she knew there would be a mess waiting for her at home. She then proceeded to point to a small morsel of peanut butter on the wall and complained, "See what I'm talking about?" The smudge was so small I had to strain to see it. The problem here is she was looking for dirt and a reason to be upset. The house was orderly and neat. A chunk of peanut butter should not be such a big a deal.

To improve their communication skills, we established what I call *non-critical time*. For the first thirty minutes when the mother returned home, she was not permitted to point out any dirt. In turn, she would set the timer and give her son time to clean up. Knowing she could not say anything critical, she was able to give herself permission not to think about the dirt. Consequently, she would come home and ask her son how school went or if he had had a good day. For her son, the pressure was off. He didn't have to worry about her screaming as soon as she walked in the door. He was able to see his mother coming home as a good thing. This new communication process allowed them to think of more positive things to say. The defenses went down and so did the fighting. The old messages were erased and replaced.

When applying non-critical time, try not to caveat your praise with anything negative. For example, one mother would compliment her son's intelligence; then add a negative comment. She said in several variations, "Sam is so smart and could do anything if he just wanted to." Sam is getting the message that he doesn't want to. Because his mother ended with a negative comment, the intended message that Sam is smart got cancelled out. Bad communication skills do not make someone a bad parent. It just means these parents have to work harder to eliminate the criticism. This advice is easier said than done, but necessary. To implement this plan, during non-critical time, designate ten minutes per afternoon for talking about the day's positive events. Initially, your kids might think you are strange. They may even wonder, "Has my mother lost her mind? She never talks like this!" Don't be discouraged. Within two or three months, your children will catch on and follow your lead. One mother reported that her daughter only participated half the time when she started this process. The young girl was confused about her mother's new communication style. But as she observed her mother's continuous pattern, she accepted the change as genuine, and she started participating more receptively. Children often test their parents to see whether the new changes are real. They might sabotage your efforts to see whether you will remain consistent. If you stand fast, and refuse to cave into their criticism, the message will be clearly sent that you have changed. But if you fail the test by throwing your arms in the air and giving up, the message will be just the opposite.

How and when you choose to communicate will often determine the outcome of your interaction. Many parents fail with their communication because they are too quick to want to solve the problem, and it is often ineffective. Not only have they not solved the problem, they have added to it. When you live under the same roof 24/7 with your kids, even under the best of conditions, it can cause problems at some point. It is inevitable. Consequently, you cannot always avoid conflict, but you can choose how and when to react to it. Selecting non-critical time when the emotions are high could save a great deal of heartache.

RAVE to Your Children

RAVE, a successful communication technique that I developed, promotes healthier communication. The acronym means:

Recognizing your children's problems by utilizing the mask of anger

Acknowledging those problems because children do not want to

Validating your children so they know that what they are feeling is okay

Eliciting a response to the problems and talking out some alternatives

In Chapter 2, you learned to look beyond the anger and recognize what was really going on with your children. Now, you must acknowledge these issues for them because they absolutely do not want to tell you what their problems are. The two common responses children give when asked what is wrong are, "Nothing," or "I don't know." They look to you for guidance and you are the one that has to figure out the problem. After you understand what your children are thinking, you must validate their feelings. Adults so often say things like, "You shouldn't feel that way," or "Don't be silly, they do too like you." This invalidates their feelings and puts a communication wedge between parents and children. This type of response creates a top-down interaction that places the parent in a superior position—one that the children interpret as "You can't possibly understand what I am going through." To validate them, you must bring yourself to their level. Once children know that you recognize their true feelings, you can elicit a response that helps solve the problems. The following example occurred between an eleven-year-old son and his mother.

Son: "Can I stay out til midnight?"

Mother: "No."

Son: "All my friends think you're mean!"

Mother (using the RAVE technique): (R) "I bet it is really hard to have your friends think that I am mean. (A) That has to be really humiliating. They probably think I treat you like a baby. As a parent, everyday I have a lot of tough decisions to make about your life and I know that sometimes I am going to make the wrong ones. I make decisions based on how much I love, even though it sometimes feels like I do it to be mean. (V) I am guessing you want to grow up and you need some freedom so I am willing to negotiate and change other things that make you feel like a baby. (E) I would like you to think about other compromises we can make besides staying out late that will make you feel better. But the bottom line is that you cannot stay out until midnight. You are just too young. And in my opinion your friends that are allowed to stay out that late might not have parents that really care about their kids."

The issue here is that the child wants some independence without being teased. Growing up and separating from parents is a natural process. Children need to be guided in a manner that allows that healthy transition into adulthood without too grave of consequences.

Once the RAVE response occurred, this boy shifted from being incredibly upset to mellowing out within moments. His scowl softened immediately. This mother could have responded by saying, "I don't care what your friends think! Until they are paying my bills, I am the boss!" But would that have accomplished the same objective? Probably not. Although each part of the RAVE technique is essential, it is most imperative to validate, validate, validate. Validation takes most of the punch out of the fight because your children are trying to convince you that they are right. The debate cannot go much further if you are saying, "You absolutely have every right to feel that way." It doesn't completely take care of the problem, but it certainly knocks the anxiety level down a notch or two.

You can use RAVE with the scenario of an adolescent girl rolling her eyes at her parents. First, identify what her possible reasoning is for this blatant disrespect. Her projected attitude is due in part to her quest to become independent. She wants to think for herself and have her own independent thoughts. One way to achieve her goal is to become everything that her parents are not. Therefore, her reaction is to discount their opinions and think that they are stupid. This attitude is often displayed through eye rolling, contorted facial gestures, or blatantly ignoring adults. Adolescence can be a frustrating time for parents if they do not learn to let go. Parents must remember to grow with their children. And kids need more appropriate methods of expressing themselves. Examine the following use of the RAVE technique and determine whether it helps this situation.

(R) "I noticed that you have been rolling your eyes at me a lot over the last few days. (A) I know how hard it is to be a kid and feel like the grown ups around you don't take you seriously. (V) It is so natural to want to grow up and have your own thoughts. I bet there are times that you think I treat you like a little kid. And I am sure that sometimes I do. (E) So what I want you to do is sit down and write a list of things that I do that make you feel that way. Then I will sit down and write a list of things that I feel I have to constantly remind you to do that make me feel like you are still a little kid. Tonight, we can look at our lists and I will do my very best to respect what you are saying and work toward changing my behavior. And in return, you have to look at my list and make some changes so I can feel good about letting you grow up. However, under no uncertain terms can you roll your eyes at me. I don't roll my eyes at you and I would like the same courtesy extended to me."

This example shows the validation along with negotiation. You must make your kids think they are winning and that they have a say in their lives. They appear angry and upset because they feel that people are not listening to them. Consider how frustrating it must be to feel invisible and unheard. Compound that with the inability to communicate appropriately and you have children who think their only option is to be obnoxious. Remember what it felt like to be a kid and find alternatives that might have worked for you. They might not always work because your kids are not you, but it is a place to start.

Sherri was angry with her mother, Jennifer, for not giving her money when she "needed" it. Jennifer is frustrated because her daughter has asked for money for three days in a row and she felt she needed to set some boundaries. Sherri reacted harshly and decided to lash out at her mother by telling her that she was keeping the Mother's Day gift that she had made for her. Sherri's reaction hurt her mother. Jennifer chose, however, not to express her disappointment but rather to utilize the RAVE technique and to validate Sherri's feelings. Jennifer reported that once she verbalized and appreciated her daughter's feelings, Sherri was remorseful for lashing out. After reflecting on her behavior, Sherri asked her mother if she would still act surprised if she decided to give her the gift. To Jennifer's credit, she responded positively by saying with a smile that she would act surprised. She permitted her daughter to recover from her mistake.

Using the RAVE technique is difficult initially because you have to really practice what you want to say to your children. The propensity, most often, is to just deal with the problems by pointing them out. Think about your communication with your children and whether it is effective. If the answer is no, then try using RAVE and see what happens.

Sandwich Effect

The sandwich effect is a technique used to take a concern that you have regarding a child's behavior and place it between two positive statements. The purpose in using this technique is to lessen the blow of criticism. The truth is, your kids, coming from family violence, have been hit hard enough emotionally. They need a softer touch and the sandwich effect is just the thing to do the trick.

Kids, especially those coming from family violence, struggle with disapproval. They internalize negative comments and accept them as truths. It is possible to address concerns with your kids without hurting them. Consider using the sandwich technique for the following concerns:

1. Your child is hitting her younger sibling.
   "I noticed today at your friend's house that you were so gentle with his sister. I bet you could use that same technique with your brother. The fact that you were able to keep your hands to yourself shows that you are really maturing. Keep up the good work!"

2. Your child is disrespectful toward you after his visits with his dad.
   "Grandma told me that you were very patient with her on Friday. She says that you were respectful and that you didn't lash out at her when she asked you to take out the trash. It is great that you are trying harder to make good choices. I bet we will be seeing the

same changes at home. It made me feel really great to hear Grandma bragging about you."

3. Your child is getting a D in science.
   "Your teacher tells me you are doing very well in math. She says you are at the top of the class. You must be so proud of yourself. She is somewhat concerned about science. But, the fact that you have done such a great job in math says that your heart is really into doing a good job. So I thought we could work together on your science. I am glad you take pride in what you do."

Do you hear the concerns? The easy way out is to hit the problem head on; but is it effective? Do children gain the desire to improve their behavior? To be successful with the sandwich effect, make a relationship between things your children do well and your concern so they can make a good connection. If you soften your technique, they will be motivated to do better.

Indirect Communication

As a child, did you learn lessons by being told directly what to do or did you learn them the "hard way?" My guess, more times than not, is that it was the latter. Therefore, using the direct approach with children often does not work. It is their job, as it was yours, to grow up and be free thinkers with independent thoughts. To establish their individuality, we cannot solve their problems for them. So where do we draw the line between guiding children and ruling their lives? We hate seeing them make bad decisions. Yet, how can they learn if we do not allow them to make mistakes? We start by motivating them indirectly. To encourage children to *want* to do the right thing, we must find ways to approach them which are not so obvious. They need to think they are making the choices rather than us. It may seem ludicrous, but it is necessary.

An adolescent girl who had broken her leg strutted out of her bedroom wearing high-heeled shoes and a cast. I could have directly told her how ridiculous she looked, but she would have blown me off. So, I needed to find an indirect approach that made her think she was in charge. I pondered, "What motivates adolescent girls? (*pause*) Boys." We talked about how to accentuate her broken leg to get them to notice her. She immediately retrieved a pair of crutches to enhance the *look*. Next, I queried, "How do you think boys would view crutches with heels? Would they think that was stupid or smart?" She disappeared momentarily then reemerged wearing tennis shoes. Saying directly how ridiculous she looked makes the point, but does it work as effectively?

A story retrieved from the Internet serves as a perfect example for utilizing the indirect approach. A principal in Oregon was having problems with her female students. The girls were applying lipstick then kissing the bathroom mirror. After countless and unsuccessful attempts to use direct approaches to make the behavior stop, she gathered them in the bathroom and had the custodian demonstrate how difficult it was to clean the lipstick off the mirror. A cleaning brush was dipped into the toilet and the mirror was scrubbed down with toilet water. The girls were mortified to think their lips had touched that mirror. Consequently, lipstick on the mirror was never a problem again. Why? Because the principal found an indirect means of motivating these girls. Lessons are caught, they are not taught. Until they personally experience the revelation, our guidance doesn't work.

Children need to learn how to problem solve on their own. At some point, we will not be there to make decisions for them. We have to change our approach to one that makes us more of a mentor rather than a parent. Consider viewing them as though they were apprentices rather than children. They will make mistakes just like we did. It's a part of growing.

Children's Perception

When children perceive their world as unsafe; that is the reality for them. We must respect their perception. Using a direct approach won't change their minds. The challenge is that children process differently than we do. They do not possess adequate language skills to fully comprehend a situation in the same manner as adults. Most behavioral problems are due in part to poor language and communication skills. Children are coming from a limited language base and they must draw upon what little knowledge they have to make their conclusions. For example, a boy was preparing for a bath and yelled out in frustration, "Mom, Paige used all the cold water!" He knew from his experience that hot water runs out. When his bathwater was too hot, he deduced that his sister used all the cold water. This is his reality and the issue had to be resolved from his perspective, not his mother's. To an adult, this seems humorous; but for the boy, it was very real and frustrating.

Breaking the Communication Barriers

Nonverbal Communication

Now that we have discussed verbal means of communicating, let's look at the nonverbal ways that we speak to others. Body language is at least 80 percent, if not more, of our communication. Therefore, recognizing your children's body language is imperative. The following scenario might help you understand how important it is to watch how your children speak to you without saying a word.

Your child has had a bad day at school; you've HAD it, because your day has been filled with demands. Your child enters the kitchen and starts slamming things around while you are cooking dinner. His attitude seems disrespectful and downright rude; you lash back as you are stirring your mixture, not noticing that he has a bandage on his covered arm. He storms out of the kitchen and you begin to fume, confused about what has just happened. Later, you find out that he has been in a fight at school and his elbow was injured as he was slammed into the ground. The problem here was that you were not reading his body language. You only recognized the anger. The fact that he came to see you suggests that he wanted support and reassurance. But what he got was a bad reaction, which exacerbated his current state. Anytime a child lashes out, you can bet something is going on inside his head. He probably had an intense look on his face and agitated body language. And there is a good possibility that his eyes were not making contact with yours. These are signs of a child screaming out in silence, and you weren't listening.

One way you could have solicited information from him would have been to sit next to him; look at him intently and say, "Wow, it looks like you had a really hard day." By moving across the room and focusing on him, his interpretation could have been, "My mom is paying attention to me; she hears me; and I am important." Children need to know that you are listening even when they are not verbally saying anything. They desperately need you to see what the problem is. Children from battered homes learn early that their feelings and thoughts are unimportant. Now, you must recognize their emotions, put words to them, and teach them how to cope more appropriately with those intense feelings.

Another form of nonverbal communication is the written word. Sometimes physically writing down your children's needs is helpful. They may have learned to disregard verbal praise and cannot internalize your comments because they are incapable of hearing it. Writing their ideas on paper so their words are more concrete and *heard* can serve as an excellent way to communicate with your kids. If you are a single parent supporting the family financially and emotionally, your children may not be getting much attention from you. You are treading water like a dog in the middle of a lake, just trying to survive. You may not have taken the time to acknowledge the great things your kids have done. Now, they are in bed and it's too late. By morning you will have forgotten the good deeds, because you will be combating a new day. What can you do?

For starters, you could write a list that shows that you are paying attention. Writing is a great way to express your thoughts and it is visual. Before you pass out from exhaustion, sit down and journal your observations for the day. In the morning, leave your notebook in plain sight for your kids to see. Acknowledge them as often as possible by writing down what you feel. Here are some examples:

"I noticed you cleaned your room today. Wow!!!!"

"I saw that you were helpful today when your sister was struggling with her homework."

"It was great that you didn't complain when I made the dinner too salty."

"You handled yourself well when you found out I couldn't afford those new shoes you wanted."

Never throw away the list; just keep adding to it. The longer the list, the better. When their accomplishments are on paper, they are viable and more concrete, which makes them more real. Seeing them on paper is less intimidating and may give your children permission to privately accept what you are saying as true. Your kids desperately want to believe they are good; but when coming from family violence, the message until now has probably been that they aren't.

We have covered a great deal of information regarding communication. Learning these changes will require practicing them. Do not try to accomplish everything at once. Take one technique at a time, master it, and then move to the next. When you have achieved each of these new skills, you can break the communication barriers that have impeded your family's life. Your kids will be on their way to a healthier and happier childhood. Good luck and keep talking.

CHAPTER 4

Attitude Adjustment: Shifting the Paradigm

A stump in the road is either a stumbling block or a stepping-stone.

Much of what you've learned so far is how to recognize and understand why your children have developed distorted thinking. In this chapter, you must take your newfound knowledge and shift the distorted thoughts to more positive, healthy ones. Overcoming the obstacles your batterer created will be the most challenging, yet rewarding, feats you will ever accomplish. Children look to adults for guidance and want to believe them when they say that life can be good. They just need permission to do so. Children are conditioned to respect their elders, to not talk back, and to believe that adults are always right. Although under normal circumstances these philosophies have good intentions, they also lend themselves to producing victims. Not every adult deserves to be respected. The media regularly reports how adults are charged with abusing their position of trust. For your children, the violator was most likely your spouse. Your children believed the piercing messages he inflicted upon them. Now, you need to turn each message around and shift the paradigm. In other words, change your children's current thought process and make it better. Although the focus of this book is primarily on your children, remember the impact the violence had on you. Use the tools in this chapter to help yourself as well as your kids so that you all can begin a new life together.

Pound 'em with Positives

Inundating children of family violence with praise can break the negative thought patterns that they have developed. Remember, it takes a lot of acclaims to undo those old destructive messages from the past. So re-record over them with tons of good stuff. Pounding your children with positives may feel awkward, especially if you have never been praised yourself. It is natural to feel uncomfortable initially. This is a common obstacle that many parents experience. The concept of praise is so foreign to them that merely thinking about using it feels fake and insincere. It takes practice to overcome the discomfort that goes along with this shift. You must see your praise as a form of recovery and damage control.

How do you undo those hateful and cruel words? One way is to start establishing a targeted amount of time each day to praise your children. The praise will be accepted more easily when you apply a gentle smile and touch with the words. A warning should be made, however. Depending upon how your children have internalized their abuse, they may struggle with compliments and may sabotage your efforts. In Chapter 5, you will learn more about how to understand children's reasoning.

The following exercise helps combat your children's belief system by mounting positive input. Buy a bag of M&Ms or Skittles and tell your kids, "For every good thing you can think of about yourself, you get a piece of candy, and for every bad thing you can think of, I get a piece." Without fail, children can find things that are positive to say. If at first they are struggling, help by verbalizing to them, "Well, did you hit anyone today?" When they say no, give them a piece of candy and say, "Well, that's a good thing." When the exercise is complete, have them count the candy in both piles and ask them whether they feel bad or good. Next, explain that each time a piece of candy is consumed they must remember how good they are. Make the exercise fun by saying, "Hey, you are way ahead of me on candy, not fair!" Use a lot of animation and joy in your tone of voice. For those children who are not motivated easily, they may need help feeling good before any external reward can be beneficial. We will learn more about that later.

Attitude Adjustment: Shifting the Paradigm

Understanding the Spirited Child

Your child might be willful and spirited, but others view her as a "An obnoxious brat." Adults who interact with these distinct attitudes often misunderstand these very special children. As you attempt to overcome the effects of family violence, your job will be to teach your child how to cope with societal expectations. Spirited children's traits will serve them well in adulthood. They become great leaders: they are presidents, top sales people, and famous quarterbacks. But for now, most adults find these children difficult and challenging. One mother complained that her daughter's spirited attributes were annoying. I personally found this young lady to be refreshing and vivacious. Unfortunately, her mother did not see it that way. Without a paradigm shift, this little girl will be viewed as a "problem child." She will most likely accept the label and live up to the expectation given to her. These kids stand out in the crowd and think independently. As annoying as this may seem now, there are some advantages later in life to possessing this quality.

Some see spirited children as defiant with an unwillingness to conform. Barbara Coloroso, a renown parenting expert, professes that the benefit to children who are not adult-pleasers is that they are not peer-pleasers either. Although their inconformity is not always pleasant, it serves them well because they will not bow down to peer pressure. Therefore, a shift in the paradigm would allow you to see this trait as an attribute rather than a flaw. With the proper guidance, spirited children have an incredibly bright future. We just have to survive their childhood. An art teacher once said, "Katlin is a high-maintenance kid; but I'd rather have ten of him than one that just sits there." These were the first positive words ever spoken on Katlin's behalf regarding his spirited nature. His behavior had not changed, but the attitude of the adult had. At that point, I shifted my paradigm and viewed his spiritedness differently. If others could see his personality as good, I had to also.

Spirited children who are singled out as different will see those disparities as bad. Those differences may push them away from their family and other support groups. They might compare themselves to others and feel resentment toward them. Children need help feeling more connected to the group. Otherwise, they will feel like outcasts. Each message that reinforces that they are different moves them toward rejecting others to avoid being rejected first. One mother lamented that her son refused to eat breakfast with the family. I explained that he probably felt his family didn't want him there. Therefore, he made it easy on everyone by being indifferent and apathetic. When the family did not challenge him and insist that he participate with the family, he deduced that they really didn't love him. I suggested that she prepare his favorite breakfast and adamantly refuse to let him leave without eating. To her surprise, her son sat down and ate. She initiated this ritual each morning. What followed was amazing. This mother reported that their interaction improved, and he started spending time with his family. The changes in this young man occurred because the mother shifted her paradigm and stopped believing that he hated his family.

The Buildup in Perception

Children may spiral downward when a paradigm shift does not occur. Each reaction to their personality serves to compound their negative self-image. Children learn what they live.[1] As a result, they only live up to the adults' expectation. When a child receives the message that he is stupid and incompetent, he might resist doing his homework because of his sense of failure and inadequacy. Unwittingly and wrongly, the adults view him as lazy. When his report card comes, the grades are as bad as he expected. He skips school because he hates that "stupid" place. To avoid confrontation with his mother, he decides not to come home for the entire weekend. His problems increasingly worsened because his self-perception deteriorated. This mother's options when her son returns home are to punish him further or to try and understand how this got so out of hand. The message thus far has been that this boy is bad. Will punishing him make a positive difference or will it reinforce his feelings? In this particular case, the young man's inadequate feelings were punishment enough. Instead, a hug and some reassurance could promote better feelings. The goal is to stop the buildup in perception and shift the paradigm.

Another mother reflected on her daughter's perception buildup and realized that an educational downfall occurred in the seventh grade. Each year since that time, her grades and attitude gradually declined. This mother admitted that her daughter had complained years earlier that her seventh-grade teacher was mean. She minimized her daughter's comments, then stood by and watched her grades and self-esteem plummet. She never made the connection between that teacher and her daughter's decline until later. This experience compounded every aspect of her daughter's life and was detrimental to her emotional growth. Any teacher who is mean does not deserve credibility. The old messages must be discounted. This young girl needs to evaluate the teacher's character and determine whether the criticism deserves any acknowledgement. Undoing the buildup in perception will move her in a direction that is more conducive to healthy development.

Selective Editing

Selective editing is a process whereby individuals unconsciously choose to edit the information given to them to reflect their self-image. Children are programmed to focus on their faults. Therefore, they often edit the input given them to match that perspective. For instance, you say ten nice things about them, but their perception conflicts with that. Then you say one negative thing and they embrace it.

Throughout life, we all develop associations that generate editing and we react to those connections. An example may be that you were very poor as a child. Children teased you relentlessly. You are triggered when you see a dirty and unkempt child being pushed around in the schoolyard. You react by standing up to the kids only to find out that the girl had taken a knife and slashed one of the kid's jackets. Your association with being poor and how it made you feel edited the information. This type of interpretation is referred to as *perception goggles*. We all have a pair. We can view the same experience completely differently depending upon how we edit. Your job will be to find your children's visual prescription and make the corrections for them to edit more positively.

Making Peace and Managing Chaos

Peace is not familiar to kids of family violence. To make peace, you must understand how chaos plays a part in your family's lives. Chaos is not something abused families enjoy, but chaos feels comfortable for those who live with it. When chaos becomes an everyday part of life, it simply becomes *normal*. To change the paradigm, assess how you view chaos.

- Do you feel like you are going against the grain?
- Does your life feel out of sorts?
- Do you run around putting emotional fires out all day?
- Do you feel like you are always running and getting nowhere fast?

If you answered *yes* to these questions, you are probably living in chaos. Now to make peace, you must slow down and make some significant changes. This may require that you interpret your chaos differently. For instance, the Chinese have a symbol that represents both chaos and opportunity. Which meaning would that symbol have in your life?

To recognize chaos as an opportunity you must establish certain criteria to change its meaning. Chaos must be defined before it can be managed. For example, a clean kitchen and a neatly made bed may give you a sense of order. Everything else can be cluttered; but when those two criteria are met, you feel organized. When they are not, life feels chaotic, disjointed, and out of sorts. To reduce your chaos and then maintain peace, identify areas that calm you. Do a little each day by setting goals you know you can accomplish. Make them small so they are not too overwhelming. As the Chinese proverb states, a journey of a thousand miles starts with one step.[2] As you bring order into your life, your kids will find order in theirs.

How to Shift the Chaos

Children from family violence suffer with cluttered thoughts. They are preoccupied and constantly reliving the violence in their minds. One doctor explained it as a low-grade white noise that sounds like static in their heads. The interference makes it difficult to focus. This could explain why some children appear to be ignoring others or falling behind in school. They are inundated with stimulation and are unable to filter all the information being thrown at them. To clean out the clutter, provide structured time for them to sort things out. Their lives have been filled with chaos and anxiety. They need to take time to clean out the cobwebs.

Children with cluttered minds usually deal in the here and now. Expecting them to be introspective or to "see the light" is unrealistic. Foresight comes with experiencing consequences through hindsight.

They haven't lived long enough to develop that talent. They need your wisdom to change. They will want to lead a better life when they understand that a better life is possible. Therefore, you have to be their inspiration. Recognize, however, that just because you may have had a revelation and changed your attitude doesn't necessarily mean your kids will immediately change theirs. They have to determine whether your new shift is the right choice. Be consistent and positive in your role modeling, and you can show them how to live their lives differently. Be patient, they will get it. The lessons you give to your children are not always comprehended immediately. But as they watch them work for you, they will incorporate them. Remember, your batterer always won with his methods. Your children learned that his behavior worked. Now, you must teach your children how to get what they want without using intimidation, manipulation, and guilt. Once you provide them with other options, you create choices for them that they did not have before. But again, the clutter must be removed before learning can take place.

Having cluttered minds generates stress. For that reason, some people are more affected than others. Some worry about everything while others just seems to glide through life. People who appear unaffected by stress have chosen to not personally invest in it. In other words, they no longer want to give their energy to all the little things. They realize that by reacting to the external environment, their focus gets lost. A man on the Candid Camera show was once asked why he didn't get angry by their trickery. His response was, "I don't let anyone rent space in my head." This is a profound statement, which says it all, and I, for one, will incorporate this philosophy. It is time to remove the clutter and clear your minds.

Stress Management

Parenting is an incredibly hard job that can drain us to the point of exhaustion. To maintain a healthy perspective, we may have to start looking at our situations differently. Being vulnerable to stress could be due to having continuous negative thoughts that take on a life of their own—before the person knows it, he or she is consumed with destructive thought patterns. Essentially, he or she has given into those bad thoughts. This thought process could be compared to growing strawberries. A strawberry plant produces shoots, which spread throughout the garden. As the vines grow, they root themselves into the ground. In time, more shoots appear and root. If they are not uprooted, the vine engulfs the entire garden. The strawberries eventually choke out the other plants and all you have are strawberries (or negative thoughts). You can use this same scenario in a positive manner to shift your paradigm. Say all you want in your garden are strawberries (this time, positive thoughts). Allow the vine to spread, root, and grow until you have a magnificent strawberry patch.

To stop having negative thoughts, shift your attention to one that is more positive, and then add five related thoughts that shift your paradigm. This is not so easily done, but if you want to feel better, you will. It is a matter of choice.

The Impulse to React

You must be careful not to personalize your children's behavior and impulsively react. They are so confused as to where to lay the blame for how they feel. Their attitude toward you can fluctuate from love to hate. Reacting to those moments will only compound your relationship with them. When you stop internalizing their behavior, you can minimize reacting inappropriately to them. Their disposition, in return, will improve. Your children need your help to see themselves differently, which may require you to alter your perception of them. One way to support this would be to view today as though it was your last day to ever be with them. Amazingly, your reaction toward them will be noticeably different. When you say to yourself, "This could be the last time I see my children" you will accomplish two goals. One is that your children see themselves differently because of your attentiveness, and two, you live without regret because you were there for them when they needed you.

When you take the time to give to your kids, they will notice. However, don't expect too much because it won't be too profound. Pick one day per week when you shift your paradigm and take the time to enjoy your children. You will be amazed at how good it feels to focus on their childhood instead of your drudgery. One mother reported using this philosophy and watching her child glow. Her son had forgotten his helmet at home. Normally, she would have said, "That's too bad, you should have remembered it." But because she was viewing this as her last day with him, she returned home and retrieved it. Because she was willing to go home and get the helmet, he received two messages that day: (1) "My mom cares about my safety," and (2) "I was worth making the extra trip." In the past, she was restrictive and limited. Now, she felt good about her new outlook. I bet this young boy's attitude for the rest of the day was great because his mother's impulse to react was different.

Absolutes

Every child at some point in his or her life uses absolutes like *always* and *never*. This is particularly true of children from family violence because they develop distorted views of how the world treats them. They may verbalize statements such as:

"No one ever cared about me."

"My parents never respected me."

"My sister always gets her way."

Most children who use absolutes really mean what they are saying. These are genuine emotions that need to be guided in a different direction. Basically, there are few instances where anything in life is *always* or *never*. Your kids need to learn that life doesn't hold these absolutes. To address this problem, make the absolutes that they are complaining about the consequence for one week. Do not be cruel or hurtful when applying the consequence. Warn them in advance that you are applying this consequence, so the impact will be less when you follow through.

Absolute: "You always get your way."

Consequence: "No, I don't want to eat at Burger King today; I like Taco Bell and since I always get my way, we will eat there today. Maybe we can eat at Burger King next week."

Absolute: "I always have to go to the basement to get my clothes out of the dryer."

Consequence: Day one: "Your clothes are always in the basement, so that is where you will find your pants." Day two: "Your clothes are always in the basement, so go there to get your socks." And so on.

Absolute: "You are always mad at me."

Consequence: (Because staying mad for an entire week is unhealthy, become sickly sweet.) Day one: "Oh, THANK YOU, THANK YOU for picking up your toys." Day two: "WOW! That is soooo great that you ate your dinner." Day three (with total *ad nauseam,* they will plead): "Please stop!"

When your children can moderate the extremes, you are well on your way to shifting the paradigm. Think about it—didn't your batterer live in extremes? Weren't the family dynamics either high or low? No wonder so many children are now being diagnosed with bi-polar disorder. Living in extremes can have mind-altering consequences.

One reason people, especially children, use absolutes is because they do not know what makes them happy. It is easier to look at life and see what is missing. You don't hear children say, "I always get to do what I want." In order to shift the paradigm, eliminate absolutes as much as possible.

Making the Shift

Making the paradigm shift and modifying your attitude requires awareness. You have to recognize your misgivings, make a plan to improve them, and then practice your new behavior. Dedicate time to any given problem, find an answer, and then turn it around so your situation looks different. Do not work on another problem until you master your current one. Your problem can be in parenting, or it can be with yourself. Whatever the case may be, schedule time to work on these changes and start living a healthier life.

The following two issues can be used to begin your shift:

- You say *no* to your children more than you say *yes*. You recognize that they are frustrated and disappointed because you "never" do anything with them. To change your negative mental attitude, change the concept of "Not" to "Why not?" For instance, when your children want to stop to play in a sprinkler, rather than say, "No. Stay out of there, let's go." Think "Why not" and say, "Sounds like fun, go ahead." We get so caught up in daily obligations that we forget to have fun. But the time has come to move past the negative and embrace life.

- Your family uses criticism and sarcasm toward one another and everyone feels miserable. They have learned to name-call, berate, and taunt each other. In your new environment, you realize that this attitude is unhealthy and it creates unnecessary tension. Your children need to change how they interact with each other by practicing new communication skills. This requires learning new skills that meet everyone's needs without hurting others in the process. Give your children phrases that will assist them. For instance, say you would like your children to ask you rather than tell what they want. The shift, therefore, would be a less demanding and more humbling approach:

Old Shift

Your child: "Get me a drink, now!"

You: "Those words are too harsh for me. Say it again please and this time say it more nicely."

New Shift

Your child: "Can you please get me a drink?"

You: "Absolutely, since you said it so nicely, I'll get it right away, thank you."

As simplistic as this sounds, it takes practicing positive parenting to make the shift. A good place to begin is with praise. Unfortunately, making this shift isn't so easy. There are at least two explanations why some parents do not praise their children. Some feel children are supposed to do the right thing without any acknowledgement. Others simply feel relieved when they don't have to correct their children that they do not say anything at all. What message do your kids get when they only hear criticism? How do they achieve good feelings about themselves without the praise? Consider what you would have liked your parents to say to you and work from there.

> One young teenager complained that she had cleaned the house to surprise her mother. She was proud of her accomplishment and anticipated that her mom would be really pleased. But to her dismay, her mother criticized her for moving items around in the cupboards and demanded that she put them back in their original order. Her mother's critical attitude deflated the adolescent. If this young girl doesn't feel that she can ever please her mother, she will stop trying.

The goal for your family, I hope, is to find the positive attributes about one another and build on them. Your history has been filled with anger, disappointment, and negativism. Your family needs to find fun and positive ways to interact with one another. Learn to cook meals together, play games, and hug each other. Tell jokes and talk about funny things that have happened to you over the course of your day. Laughter is probably something that was lost in your life of family violence. Reclaim your life and shift the paradigm.

One mother reported that her son was putting himself down. He was frustrated and began complaining about how bad his life was. She decided to add what she saw in his life that was good. She turned the conversation around and reminded him that in one month, he received a pay raise, bought a car, and started back to school. By the end of the conversation he was announcing his other accomplishments to her. This family suffered from critical comments for more than fifteen years. This young man was simply repeating the messages his abuser gave him. That day, this mother realized that when she thinks positive, her kids listen.

Each night determine whether your day was well-spent. Did you do anything positive to change your life? If the answer is no, then do something about it—yesterday is gone and tomorrow is never promised. Today is all that matters. When your life has meaning, then your energy level increases and your outlook improves. When your attitude is positive, your children's will be too.

A little boy is telling his Grandma how "everything" is going wrong. School, family problems, severe health problems, etc. Meanwhile, Grandma is baking a cake. She asks her grandson if he would like a snack, which, of course, he does.

Grandma: "Here, have some cooking oil."

Boy: "Yuck!

Grandma: "How about a couple raw eggs?"

Boy: "Gross, Grandma!"

Grandma: "Would you like some flour then? Or maybe some baking soda?"

Boy: "Grandma, those are all yucky!"

Grandma: "Yes, all those things seem bad all by themselves. But when they are put together in the right way, they make a wonderfully delicious cake!"

This example, circulated on the Internet, serves as a reminder that attitude is everything. Start looking at the big picture: you left the abusive relationship, your bruises are healing, and your kids are more relaxed. The small things will work themselves out, one at a time. Start focusing on and being proud of your accomplishments. When someone compliments you on a job well done, do not minimize your efforts with the phrase, "Yes, but . . ." It does not give you the opportunity to feel content. Embrace your successes as often as possible. Enjoy those moments; you deserve them. You will recover more quickly from the drudgery of the past when you take care of yourself and have a sense of purpose. Reflect on the following questions:

Are you just getting up and breathing, or are you driven by a cause or purpose?

Do you have goals that move you in a direction other than your current path?

Life beyond abuse starts with change. You must create a paradigm shift that allows you to look at life's obstacles as though they were simply interruptions rather than roadblocks. Usually what happens is adversity rears its ugly head and gets in the way of your goals. Life happens and obstacles occur. You have two choices: You can succumb to them by curling up and getting kicked, or you can assess the interruptions, then change your strategies to incorporate your new challenges. The trek you are on might be difficult, but you will still get where you need to be.

I heard a speaker at a conference address the variations of personal journeys with the following analogy. There was a vertical road on a steep hill. One bicyclist at the top of the hill and one at the bottom were each trying to reach a bike path, which ran horizontally and crossed through the center of this road. One bicyclist coasted downhill to get to the path while the other labored uphill. Both met on the path and road along side one another. Although they met at the same place on the path, their journeys were different. Once the goal was reached, it did not matter how the cyclist got there, only that they did. The harsh reality is that you have an uphill battle to climb. But, I can tell you from experience that it is all worth it. Find your purpose. Seek peace in your life. Start by changing your attitude and making the shift. It will allow your children to start making the changes in their lives as well.

Childhood Depression

When we think of depression, we rarely consider it as a childhood problem. It is an illness that is generally viewed as an adult issue. Some believe that people who suffer from depression are mentally ill or crazy. It is probably one of the most misunderstood illnesses out there. My theory is that depression starts in childhood. It is a feeling that is produced because we lack control and purpose in our lives. We don't just wake up one day and feel depressed. It is a gradual thought process that is learned. Think about someone you know that suffers from depression and look at his or her childhood. Most often you see that they were sad as children. Depression builds as the feelings of hopelessness and helplessness become more real. Everything in childhood is transferable to adulthood. How we cope is based on the interpretations of our childhood experiences.

To explain the sense of despair created by depression, evaluate the following experiment. A group of rats was placed in a tank of water. Half the group was given a rock to retreat to when they were tired; the other half was forced to continue swimming. After weeks of conditioning, both groups were placed in the tank where no rock was available. After several hours, the group that had been given the opportunity to periodically rest continued swimming even though they were exhausted. But the group that had not been given a rest plunged to the bottom of the tank and drowned themselves. They simply gave up because they had learned that they could not help themselves. Could your children keep going under these conditions? To determine where your kids fall in the spectrum, ask yourself:

- Are they doing okay academically?
- Do they handle peer pressure appropriately?
- Do they give up easily?
- Do they take pride in anything?
- Do they participate in extracurricular activities?
- Do they appear lazy or unmotivated?
- Do they look forward to their day?
- Are they more irritable than other kids their age?
- Are they showing interest in their family?

These questions can help determine whether your children suffer from childhood depression. Berated children usually buy into their batterer's input. When this happens, they may display signs of depression or deep sadness such as listlessness, severe emotional swings, agitation, and lack of concentration. The bottom line is, in general, they simply do not care. Mostly, they do not care about themselves, which trickles down into every aspect of their lives. They may experience different degrees of sadness; so, they may be selective in what they do or do not care about. Depression is caused from not being in control of your life, not feeling hope, and not knowing how to change it.

These symptoms may be temporary, or they may be long-lasting. There were times when I suffered severely from depression. Then I learned how negative thoughts build upon one another, causing sadness. I recognized that much of my sadness came from my upbringing. The revelation I had was that my circumstances took away my childhood, but that did not necessarily mean it had to take away the rest of my life. I decided to take control of my life and make up for all the childhood activities that I missed. My dear friend once said, "It is never too late to have a happy childhood."

Clinically, depression is caused by the release of chemicals that slow down the body and actually assist in developing negative thought patterns. When you can change your children's thoughts, you minimize the secretion of this chemical. According to Medscape Health,

> The basic biologic causes of depression are strongly linked to abnormalities in the delivery of certain key neurotransmitters (chemical messengers in the brain). . . . Some experts theorize that low mood is an adaptive response to situations in which expectations fail to match achievements and active efforts produce no benefit. . . . Depression as a disorder [characterized by pervasive pessimism, low self-esteem, and total lack of initiative] may develop if there are constant unachievable objects or goals and there are no positive relationships to help a person change direction.[3]

In simpler terms, one must feel successful so that a level of achievement is possible, which in turn minimizes the release of those "yucky" chemicals. In the past, your children's lives have been limited emotionally and physically by your batterer. Therefore, your children need to recognize that life can be fun, exciting, and worthwhile. Overcoming depression is not easy, but it is possible. If you find that you cannot help them, seek medical or mental health treatment.

Children's Self-Esteem

As mentioned previously, low self-esteem contributes greatly to depression. Depending upon the severity, length, and exposure to the abuse, children can feel unattractive, worthless, and inadequate. They cannot see how great they are without encouragement. As victims of family violence, their self-images may disgust them because of their abuser's damaging messages.

Self-esteem is often based on a sense of love. If a child's perception is that he is unloved, then that is the reality. In order to shift this paradigm and build the love, find ways to share hobbies and interests that both you and your children enjoy. Sing, draw, brush each other's hair, or just eat popcorn on the couch together while you tell stories. Do anything that builds the bond between you. Use lots of eye contact and touch. The goal is to get your children to feel good from the inside out.

Projective Positives

Projective positives occur when you forecast the future in a positive manner. Projective positives teach your children to look at the brighter side of life. Unfortunately, throughout life, everyone will at one time or another have to contend with negative forces. External sources such as your abuser, school, and other peer groups may cause your children to be cynical. Your job will be to ensure that they get an attitude adjustments. Using projective positives solicits your children to focus on all that is good. Ask them questions such as the following:

"What was the best thing that happened to you in school today?"

"What was the funniest thing you heard today?"

"What was your favorite thing to eat today?"

Initially, your children will have no idea how to respond to this line of questioning. They will give you short and sweet answers like, "I dunno." This is where role modeling comes in. Tell them something great that happened to you:

"I saved $5 at the store today. I thought we could use the extra money to rent a movie."

"I was excited when I heard that our company was having a party."

"I had broccoli for lunch, what did you have? Pizza? Wow, you're so lucky."

Using projective positives help identify good aspects of everyday life. To accomplish this, establish a scheduled routine in which you practice thinking positive. Talk daily for ten minutes about the good things that occurred throughout the day. This helps change their focus. They may be somewhat resistant and anxious about this exercise, because this attitude is foreign to them. Implementing this new concept can bring your family closer together once they become comfortable with the change. It will give them something to look forward to. Using projective positives serves to redirect negative thought patterns and change the focus to one that is more optimistic.

Perhaps practicing projective positives may also help you see the benefits in your life more clearly. I remember once, as a waitress, complaining to a customer, "I hate this stupid job, my classes in school suck, and I hate my boss in the navy reserves." Without blinking an eye he retorted, "No one is making you work at this restaurant, you don't have to go to college, and you certainly don't have to be in the reserves. If you don't like the choices you've made, change them." His words felt like a slap in the face. He was right. I created these choices. Within the week, I switched to another restaurant, accepted that I could finish the remaining six weeks in the semester, and I transferred to a new reserve department. My paradigm shifted immediately. I realized that my life belonged to me.

When you lived with family violence, your choices were taken away. Now, it is time to take them back. Find the positives in your life either by looking at things differently or by changing your circumstances to reflect the way you want to live. How you view life is a choice. When you have experienced family violence, it may seem as though you have nothing to look forward to and that nothing is good. But the fact that you had the courage to pick up this book and learn about what this has done to your children says you can make it. There is a lot to overcome, just never give up!

Knowing Yourself

When thinking of a paradigm shift, it may be important to revisit your perception of the abuse in your life. You must understand yourself before you can help your kids. This way you will serve as a better role model for them. "Children have never been very good at listening to their elders—But they have never failed to imitate them."[4] If you are unconsciously accepting responsibility for the abuse, your children also learn that they caused their batterer's outbursts. It is imperative in this stage of change that you take a hard look at your life and place the onus back where it belongs: on the perpetrator.

The common denominator with many victims is that they often contradict themselves. Invariably, they say that others blame them for the abuse, only to turn around and justify their batterers' abuse. The victims complain that their batterers need treatment more than they do, yet they say, in the next breath, that it is their fault for staying in the relationship too long. Victims need to recognize what they are really feeling. They need to know that they are not to blame before others can be convinced. That requires treatment or some education. Many victims feel resentful when they are forced into treatment while their batterers are free to do as they please. But knowledge is power, and with that power the recipient has other options.

Training taught me that the abuse was not my fault and that I was not the only person going through this. Therefore, education is key. Women approach me after seminars and say, "You described my ex-husband to a T." The revelation they have is healing. Some victims' advocates feel that it is unfair to force victims into treatment. I repeatedly hear from class participants that they would not have voluntarily taken my course; but that they were really glad they had.

Simple things like classes and support groups really can make the difference in the paradigm shift. You may hear something that seems insignificant to others, yet it has life-changing meaning for you. One such insight for me was the saying of unknown origin, "When a pick-pocket sees a saint, all he sees are the pockets." That one sentence changed my life. I was able to let go of the idea that I caused the abuse. My batterer saw an opportunity and he took it. It did not matter who I was or what I did. He wanted to control someone, anyone, me. Without that one piece of knowledge, I may have continued to blame myself for the abuse. If you do not have time for classes or groups, go to the library and check out audiotapes. Listen to them in the car, in the kitchen, or in the breakroom. You can gain a lot of insight into what you have experienced by learning all you can.

In the end, you only answer to yourself. Learn as much as you can about how to feel and think differently. Do your children a favor; change your attitude, own your feelings, and shift your paradigm.

CHAPTER 5

Sabotage: A Positive Experience

Extreme remedies are very appropriate for extreme diseases.
—*Hippocrates*

Children from family violence develop negative self-images from the constant brow beatings they get from their batterers. The volume and intensity of the abuse can emotionally debilitate anyone, but it particularly affects children who are indoctrinated to listen to and respect their elders. The problem lies with the lack of regard most batterers have for their children's emotional and physical safety and society's ignorance toward the abuse. Adults, who are not familiar with the extent of torment these children face, minimize and send the message to them that they must tolerate the verbal "correction." As a result, kids are forced to accept what the batterers say about them. This chapter will focus on how children from family violence develop their self-images and introduce the process it takes for them to heal from the abuse.

As we learned in Chapter 2, children often appear angry when they really feel other emotions. Unfortunately, children who do not cope well get labeled and judged based on how they react. As a result, an increased apathy toward these troubled children makes healing diffi-cult. Society's "zero tolerance" policy punishes them for acting out without considering the reasons behind the behavior. These new restrictions do not permit educators and other professionals to use their judgments anymore. Consequently, taking each child's behavior on a case-by-case basis is no longer an option. This attitude leaves kids feeling not only physically assaulted by their batterers, but emotionally beat up by society as well. It is crucial that adults recognize how important their roles are to the lives of children experiencing family violence. When kids get the message that they are "losers" because of their behavior, they can only live up to that expectation. Your job, as a parent, will be to undo these damaging messages so your kids can feel good about themselves. In this chapter, we will review how children take these messages and use them to sabotage their lives. Gaining a better understanding of this process might help you see your children's sabotage as a positive experience.

But first, you must understand your children's attitudes and behaviors before others can. When children have negative self-images, they have belief systems that say they are bad. This system includes a combination of what the head thinks and what the heart feels. When your children were first removed from the violence, these feelings were congruent with one another. They genuinely believed with both parts (head and heart) that they were bad. The residual effect is that the behavior rarely rises above that expectation. They were constantly berated for things they did wrong. The positive things they did went unnoticed or were overshadowed by the criticism. The intensity of the input gradually made hearing the good things impossible. Consequently, they learned to accept the negative input as true. Now, every piece of information they receive is filtered by that perception.

You need to change your children's belief systems so they realize that the information inflicted upon them was distorted and false. Although this task will not be an easy one, it is an important part of healing. You will suffer a great deal while overcoming this obstacle, but it is well worth it. You can anticipate confusion and incongruent emotions as you introduce this new set of values. The psychological term for this imbalance is *cognitive dissonance*. This is when your children's hearts feel one way, and their heads think another. Although they do not want to feel badly, the negative feelings are what they know and are comfortable with. In the past, both head and heart felt badly, so they may unconsciously sabotage your efforts because you have contradicted one of the two belief systems. This may be a time when you feel like giving up because what you are doing does not seem to be working. But the opposite is true. When they are sabotaging, they are actually on their way to changing how they feel about themselves.

In the third grade, Katlin could earn "caught slips" for having good behavior. These awards were for getting caught doing the right thing. It was an absolute guarantee that if he got a caught slip he would be in the principal's office for the next three days for bad behavior. The school didn't understand his reaction but I did. He couldn't handle someone praising him. He needed to prove that the information from the outside world was wrong because it did not match his belief system. One day, as I explained that he was sabotaging his efforts, he retorted, "If you know telling me that I am good is going to make me act out, stop telling me that I am good!" With a deep sigh of frustration, I proclaimed, "I don't care if it is the last thing I do, you are going to believe that you are good!" This has been a lifelong process. Although there are times when he doubts himself, there are also time when he feels good about himself. Only time will tell whether he makes it. All parents can expect both successes and setbacks when it comes to their children regarding this area.

The next step is to examine how messages are delivered to children. As mentioned in Chapter 3, children understand clearly what makes us unhappy with them. Because of the frustration, often what happens with parents is that they stop believing that their children can change because they see the sabotage as failure. This is absolutely the biggest mistake ever. If they are sabotaging, you are moving in the right direction. The sabotage indicates that you have challenged their view of themselves. As frustrating as it seems, you have to look at their mistakes as a good thing. You instilled doubt about who they think they are.

Dr. Kendall Johnson describes this change as reorganization. He says that you have to rebuild an adaptive set of beliefs, assumptions, and perspectives necessary for the resumption of normal life.[1] He believes that there are a negative set of expectations and internal dialogues that children buy into. They also experience self-defeating biases and judgments. What many adults do not understand is that when children feel defeated, they lack the desire to want to learn or aspire to be greater. Your batterer programmed your children's thoughts—the messages are burned into their memories and last long after the abuser is gone. They repeat the programming through self-talk and say statements such as, "You stupid idiot!" They emotionally beat themselves up and buy into the criticism they have recorded in their minds. Consequently, the emotional abuse lingers on for years and sometimes for entire lifetimes.

The majority of children from family violence feel this way about themselves. As a parent, this is one of the most heart-wrenching experiences you can ever have. You ache for them because you know the pain is so great. You want to assure them that everything is going to be okay, but you can't find the words to comfort them. They have learned how to graciously accept the negative, and rarely can they embrace the positive things they do. As a result, their self-perceptions play a very significant role in how they make their choices. And each choice leads to another consequence that basically creates a snowball effect on how they feel and behave.

Because cognitive dissonance suggests that words and actions are conflicting, you must internalize the behavior differently. This could be one of your toughest challenges because you are trying to heal yourself. Try to see your children's behaviors for what they are, cries for help. Rather than punish them, try to support them. Use understanding and validation rather than condemnation. They will eventually regard your words as true if you become relentless in your attempt to change how they feel. They want to trust adults who say there is hope for a better life. They want to believe that they are good. Once I professed to a young man that it was possible to have a better life and he retorted, "I hope you're telling the truth lady. I really do." He really wanted to believe that a good future was possible. He just needed an adult to give him permission to hope. So show your children that there is life after family violence. When they understand that a better life is possible, they can gradually work toward improving their self-images. Just understand the time and energy involved for healing comes at a cost. But it is worth the investment.

The Calm Before the Storm

As your children become more comfortable with their new self-perceptions, they may recoil. They will experience anxiety, and setbacks may occur. You can have periods of calm, when all seems to be going well, then a trigger occurs and they might sabotage the new sense of peace. Everything that you feel you've accomplished seems gone by the wayside. This is the time when you have to be more patient. You might feel discouraged because you thought the relief meant they were over the trauma. The resurgence of old patterns makes you feel like a failure.

Sabotage: A Positive Experience

When your kids had bad behavior all the time, you understood them, and you knew what to expect. But the period of calm gave you a false impression. For the first time, they were making good choices, which felt great. But then the sabotage occurred, and when you weren't looking, you got cold-cocked. Now you worry that you are back to square one. The setbacks leave you feeling discouraged, unprepared, and frustrated. You were enjoying the peace, and the resurgence of bad behavior catches you off guard. As weird as it sounds, the constant bad behavior made you ready for anything; your expectations were lower, and you weren't hopeful. But now you feel like their misconduct is from out of nowhere, and you are not as prepared to deal with it. Not being able to predict the behavior may make you feel out of control and hopeless. The key here is to stay alert; anticipate the worst, yet hope for the best. Just be on your guard while embracing the good times and hold on tight for those unpredictable moments. You will make it through if you take it one day at a time.

Children may be uncomfortable with the good feelings they are having toward you, and they may try to sabotage the relationship to return things back to "normal." They don't do this because they like turmoil; they do this because of the imbalance the new information creates. The internal conflict is too great. Children who believe that they are unloved will continuously try to sabotage any goodness that they are experiencing. As long as their actions reinforce the belief that they are unloved, they can support their perceptions and make that belief a self-fulfilling prophecy. Therefore, your job will be to discount those feelings. However, this cannot happen by invalidating their emotions. Simply saying that they shouldn't feel like they are not loved does not work. You must validate and empathize with those feelings in order to discount them. Recognize that love is a verb, which requires action. Show them more than tell them that you love them. You have to take away the desire to sabotage in order to improve their self-images.

The Big Picture

Children from family violence do not see the big picture. Their thought processes are compartmentalized, and they can only view events in a situational manner. What this means is that they see each event and situation as separate. It doesn't matter whether they have ten nice things happen to them over the course of the day, their

83

moods can change in an instant if something negative pops up. They do not cognitively think, "Overall, I had a pretty good day." The positive aspects of the day are most often overcome by negative events. Because of this inability to view globally, they can work toward sabotaging their behavior without realizing it. Helping them look at all the pieces of their lives will be the most effective. Finding the good in what they do and focusing on the positive works best. Once they learn to put all of the pieces together, they may find comfort in feeling good about themselves.

Solving Sabotage

To help your kids continue to move toward better self-images, sustain a level of praise even when they mess up. For example, your child might hit other children; take the opportunity to say, "You know son, two months ago you were hitting kids everyday and this is the first time in over a month that you didn't keep your hands to yourself. I am sure you just forgot what you were supposed to do. I am confident that it won't happen again." Whether your heart believes this or not, your child needs to hear what he is doing right. If you want to see change, your communication must reflect what your children need, and not what you believe. When you can convince them that they are intrinsically good, they will be. As they learn new personal messages, they may get anxious because of the unfamiliarity of it all. If this sabotage occurs, consistency and patience will be key to their success. If they can see that your love is unconditional, they will eventually feel secure enough to trust you. When you have built that trust with them, they will follow your lead. They will believe in the changes if you do.

Cognitive dissonance is a hard concept to understand. Verbalizing the imbalance to your children will be important to the process of changing their belief systems. As you learned in Chapter 3, you must share with them what they are feeling because they are unable to verbalize for themselves. Therefore, they need you to define their emotions for them. Then your next step is to teach them how to think and react differently. The objective is to give them a gamut of choices to pick from. In the past, violence was the only option they were given. Now, parenting in the aftermath of family violence, you have the opportunity to open their minds up to a whole new world.

Sabotage: A Positive Experience

A mother has been frustrated lately because her son continues to hit a little boy that comes over to visit. She decides that instead of reacting to him by correcting his bad behavior and reinforcing his self-image, she instead hugs and coddles the other child. Her son is looking for attention (negative affirmation), and he will get it any way he can. He becomes confused when she ignores him. He grows annoyed with her and throws himself into a rage. He does not understand what she is doing and why she isn't responding the "right way." In the past, this type of behavior always made him center stage. Now the other child is stealing his thunder. He absolutely hates that the other child receives the attention. If she stays strong and continues with this course of action, he will eventually learn that hitting doesn't get him what he wants. Of course, there must be limits to the degree to which he hurts others. Punishment may be needed, but it should be used as an absolute last resort.

Children's emotions and reactions are due in part to the recurring memories that have been burned into their psyches. Although they are now free from physical harm, the ghosts from their pasts still haunt them. They can fluctuate between occasional flashbacks to obsessive fears, depending upon the significance of the triggers that spark the memories. These triggers provoke feelings of inadequacy and worthlessness. What follows is that they may react inappropriately due to these perceptions. The triggers can vary according to the associations they have made with them. Unfortunately, you may not be fully aware of what they are, and you may become the scapegoat for their frustration. You are an easy and safe target. In the abusive relationship, they were not permitted to act out or express their feelings. Now, they may unleash all of their pent up frustrations and anxieties on you. The floodgates may open, and emotions may soar to levels you never thought possible.

Being the Protector

As the parent and the victim in your family, you may have lost credibility with your children. Because you were unable to protect them in the past, they may view you as weak and undeserving of their respect. Their concept more than likely will be, "You didn't protect me before, why would you protect me now?" They may even continue where your batterer left off by abusing you also. To minimize this attitude, make clear and distinct boundaries to prove that you are in control.

An internal conflict is created by your new emotional boundaries, which confuses them. Redefining roles and philosophies will be challenging to say the least. This would be a good time to call in the reinforcements. Find someone outside your family to assist with the changes. Amazingly, an unbiased person greatly contributes to this process. It is not enough to be the "greatest" parent in the world; your children need others. Particularly important is someone from the opposite sex, to counter your female position. Because your children's male role model was dysfunctional, they could benefit from having a healthy man that they can count on. He should be a neutral party, someone whom you are unemotionally involved with. It could be a teacher, coach, or platonic friend. Our family was fortunate enough to get a terrific man from the Big Brother program to be a part of Katlin's life. Although not all volunteers take their role as mentor so seriously, Katlin's did. There were many times when I believed that I made it through the parenting process because this man provided Katlin with messages that I simply could not get across to him. Professionals are stating now that it takes approximately eight to ten adults to contribute to a child's development. Do your kids have that type of support? If they do, great! If they don't, then do something about it. Parenting alone is just not realistic. This means, however, that you will be required to trust someone again. Needing others can be extremely difficult during this time, but for your kids' sake, you must try.

Solidifying Your Children's Beliefs

Children are concrete thinkers that believe in symbolism. Anytime you can write down how great they are and they can physically see their accomplishments, there is a greater chance that they will internalize their goodness. Solidifying their beliefs makes what they have done more real. You will be amazed at the remarkable results. There are many ways to acknowledge their achievements using symbols. You can have a certificate or trophy made up that tells them how good they are: the bigger, the better. The representation serves as a reminder that they are worthy.

The primary problem with cognitive dissonance is that most children are afraid to care about themselves or others. The thought of rejection is so overwhelming that they would prefer to avoid developing relationships rather than opening up to the potential pain.

Sabotage: A Positive Experience

Most kids secretly want to care, but don't know how to protect themselves emotionally. The risk becomes too great.

At this point, you cannot be too discouraged because your children are just trying to sort out their *real* emotions in a manner that keeps them safe. Their attitude appears conflicting: on one hand they appear to want help, yet they are resistant and afraid on the other. Most children want their parents to identify the problems and fix them. The hard part is that you cannot really help them until they learn how to let you in. Your effort seems like a double-edged sword: darned if you do, darned if you don't. You will have to make tough decisions based on what you know is good for them rather than what they feel is right. You might have to make choices that don't feel so good right now but deep down you know it is in their best interest to do so. Your job will be to solve the problems for them because they are not mentally capable of doing so.

Failure is a huge part of cognitive dissonance. Children from family violence fear failure. They personalize losing or being wrong much more strongly than the average nurtured child. Any failure reinforces those bad feelings, and contributes to further acting out. When children's sense of self is weak, their tendency is to sabotage good feelings. In order to help them be successful, you must appeal to their strengths and create a sense of hope. Therefore, you must focus on what they are doing right.

Dangerous Behaviors

Some children have no regard for their own personal safety. They will participate in behaviors that are unhealthy and dangerous. They appear to have no regard for the consequences of their actions. One young man crashed a car and wrecked a motorcycle, which required hospitalization in an intensive care unit. Yet, he remarked that he was invincible and considered the danger as an adventure. He, like many adolescents, may genuinely believe that life is forever, or he may simply not care about his personal safety. At this point, he does not recognize danger as a problem. He may be getting his sense of importance through thrill-seeking events. If you are dealing with children who participate in reckless behavior, teach them other ways to "find" themselves.

Your Own Sabotage

Now that you have learned about your children's self-sabotage, think about your life. Do you find that when things are going well, you feel uncomfortable? Does chaos seem to break out when things have been relatively calm? If so, you may be unconsciously sabotaging yourself. Victims commonly struggle with tranquility because peace was never an option, and they simply do not know how to respond to it. Some victims sabotage due to the lack of confidence they *think* they need to make it. They may fear being alone, so they desperately search for ways to rationalize why they should return to the abusive relationship. They start using "What if . . ." statements that allow them to justify why they need to go back, such as:

"What if my husband is sorry?"
"What if I lose my job and can't make the house payments?"
"What if the kids really miss their dad?"

This damaging self-talk often contributes to reconciliation between victims and batterers. If you find yourself participating in this destructive communication, do your best to change it. Avoid the "What if . . ." statements as much as possible because they serve to sabotage your progress. As uncomfortable as it feels, work past the anxiety and embrace the fact that you are doing the best job you can. You are bound to make mistakes simply because you are human. If you feel compelled to use "What if . . ." statements, I would recommend the following as a guide to reevaluating your situation:

"What if I become a success at my job?"
"What if I am able to qualify for that home loan?"
"What if I realize that I am a capable and good parent?"

Try to reach beyond your past and look toward the future with hope. Happiness is possible if you choose not to fear it. Ask yourself whether or not you truly want to be free from the violence that you have endured. Then decide if getting healthy will give your kids a shot at better lives.

Sabotage: A Positive Experience

Beyond the Point of Sabotage

Some families have lived in violence for so long that they may not have any positive moments in their lives. Their behavior and choices are severely destructive. Examples would be the families that appear on the Jerry Springer show. If you or your children display similar behavior patterns, you will need some serious counseling. This is beyond the point of sabotage; this is self-destruction. Cognitive dissonance only occurs when one of the two belief systems feels that some behavior is good. If you feel that there is nothing positive about your family's behavior, then seek professional help right away. Sometimes the severity of abuse is just too great for anyone to deal with alone. Don't beat yourself up over staying in the relationship too long. There is a time and reason for everything that you do. The important thing is that you did leave, and your kids now need you to look forward and not back.

There is no single way to parent and it is impossible to always anticipate the outcome of your decisions. Give yourself a break and believe in what you do. As you begin to feel good about your parenting, you can embrace the great accomplishments that you have made.

CHAPTER 6

Just Behave Yourself

Children act out most when we need it least.

—*Christina M. Dalpiaz*

"Behaving" is more than just stopping or avoiding inappropriate actions. It is also doing the appropriate or "right thing." In this chapter, we discuss *behavior modification* and what it takes to get your kids back on track. It involves not only correcting bad behavior but also internalizing rules of good behavior. Put aside your old concepts on parenting and let's focus on a new plan: Your children's behaviors and values are *skills*, and they can unlearn the bad ones and replace them with good ones. Your job is to guide them in new and challenging directions. This chapter offers ideas and mental strategies to assist you.

Goals and Objectives of Behavior Modification

In order to get children to want to do the right thing, parents need to build a strong foundation for them. The following are some basic rules to remember to assist in the behavior modification process:

- Reduce your expectations to a lower age, because abuse has probably delayed your child's development.
- Start small and increase your applications slowly. Move from short-term to long-term goals. Don't overwhelm them with too much.

- Be patient and recognize that it takes approximately three to six months of practicing new behaviors before changes happen.
- Use love and respect in your discipline.
- Continue intermittent reinforcement after behavior modification has taken root.

Good behavior is a skill. It takes practice to get it right. You can learn all the ideas in the world, but if you do not implement them through practice, change will not occur. Let me stress that you cannot expect instant improvement. It may take several attempts before your children respond. For one thing, they must recognize that you are actually *making changes,* not just having a weird day. To help you get started, the following behavior modification goals for your children are provided:

- Keep hands to self
- Use manners
- Take turns
- Share
- Respect personal space

Consistency

Consistency is key to behavior modification. Children's behaviors suffer when parents are unwilling to follow through. Parents may make threats and conditions, and then forget about them, or simply give their children yet another "chance." Then parents are surprised and frustrated that misbehavior continues. Frustration builds into anger, which confuses the children. Kids do not understand how they may get away with improper behavior five times, and then get into trouble for it the sixth time. Some parents say, "I really mean it this time!" What that says to their children is that they didn't mean it the other five times they said it. The best way to combat this problem is to say internally before you correct your kids, "I mean it the first time." To be an effective parent, you must say what you mean and mean what you say.

Preparing for Behavior Modification

Before your children can modify their behavior, they must be in a good emotional place. Chapter 1 showed the need, first of all, to be sensitive to the stages of healing. We should also understand that trauma victims develop physiological responses that need addressing before children can learn how to behave. This is critical to successful parenting. There are three crucial physiological responses standing in the way of behavior modification: *visual motor problems, anxiety,* and *poor impulse control.* Once these concepts are understood clearly, you can work on changing behaviors.

Developing Visual Motor Skill

In my experience, most children from family violence do not visually focus well. They struggle with coordination of fine motor skills, such as tying shoes, organizing, sorting, and writing. Their eyes vacillate, making prolonged eye contact difficult. As a result, these children have difficulty concentrating, learning, and bonding. They have been conditioned to avoid connecting with others because their batterer made attachment incredibly scary. Your task is to make them feel safe enough to participate visually. Behavior modification is more likely to succeed when you can make that emotional connection from eye contact.

There are many ways to develop better visual motor skills for your children. For instance, they can sort the contents of closets, cupboards, and dressers to learn how to focus and reorganize. Past abuse has likely left them hyper-jumpy, unable to focus, their minds cluttered. They need help to slow down, learn how to arrange, and categorize. Provide any activity that promotes focusing. Puzzles, Lego toys, or models work well. Initially, they may experience some anxiety, so your participation would be helpful. Confidence in mastering visual motor skills will affect other areas of their lives.

Eye Contact

Eye contact is important to learning focus, and needs practice. At first, I don't recommend a major staring contest. Take "baby steps" for this and all the other techniques in this chapter. Your goal, the first week, might be to look at each other for a period of three seconds, five times a day. Maintain this consistently until your children feel comfortable with the contact. The following week, increase the time to five seconds, and so on. Keep it brief and make it fun. You don't want to use this exercise for correction (i.e., "Look at me when I'm talking to you!"). The idea is to make a positive connection. When your children feel safe looking you in the eyes, they will be able to empathize with your needs, and behavior modification is more likely. Here is a short list of activities that can enhance visual motor development:

- Stringing beads, macaroni, or popcorn
- Reading maps with your fingers
- Tracing pictures
- Cutting-out coupons
- Making a rubber-band ball
- Making designs out of glitter and glue

Improving visual motor skills requires some creativity and the willingness to have fun with your kids. Katlin and I used to have a contest with his friends to see who could focus the hardest on our walks to the park. We would kick a rock along the sidewalk, trying to avoid the grass. If it went into the grass there was a one-point penalty. Whoever made it to the park with the lowest score won. This exercise served two purposes: (1) it made the boys focus on using their visual motor skills, and (2) it kept them busy so I didn't have to stop them from running off. The boys never got tired of this fun exercise and their behavior was great.

Overcoming Anxiety

Trauma causes anxiety that lasts. For your children, it is like they lived in a war zone. You could think of their exposure at home as something like a soldier trapped in a foxhole. The threats were imminent, terrifying, and very real. And although many times the violence was predictable, there were also many times when it was not. This creates a high state of anxiety. You must help reduce it by teaching them how to anticipate what the world expects from them.

Calming the anxiety within your children may take time. Some of their experiences were so horrific that the average person has no idea how anyone could survive such an ordeal.

Nine-year-old Stacey has nightmares about the violence she witnessed against her mother Val. Val says Stacey has become overprotective of her. Val is concerned because her daughter displays behavior that is not age-appropriate. She alternates between acting either much older or much younger than her chronological age. One minute she cradles a baby doll like a frightened child, the next she dresses and carries herself in a manner that is provocative and unhealthy for her age. Stacey's experience has paralyzed her development. Still too young to cope with these issues, she wishes to be mothered, the way she was when she was younger. But she also feels compelled to grow up quickly to protect her mother.

Children who witness violence against their mothers may not trust that the victims can handle parental responsibilities. They can feel that it's their responsibility to take care of the family (that's enough to make *any* child a little anxious). One mother's son consistently got into trouble at school for fighting. The students called him names and bullied him. Not only did he have to cope with his family's past, but also, he had to deal with an uncertain future. His distress grew. He felt alone, afraid, and unsure of his environment. His anxiety left him permanently on edge, ready to react. As a consequence, he was always in trouble.

The *fight or flight* response is an instinctive animal survival mechanism accessed during danger situations, where all the body's muscles and chemicals are primed for the spark of a threat stimulus. The physical and emotional effect is like a car engine revving full throttle while the clutch is engaged. Pop the clutch and look out! The body is revving, pumping adrenaline. Eventually, the body and mind wear down from the internal tension, and a person reacts inappropriately (pop! goes the clutch). Adults commonly refer to this event as a *meltdown*.

Kids from family violence use the adrenaline to stay alert and ready for attack or flight. As a result, they are left in high states of physical and mental excitement that may cause bad behavior. Your task is to prove that you can now protect them. They need to pass the torch to you and trust you enough to relax.

You can start by verbally communicating that you are the protector. Then you must show them through your actions that you are there for them. One way that words and actions can go together is by generating scenarios with your kids regarding their safety, and working out solutions. Kids are usually unable to forecast and create solutions on their own. They need your guidance. You can make up, "What if . . ." stories to provoke their thought. Then give them some solutions:

Scenario: "What if a teacher calls you a loser?"

Solution: "You can either wait until you get home and I will call the teacher to straighten things out, or you can ask to call me and I will come to the school."

Scenario: "What happens if a student beats you up on the bus?"

Solution: "You can tell the bus driver, and if that doesn't work, I will call the kid's mother and address our concerns."

You must be careful when generating solutions, because your children may interpret them differently from what you intended. Don't assume that they have the same compilation of ideas as you. They have different experiences, which can alter the information that you provide to them. I recommend that you keep the lines of communication open in order to learn what is running through their minds. Encourage your children to also generate "What if . . ." questions to accomplish this task.

Anxiety is an incredibly difficult thing to overcome simply with practice. It may be necessary to seek professional help. One such therapy that I would highly recommend is Eye Movement Desensitization and Reprocessing (EMDR). This is a relatively new therapy that is having profound results. The therapy lets trauma victims revisit their abuse in a safe environment. The therapy permits victims to reprocess the events and accept their past. Therapists are using this procedure to help severe cases of trauma, including war veterans. Ask a therapist or go on-line for more information.

Improving Impulse Control

Another effect family violence can have on children is that they become unable to control their impulses. They act without thinking, doing absurd things without regard for the consequences. A doctor during a conference reported that traumatized kids do not use the frontal lobe of their brain, making them unable to recognize the "big picture."[1] So basically, adults are partly right to say these kids "don't use their heads." A loss of impulse control is a physiological response to prolonged traumatic experience, and it is a good indication that a child may be suffering from an anxiety-based disorder. Reducing their nervousness, discussed earlier, is key to controlling some of the impulse issues. Poor impulse control is probably one of the most frustrating parts of parenting traumatized children. The outside world is intolerant of this deficit and they tend to label your children. You are left frustrated because you are trying to teach your children to cope, and you are fighting the societal labels at the same time. (We will learn more about dealing with society's perceptions in Chapter 9.)

Perhaps it is a good idea to understand why children have poor impulse control. The problem is twofold. We have discussed anxiety, which pumps them up and makes them over-ready to *react.* The other problem stems from severe emotional and physical deprivation: they do not believe that the world can meet their needs. As a result, every new opportunity or stimulation has a *now or never* quality, a *get it while you can* need that the average person just cannot comprehend. Their perspective is that they *have to have* it. This need is not exclusive to kids from trauma, of course, but it is greatly exaggerated among them. The urgency to have these items prompts them to beg or bully to the point of extortion. To combat this issue, create opportunities for your children that reduce the impulse while helping them satisfy their needs without other kids losing their stuff. Have them write down everything that they saw during the week that they liked, and tell them that if they don't beg anyone for anything all week, they can go to the store on Fridays with a certain dollar limit and get what they want. They will eventually learn to reduce these impulses.

However, such a method is only good to get them to *start* slowing down. You don't want them to rely on external gratification of needs and not get to the point of dealing with their real, internal needs. In the book *Emotional Intelligence,* Daniel Goleman suggests that external impulse gratification only serves to debilitate personal growth.[2] Children must not be permitted to always have immediate gratification to meet their emotional needs. Otherwise, they will constantly be searching for stimulation. The biggest problem with instant gratification is that it is only temporary. Unfortunately, another external source will usually be required to meet the emotional needs shortly after the first. The sad part is that the need can never be satiated.

So what do you do? Let's start by recognizing that poor impulse control, because it is reactive, is like a reflex. A person is not aware of what is going on, making it hard to address impulse control safely and constructively. Videotaping is a great way to help kids correct themselves. You can tape them playing or working in social contexts, and then give them the tape later to view in private. They can watch their own behaviors and not feel like they are being confronted. They can see for themselves that they are being impulsive, intrusive, or unfair.

Sometimes parents feel that they need to give on-the-spot correction, and sometimes they're right about that. But often it is not the case. If your child is geared up because his anxiety level is high and you lash out, the situation will get worse. My advice is to wait for a better moment, when both of you are calm. You have to anticipate outcomes, which means being selective about confrontation. Your goal is to change the behavior, not add to the problem.

To help your children cope with impulse problems, create situations where they can see what they are doing. The video technique is a good way, but there are others, too. For example, if your child races to be first in the water fountain line, make her let two people go in front of her. This will show her that she will get a turn, and so will everyone else. Let her know in advance the point of this exercise so that she knows her needs will be met.

Another impulse problem that you may face involves spending money. When they get a chance, kids with impulse issues will spend every last dime they have in their pockets. To eliminate this urge, work out a rule that they are not permitted to spend any money for three days after they receive it, and then they can only spend half. This helps them reduce the impulse to spend it all at once. Another impulse to curb is begging for more (of whatever they want). The rule for begging needs to be that if you bought them something they asked for, they are not permitted to ask for anything else for a month. If they ask too soon, then tack on a longer wait. This will be painful for them but in the long run they will be much better off. Some of the impulse issues will dissipate with maturity and experience. But for now, let's discuss how to use stress management techniques to better improve your attitude and your children's impulse control.

Stress Management for You and Your Kids

There are many times when children's behaviors are definitely the problem, but then there are those when they are not. Sometimes we have to stop and admit that the adult's behavior may be the problem. There are many different stress factors that play into the life of *any* parent, let alone for parents coping with family violence. You can see why some families are stressed out. For example, those who escape their violent home will most definitely experience financial stress, which carries over into parenting. One mother admitted that she would work herself up before she got home just thinking about the bills. Her thinking was so negative that she found herself constantly disappointed in her children's behavior.

She realized later that it was her financial situation and not her children that was the problem. She had to work really hard to separate the two.

"Mommy, why am I on your last nerve today? I act like this everyday."

What most parents do is let their stress build, until it wears them down and they explode. Often, unfortunately, it is the children who trigger such explosions. Stressed-out parents may ignore children's misbehavior over a period of mounting tension simply because they don't feel like coping with it. They want to believe that their children are not struggling because they just can't deal with the ramifications of that. But part of managing the stress is keeping many little problems from accumulating into one gigantic problem that causes you to blow up. In other words, deal with problem behavior as it crops up. You must *lovingly* challenge your children constantly, letting them know you are there to keep them on track. (This may mean shadowing them at school when they misbehave, or monitoring their social interactions to ensure that they are acting appropriately with others.) It also requires you to establish consequences for misbehavior in advance—consequences that your children understand and that you follow through with when rules are broken. Your kids need to know the boundaries they may not cross. Do not personalize their reactions. It is their job to push the limits and yours to continuously reestablish them. You just have to be able to keep your cool and maintain control.

Stress management techniques will make coping easier. The first place to start is breathing correctly. It is probably one of the best stress-busters out there. Mental and emotional tensions create physical stress, which in turn restricts blood flow. Oxygen in the blood stream doesn't move as easily through our systems. Without the appropriate levels of oxygen, our bodies obviously struggle more, creating even more tension, and so on. Focusing on calm, deep breathing when you're tense relaxes the body *and* the mind. You can feel muscles start to relax once you master some breathing exercises. Inhale slowly through your nose then exhale slowly though your mouth. Continue for two or three minutes. You will be amazed at how much better you'll feel.

Focused breathing works well with children too. Adults rarely recognize that their kids may also be stressed out. Think about their lives for a moment. First, there are the ordinary anxieties we may remember from our own childhoods. Then, consider that their world is so much more different from ours when we were their age. Lastly, add to the picture the violence they have witnessed or experienced, and the associated concerns about the present and future. You can understand how they may be just as stressed as you, just in different ways.

A great way to help kids relax is to use their imaginations along with the breathing technique. For instance, when my nephew Katlin was younger, I would take him on imaginary journeys. We started with breathing deeply, with our eyes closed. I'd ask him then to visualize trips to wherever his heart desired. We would ride the winged horse Pegasus across the sky or glide through the ocean on a whale's back. The key was that he had to breathe in and out in order to move through the journey. For example, the horse's wings or the whale's tail could not move without Katlin's breaths. We would also use the breaths to change the color of the fish in the ocean. With each breath in and out, he changed their colors however he wanted. This exercise often put him, and occasionally me, to sleep. One day, Katlin was starting a new school, and he appeared to be resting during the drive. I asked if he was tired and he said, "No, I was taking myself on a journey because I'm nervous." He was using our strategy to regulate his own stress.

Another stress reducer for your family is for you to prioritize. Face it, there's never enough time to accomplish all we want and need to do. Therefore, picking the real priorities, creating schedules, learning time management, and delegating some of your responsibilities are vital strategies. If you are overwhelmed by your life, it will be difficult to work on behavior modification. In his book, *The Seven Habits of Highly Effective People,* Stephen Covey notes that you have to stop from time to time and sharpen your saw in order to work faster and more effectively.[3] You have to make the time to organize your life so that you can work *smarter,* not *harder.* Say, for example, you need to get $20 from the ATM for groceries, but then the next day you have to go back and get $20 more for a trip to the movies, and then $20 more the following day to pay for lunch. Instead of making three trips to the ATM, you could think ahead and estimate how much money you will need for the next three days. When you can recognize what you need in advance, you will be working with a sharpened saw.

Delegating some of your responsibilities to your children can reduce your load and your stress—but only if you're ready to be flexible about the results (hint: you should be). Make a list of chores you're willing to let them do (good examples include making beds, taking out trash) and have them pick which ones they can accomplish. Each week have them choose different ones, to keep it fair. If they do the trash one week, the next week they could do the dishes. When you allow them to pick, they are likely to be more receptive to doing chores. Too many parents worry about a clean house. Expecting, or even desiring, total cleanliness while raising children is unrealistic. On your deathbed, you will not say, "I wish I would have mopped that kitchen floor one more time." You are going to wish you took the time to be with your kids. Of course, filth is not the answer, either, so if you can get your kids to pitch in, it is better to have a halfway clean house than the unrealistic expectation of a perfectly spotless one.

You can now understand how to better manage your time and minimize your family's stress. Start evaluating your life and decide what you can do to reduce the hassle and create more time for yourself and your children.

Changing Behavior

With your understanding of the obstacles in front of you, and armed with stress management techniques, it's time now to begin acquiring and using new parenting tools to get your kids to modify their behavior. The rest of this chapter lays out techniques and shows how to use them in various common situations.

Behavior modification should achieve two things. First, of course, is a correction of difficult or antisocial behavior. But it should also show a child that the problem is his *behavior,* not him as an individual. In your mind and in your child's, you must separate the behavior from the person, while still holding the person accountable for his actions. It will be easier for them to change *what they do* rather than change *who they are.*

When your child asks whether she has been a bad girl today, you might say, "You are always a good girl, but your behavior really stunk today" or "You are always a good girl, but your behavior was outstanding." Can you see the difference? Helping kids depersonalize their behavior will motivate them to change it more quickly by giving them hope (e.g., "It's not me that's the problem! It's my choices").

It's not enough to just motivate them; you need to take the time to practice the changes. Some parents say there isn't enough time to work on these changes. But the reality is you either pay *now* or pay *later*. If you wait until later, you are going to be tired, frustrated, and burnt out. Behavior modification requires you to manage your time more effectively so you can use your new skills. Your past may have left you with a box of faulty parenting tools. Physical aggression may have been the only tool your children have ever been exposed to. Think of the old adage, if the only tool you have ever had is a hammer, then the world starts to look like nails. Now, you will want to go out and purchase a new set of tools in order to get the job done right. You may need to look at your parenting style and determine where you fall in the spectrum and work to improve or change your strategies.

Parenting Styles

There are three well-known types of parenting styles used when disciplining children: authoritarian, passive, and authoritative. Understanding these three styles will help you make better choices regarding your parenting and help your children learn how to behave. Many adults haphazardly use these styles at different times, which confuses their children. Only one, however, genuinely serves your children well when it is overused. Read the following and decide what parenting style you are currently using and assess whether you should change your approach.

Authoritarian

Children need to feel loved and regarded in a manner that encourages them. In your violent home, there is a good chance that your batterer was relentlessly uncaring. This type of parenting is referred to as an authoritarian approach and uses the mental concept, "Do as I say, not as I do." Children are parented through intimidation to do what is right, and basically, their abusers do not care how badly they hurt their children emotionally. Authoritarian parents use the old-school philosophy that children should be seen and not heard, which essentially sends the message that kids are nobodies.

This approach is very damaging. It destroys children's egos and really teaches them nothing. They will behave themselves all right, but they will do it out of fear, and not because it is the right thing to do. They will not learn from what they have done. Authoritarian parents use statements like, "I will knock you into next Tuesday if I ever catch you with a cigarette hanging out of your mouth." The whole time they are sitting there pointing with a cigarette between their fingers.

Although there are times when you should be able to recite, "Because I said so." It would be beneficial to be selective with its use. When children feel that you are not considering how they feel, they develop resentment, and they will eventually fight back. Authoritarian parents teach their children to be disrespectful, unfair, and selfish. The lesson they learn is that "I just have to wait to grow up, then I can do what I want."

Think about what you really want from your children. If you want kids who are kind and loving, minimize this approach as much as possible. Save your position of power for when you truly need it.

Passive Parenting

Children need and want boundaries although it appears as if they do not. They need to feel safe and the most favorable ways to make that happen are to create strict and loving boundaries. I should warn you, however, that the restrictions will hurt you much more than they will hurt the children. The reason is that adults understand loss and consequences. We think, by giving into our children's whims, we love them. The opposite is true. When we do not teach them how to set limits, they go out of control. As my saintly Grandmother says, "Sometimes you have to love them enough to hurt them." I appreciate parents who do not want their children to experience anymore pain and loss, but it is really not preparing them for the world. Although they are disappointed when they don't get what they want, they don't feel as badly as we think. Children want help making the right choices. Adults understand loss and disappointment, and they do not. They can only learn how hurt feels by actually experiencing it. We have to let them learn what that means. They must learn for themselves what life brings. If they do not learn this valuable lesson, we will retard their growth. The consequences will be devastating. Do your children a favor, and do not compensate for the abuse. The violence had no boundaries and being a passive parent does not either.

We cannot be afraid to correct our children. Years ago, I witnessed a woman purchasing a stereo for her teenage son. He was standing in the line berating her and using aggressive body language toward her. She kept her head down in the line. I sat there whispering under my breath, "Take the stereo back . . . don't buy it . . . walk away." She stood in the line patiently and purchased the stereo. Her son stormed off, leaving her behind to carry his new stereo. That image has been burned into my mind for many years. I asked myself, "How did they get to this point?" Was her kindness effective, or did it serve to worsen her son's behavior? Remember there is a difference between enabling your children and supporting them. How will this young man act as an adult? Will this mother be proud of what he becomes?

This year, while standing in another line, I witnessed a young mother with her three-year-old son. He was carrying a large box with a toy enclosed. He began jumping on the box, which had not been purchased yet. She put the box on the counter and quietly asked the cashier to hide it because she couldn't get through the store without it. She paid for the other items; the boy noticed that the box wasn't there and made an inquiry as to its whereabouts. She said, "Oh, it's in the bag." She blatantly lied to avoid confrontation. What she taught her son was that she is afraid of conflict; she is not in control; and lying is okay. When I saw this event, I recalled the teenager and his mother. Now, I understood how their interaction got them to this point. She too probably used passive parenting when she was a young mother.

Being a passive parent is as damaging as being an abusive, authoritarian one. Be careful that you are providing the right guidance for your children so they have the opportunity to grow up healthy and happy.

Authoritative

Children need guidance, strength, and protection. An authoritative parent is firm yet fair, strict yet yielding, and tough yet loving. The best way to describe this type of parenting is to see that the corrections are less harmful than the consequences of your children's actions. For instance, if you let your kids eat ice cream every morning for breakfast, cookies for lunch, and chocolate cake for dinner, rather than something nutritional, they are going to develop poor eating habits. The consequences are that they might be obese, or worse, that they might develop diabetes and other health problems.

Your kids may really love all those things, but does it serve them well to let them have it?

Be strong for your kids' sake. You know more than they do about what they need. As an authoritative parent, you have to motivate them in a supportive way to do the right thing. Discipline is a loving way of showing your kids what they need to do. Disciplining children usually means correcting in advance. Teach them values and morals before they mess up. Whenever possible, use others as examples, rather than waiting to correct your children's mistakes. The impact is always greater when your children can internalize right from wrong through the mistakes of others. Don't be afraid, however, to show your kids the way. You need to be their backbone.

If at First You Don't Succeed

One problem I see with most parents is that they only give behavior modification one shot. If it doesn't work the first time, they quit. But you must realize that these kids have been through a lot and may not be capable of "getting it" the first time. They may require extra attention to sort out what they need to do. Using parenting tools that establish routines and expectations that your children can count on will help.

Behavior = Consequences

Your first new toolset to build with is consequences. Your children must understand that their behavior has consequences—they could be good or bad, depending, but there will always be consequences. This is something you can learn to use to modify their behaviors.

There are essentially two types of consequences: *natural* and *logical*. Natural consequences are basically effects or results of an action. For instance, you throw a toy on the ground and it breaks. Or, you go to bed early and get up well-rested.

Logical consequences are also results. But these are implemented or established by someone else. The consequence of speeding on a highway is a ticket, for instance. In the case of parenting, the person establishing the consequence is you. The downfall for most parents is *not following through with consequences*. Commonly, many parents respond that the consequence of their child's bad behavior was simply, "I got mad."

Developing logical consequences with and for your children lays the groundwork of better behavior. They will know what you expect of them, and they will also know what they can expect as a result of misbehavior.

Establishing rules in advance is the first step. Make the changes slowly; do not try to apply all of the new rules at once. Otherwise, your children will be overwhelmed. Start with two goals per week. For example:

Behavior: Clothes dropped on the floor

Consequence: Kids get ten minutes of cleanup time

Behavior: Not getting up on time for school

Consequence: Bedtime is an hour earlier

Ideally, the consequences for inappropriate behavior should match the offense. A good case of matching the punishment to the misbehavior concerned my scissors, which were always disappearing from their designated spot. I was constantly annoyed and frustrated because they weren't there when I needed them. It could take me fifteen minutes to find them, and by then I was agitated. I decided that Katlin needed to recognize how frustrating it was to go to use something and not have it be where he expected it to be. I told him that the next time the scissors were not where they were supposed to be, I would hide his telephone cord. The logical consequence was that he could not use his phone until he could find the cord. It only took two times before he realized how important it was to replace the things he used. The punishment fit the case so perfectly that it made sense, and he got it right away. Now my scissors are always where they are supposed to be. Children can internalize corrections more readily when misbehavior and punishment match up. Say you ground them for not getting up in the morning when you tell them to. What does that punishment have to do with anything? They will think it is stupid because it doesn't relate to what they have done.

Too Much of a Bad Thing

Overusing one punishment sets children up for failure and makes them stop caring. They will believe that no matter what they do, they cannot achieve the goal. One family I worked with used television privileges as a punishment. During our initial visit, I learned that they had not allowed their son to watch television for three months. This is too extreme, especially because the punishment was not resulting in improved behavior. I recommended that they find something that he had done right and reward him with an hour of television. To their surprise, his behavior instantly changed. What he had learned was, "Why should I try to behave, they'll find something wrong with me anyway and I won't get to ever watch TV again." Find different rewards and punishments for different behaviors. This gives kids a chance to win even when they have made mistakes in other areas.

Whenever possible, use positive consequences to motivate your children to behave. They will learn more from reward than from punishment. For example, one young girl wanted to redecorate her room. Her mother thought that she could earn the décor by using more appropriate language when talking to other family members. Each week her mother established a list of expectations. When her daughter used appropriate language, her mother bought her a new item for her room. As the weeks went by, the room took shape and the young girl was excited. The more excited she got, the more she complied with the new rules.

Some parents feel that kids should be punished for their bad behavior, rather than rewarded for their good behavior. Yet, adults do not abide by the same set of values. Take, for instance, working forty hours a week. Would you give your time if you didn't get paid for it? Probably not. The reward for working is that you get to live in a house, go on vacation, and buy nice things. Being respectful to the boss also has its rewards. You get to keep your job, and sometimes you may even get a raise for your efforts. Parents who believe that children can only learn through punitive measures will create children who are unwilling to grow. Let's face it, adults can always find something wrong with their children's behavior. But is that where the focus should be? If all your children know is criticism, they will develop a low sense of self-worth, and they will lose their motivation to do well. It is too easy as parents to administer punishment on a whim. Create a chart to help provide alternatives to their current disciplining procedures. If they can visualize the consequences, they will have a better shot at achieving the goals.

Ultimately you want your children to be internally driven to do what is right. But when children come from family violence, there may not be much internal motivation. So, you may need to start with external gratification to raise their motivational levels. Through intermittent reward you can then gradually move toward a more internal reward. It is important to move toward internal motivation so that children do not feel that there is always an external reward. Always use praise with your reward. This will help them become more internally driven. For example, "You did such a great job cleaning the garage, you must feel good about how hard you worked.

Just as it's possible to overuse punishments, you can also overdo rewards. If children always expect material gratification, they will develop a sense of entitlement. Rewards are a privilege, not a right. Some parents who consistently give to their children may begin to feel that they can only get their kids to do the right thing for a price. It may be difficult to know where to draw the line. Foster Cline and Jim Fay from the Love and Logic Institute explain the difference between reward and bribery as a parent's attitude.[4] When a parent *enjoys* giving to her children, the incentive is a reward. But, when a parent feels forced into giving to her kids, it is bribery. Review the following two situations and determine which is reward and which is bribery.

"I promised to take her to the park as soon she straightens up the house."

"She won't do it unless I take her to the park."

Do you see the difference? The first example frames the reward and shows the good consequences of helping out. The second expresses the sense of helplessness the parent feels. The best way to check your situation on this is to consider whether you are able to get your children to cooperate sometimes. If they will never work without money or incentives then you have used the reward system incorrectly.

Many adults think punishment has to hurt if it's going to work. This is absolutely not true. Your children have been literally beaten into submission by your batterer. They need a more positive healthy approach. Children can learn how to behave themselves without intimidation and an authoritarian approach. Children will change their behavior more easily if they are the ones making the decisions regarding outcomes. For example, a mother asked me what she could do about her two adolescent sons fighting non-stop. I suggested she have them sit down until each one gave the other permission to get up. However, each had to agree to stop fighting for the rest of the evening in order for the punishment to be over. The next week she told me:

Parent: "Well that didn't work. They sat for one minute and got up."

Me: "Did they fight anymore after that?"

Parent: "No."

Me: "Well then, it worked."

Because she was focused on the punishment side of it, which was supposed to make them suffer in order for the lesson to sink in, she had missed the real issue: their behavior improved.

Making Consequences More Real

Children are concrete thinkers and do better when they can see what is going to happen. A great way to help your children understand consequences is to show them what they can lose or gain through their behavior. For example, you may not like that your children tattle on each other. To minimize this problem, create tickets that you can physically give to them each week. Then assign a reward value to the amount of tickets they are able to maintain,[5] such as:

5 tickets = Having a friend over

4 tickets = Getting a movie rental

3 tickets = Staying up late on Friday night

2 tickets = Going to the park on Saturday

1 ticket = Getting a candy bar

Now that you have established a value, explain to them that they cannot tattle unless they are willing to sacrifice a ticket. This will force them to forfeit one each time they tell, which reduces their reward. They will be more inclined to think about tattling if they know they will lose the top prize. Reward them at the end of the week for the remaining tickets. (It is important, however, to make sure that you explain the difference between tattling and keeping others safe. If your children see their sibling playing with matches, that is not tattling. That is a safety issue. Don't assume that they know what the safety issues are, explain as many as possible.) Of course, this ticket approach works for other behaviors as well, and you can use whatever rewards you think are appropriate.

Motivations and Consequences

The best way to get your children to behave themselves is to learn what motivates them. Each child responds differently to discipline. What works for one child will not always work for another. If you have three kids, you may need three different parenting approaches. Because you lived in family violence, you may have developed only one style, and now you see that it wasn't healthy for your children. Learning new parenting strategies may seem overwhelming initially, but once you understand the natures of your children, you will see that your predictament isn't as bad as you think. Learn what makes your kids tick. Then establish consequences that match those motivations.

Motivating children to do the right thing can be as simple as establishing the right consequence. When your children have the potential to gain or lose something that is important to them, they will respond. Getting kids to buy into what you expect requires that they take some sort of ownership or responsibility for changes. Whether you like it or not, they have to choose to *want* to make the changes. Butting heads with them isn't going to make that happen. Therefore, you must find what motivates them and work from there.

Boundaries

All children learn about personal space as they develop. Children from abusive environments, however, haven't been allowed to develop properly, so they have a hard time understanding appropriate boundaries. They may use rough play that hurts as a form of interacting with others. When they are told to stop, they almost always respond with: "I was just playing/kidding/joking around." And they will be sincere. You need to work with your children to remove the phrase, "I was just . . ." from their vocabulary, because what it says to others is, "I am the only one who counts." They don't understand how others perceive such an attitude. People who are pestered by intrusive children will avoid them, a response that will eventually spread throughout the peer group. If children can't get acceptance from their peer groups they will begin to feel invisible. Their behavior will spiral downward in a self-reinforcing cycle. This can hurt children from abusive backgrounds by echoing the abandonment they have already received. These kids do not understand the boundaries. So your job is to teach them how to change their intrusive behavior. They need to learn that *no* means *no*, *stop* means *stop*, and *don't* means *don't*. This lesson is vital to their development.

Children are very concrete and visual learners. Perhaps they won't grasp the meaning of the word *boundaries*. If this is the case for your children, buy hula-hoops and walk around the house playing a boundaries game. The hula-hoops represent each person's personal space. Have the children learn to respect those boundaries by not bumping into each other. When the children can see physically where to move about, they may be able to better comprehend what they are supposed to do.

Attention

In Chapter 2, some possible reasons for your children's behavior were discussed. One reason may be the lack of attention they experienced in the past. Children need attention and, consequently, if they think they have to, they will seek bad attention, because it is better than none at all. If your children are acting out, they think they need attention. If you want to see change, you must address this need. They have been invisible for far too long. Make the time to notice and listen to your kids; they will likely respond better to your positive attention.

In other facets of their lives, children who demand attention often find themselves ostracized by their peers. To make them understand how this impacts their social skills, you have to address the issue by helping them cope more effectively with their environment. They need to learn how to be noticed without demanding the center stage.

Teaching Empathy

You know that abuse has severe consequences. One such consequence is that children may lose or not develop the ability to empathize with others because they have shutdown emotionally. Recognizing how others may feel—so vital a virtue in society— will be a foreign concept to your children. But you can reverse this consequence of abuse by deliberately practicing kindness to others. Make caring an assignment by having your children do five nice things for others, at school for example. It could be as small as opening a door for the teacher, sitting with someone during lunch, or giving someone help with homework. Have them report the recipients' responses to you, for example:

Child: "This girl didn't have a pencil today in math class, so I gave her one."
Adult: "What did she say?"
Child: "She said thanks and smiled at me."
Adult: "I bet she felt glad that she had a pencil."
Child: "Yeah, she was able to take the test."

Within three months, they should be able to empathize without the exercise. What do you do if your child resists initially? This is where motivation comes in. Tell the child that if she "forgets" to do the five nice things, then she will have to do ten nice things the following day, *and* that you will come to school to make sure she does them. That will be so overwhelming to her that she might decide to write down what she did so she doesn't forget. The idea here is to get kids to practice recognizing what others need and to see that the world doesn't just revolve around them. This belief is a major flaw in your batterer, and it may have been passed down to your children.

Another way to teach empathy is to practice on yourself. Because parents do so much for their children, they sometimes take themselves for granted. It seems as though the parents are doing everything and getting nothing in return. To combat this problem, children must learn that parents are people, too. I sometimes have parents announce to their kids that they are going to practice being nice to one another. The parents agree to do three nice things for them, and then the kids have to do one nice thing for their parents. Because kids do not realize that their parents currently do everything for nothing, they gladly accept the challenge. Parents who have tried this feel better because their kids are helping them out more, and the kids think they are getting away with something.

Eliminating the Word *Why*: Don't Ask, Don't Answer

Whenever you ask your children why they did something you don't approve of, you are setting them up for failure. Think about it. Are you ever happy with the answer they give you?

"Why did you hit your sister?"
"Why did you take $5 out of my wallet?"
"Why did you talk back to the teacher?"

Asking your kids *why* is futile because, generally, your children will be unable to come up with an acceptable answer. If you're already angry at what they have done, then their responses only increase that anger. The result is they get hit with a double whammy: one for messing up in the first place and two for trying to justify their actions.

Rather than asking why they did something wrong, suggest or ask what they could do next time so the behavior doesn't happen again. This allows kids the opportunity to problem-solve and take some responsibility for their future. Asking *why* achieves nothing. There is no resolution. As parents, don't we really just want solutions to the problem? If so, stop asking *why*. Initially, it will be hard to stop, because *why* is an automatic response. Be conscious and change how you address your problems.

Similarly, do not answer or explain yourself to your children when they ask *why*—if their questions really only mean that they're complaining about your instructions, for example:

"Why can't I stay out until midnight?"

"Why won't you give me $40?

"Why do I always have to do everything?"

When you do this, you are also trapped into giving answers that won't satisfy. It won't solve anything, and you will have given away your power. John Rosemond, an author on parenting, suggests making a *Why jar*. On slips of paper, write out five or six silly reasons why your children are not allowed to do something, and put them in the jar. Next time your child asks *why* he has to pick up the dirty clothes he dropped outside the shower, hand him the jar to choose an answer. It could be something like "Because I am mean" or "Because I don't like kids." The fact is, your kids will never like the reasons you give them either, so stop trying to explain yourself needlessly. Who knows, if you strike a funny bone the tension just might dissipate.

Getting Your Kids Ready for School

Many parents struggle with getting their kids ready for school in the morning. Often, the reason is that children suffer from separation anxiety. Home has familiarities that school cannot provide, and the thought of going out into the world can be overwhelming and scary. Kids from family violence experience this anxiety to a much greater extent than other children. A "normal" child hesitates because she knows that kids may call her names, the teacher may not respond to her the way her mother does, and she knows how to push her mother's buttons to get her needs met. Her safety net and comfort zone are gone. A kid surviving family violence experiences all of this, plus much more. Her world is complicated by the fear that others will find out about her family. She is afraid to leave her mother alone because she is worried that another beating could occur, which makes her fearful, clingy, and protective.

To reduce the fight to get your kids out the door for school, you will have to address the same issues as "regular" families, with a slight twist. This section only looks at the "regular" stuff. For the not-so-normal stuff, you will have to work on making them feel safe before they are comfortable about leaving you, which we'll learn about in Chapter 7.

If getting ready for school doesn't motivate your kids to get moving, maybe getting them ready for something else would. Tell them if they could get ready fast, you would take the extra time to go to the park and play basketball, or go out for a donut. The goal is to get them up and out of the house. Never have the donut at home. Set up a pleasant process to actually leave home to go somewhere else.

Some children, especially those age ten and up, don't want their parents telling them what to do. You may feel that you have no other option, because they won't get ready unless you are constantly nagging them. One technique I've learned is to make a *to-do chart* for your children with all the tasks that need to be completed before they leave for school (e.g., brush teeth, make beds, and so on). Have the kids check the items off as they accomplish them. Your objective is to get these tasks completed without continuously nagging, and your children's objective is to accomplish their tasks without being reminded and "treated like a baby."

Sharing

Most parents will catch their child taking a toy from another child and shout something like, "Give that back! You need to learn how to share." Then the child reacts by getting upset and throwing herself down onto the floor in a tantrum. I compare this interaction to a small flame; you can either put the fire out with water (effective parenting skills), or you can blow it up with kerosene (inappropriate parenting skills). If you or your children are yelling or getting angry, you're only fanning the flames instead of putting them out.

Even better than putting the fire out, though, is preventing it from starting. Do this by being proactive. For example, if there are kids coming over to play with your children, ask them ahead of time to put three toys away that they do not want to share with their friends. You and your kids agree that the rest of the toys are fair game. Many times, children just want to have some control over their things, and there are probably some toys that they genuinely worry about. If you establish some boundaries so they can anticipate what is expected of them, while also giving them some control, you will have much better results. After you explain that the rest of the toys must be shared, explain what happens if they do not comply. Verbalize the consequences to your children in advance so they know exactly what to expect. A positive consequence might be to reward them for every toy they share. Get a pack of stickers, and tell them that they can earn one for every toy they are willing to share with others. If you make a game of it, they will be much more eager to give up their toys.

Bedtime

Parents, particularly ones from family violence, often have a hard time getting their children to bed. There are many reasons why children have difficulties being alone in their rooms, including reasons related to past family violence. But also, bedrooms can be where they were sent as punishment, and they equate bed with being bad. Consequently, they will avoid their bedrooms as much as possible. If you want them to like their rooms, try sending them to different area of the house when they misbehave. Try making the bedrooms a fun place to be. Read them stories and play games with them in their rooms. Make their bedrooms a place of refuge.

Household Chores

If you are not getting cooperation with housework, make a daily work chart for each family member. There are several ways to handle this. If possible, start with a reward system. Rather than allowing your children to have unlimited television time, start having them earn their time by doing their chores. For every chore that is completed, they earn ten minutes of time. If they do the chore without being reminded, they earn an additional five minutes. Another method could be that you assign fines next to the chores that are not completed. The money will then be distributed to the family member who chooses to complete the task. One method that works is handing out an extra chore if they do not do the one assigned to them. To motivate them further, tell them that they cannot do anything until the chores are completed. So if they have soccer practice or a birthday party, they have to get the job done first.

To motivate your kids, use language that encourages self-respect, pride, and a sense of accomplishment. Because as parents we are tired and fed up, we often give up on making our kids help out and just do the work ourselves. We are not doing them a favor by doing everything for them. This will send two messages: (1) that they are incapable of contributing to the household, and (2) that you are there only to serve them. In both cases they will develop unrealistic expectations about the roles each of you plays, and there are no winners.

Resolving Conflicts

Conflict between parents and children is inevitable. Children feel frustrated and overwhelmed by their lives. You will have to help them sort those emotions out and find better ways to cope. The best way to minimize the conflict is to stop and redirect their emotions. This may mean that you have to listen to each other. One daughter complained that her mother would not help with her school project. Yet, the mom argued that when she tried to give her daughter assistance, her daughter would criticize her. They had both tried to bring up the past to defend their position. What we realized was that this project was huge and overwhelming. The girl was trying to work on too many sections and simply did not know where to start. Initially, we began by separating her papers into four categories. I physically handed each sheet of paper to her and had her place it into the proper pile. After she had sorted half the pile, I began talking to her mother while handing her the papers, giving less attention to the teenager's work. She interrupted us: "Can I have the rest of the papers? You're going too slow." She then retrieved another set of papers from her room and completed the project independently, receiving an A. She had needed nothing more than help sorting papers. The problem was that these two were too stuck in their conflict to resolve the simple issue at hand.

Another area where conflict can often arise is when children fight over the front seat of the car. In order to stop this, assign your children a day that is theirs to ride in the front. For example, Jimmy gets the seat on Monday, Wednesday, and Saturday; Sammy gets Tuesday, Thursday, and Sunday. You can give the seat a break on Friday if you like. The following month, switch the schedule so they understand that things change. If your children still insist on fighting, tell them in advance that they will lose their privilege for the day if they continue, and you get the front all to yourself.

Adolescence

Adolescence is a time of self-discovery and emancipation. It is the job of adolescents to grow up and grow out. In order to have their own independent thought, they have to be everything that you are not. This explains why they may think you're a naïve idiot. *Try not to personalize this.* They will come around again once they have moved on and discovered the reality beyond themselves. Growing up is really hard to do, and they need you to get them through this process. It may help to remember your own teenage years.

Most adolescents listen more effectively when voice tones are low, and when adults reason with them. Validating their feelings, rather than discounting them, will be the most effective way to get past the inappropriate attention they are seeking. Negotiation and compromise are important to helping them move on with their lives.

Mutual Respect

I hear parents complain that once their adolescents grow bigger than them, there is no way to "make" them do anything. Physically this may be true. However, in your quest to parent in the aftermath of family violence, you must ask yourself how to handle your situation differently. In the past, discipline and correction were done through intimidation and fear. Now you want to show your children a new and better life. This requires mutual respect. Ask yourself whether or not you really care how your children feel and if they care how you feel. Do you give each other a voice in the decision-making process? Are you both allowed to express your needs? Do you genuinely like each other?

Without mutual respect, children won't buy into discipline—this is especially true of adolescents—and you won't be as loving and patient as you could be. Showing mutual respect might feel foreign to everyone involved at first, but the new skills you are learning in this chapter will help you move in the right direction.

Role modeling is key to mutual respect. The rules for your children must also apply to you. This is an issue of double standards, which kids see through just as quickly as adults do. Some common examples of parental double standards include: smoking while forbidding your teenager to do so, and snacking yourself but keeping snacks from your kids. There are plenty of others. If you adopt such attitudes regularly, you'll lose their respect as quickly as you can say *double standard*. Especially because they may be accustomed to such parental disrespect from the past abusive relationship. One batterer expected his children to abide by the chores chart, but refused to participate in the housework himself. The message the children got was that he was above the rules and better than everyone else. If you take this approach you will not get cooperation or respect from your children.

Your kids must believe that you genuinely regard them as worthy of respect, which will make it possible for them to respect you in return. You may have to start each day reminding yourself, "I really like and respect my children." In our grown-up haste to get through the day, we sometimes forget what's important. We know we love our kids, but do we respect them? How you respond to them will improve with this simple reminder. Ask yourself if you treat other people's children more politely than you do your own. If so, you may need to remind yourself more often that you like and respect your kids.

Conclusion of Some Sort

Parenting in the aftermath of family violence requires that your kids believe that you are a powerful figure in their lives. Your abusive partner may never have listened to you. That may be the legacy he has given to your kids, to make you appear powerless. Consequently, you may think your children will not listen either. You have to recognize that your children need your input to discount what they have learned. They need you to be strong and protect them. You may not believe that you can make a difference, but *your kids are counting on you*. If this is the first time you have taken an active role as the authority figure, your kids will need to adjust. Be patient, loving, and understanding. As you grow more confident, they will follow your lead.

CHAPTER 7

Control: It's a Trust Issue

> You can build a shell around you to keep others out, but you become a prisoner of your own shell. Consequently, no one can get in and you can't get out.
>
> —*Unknown*

The buzzwords for family violence awareness are trust and control. In any literature reviewed, you will invariably hear a combination of the two. They are often viewed as two separate issues with distinct differences. It has been my experience, however, that the two are enmeshed in one another so that they appear to be one and the same. You cannot have one without the other. In essence, you cannot genuinely have control over your life unless you trust others, and you cannot trust others without giving up some control.

The objective for this chapter is to develop a sense of control by trusting your environment without the fear of being overpowered by it. As frightening as it may be to relinquish some control, it is necessary for regaining your life. Your children also need to let go of the control to lead healthier lives. At some point, everyone needs to depend on others for emotional support. No one should fear love, or feel that it has to hurt. You and your children deserve to be free from the prison your batterer built for you. It is time to be paroled.

Victims were forced to control their worlds to survive. Their abusers violated and hurt them, so they could only imagine what the rest of the world had in store toward them. Suspicion toward others keeps them enmeshed in the cycle of violence. They are too embarrassed to reach out. They fear being judged because outsiders just don't understand. Until you are able to trust, life will have its challenges. Your problems are compounded by the fact that your children must learn this lesson as well. This process is not an easy one; but with time and tenacity, you can protect your family and provide them with a safe and violence-free future.

Protecting children can be described in varying degrees. The most obvious is to protect them from physical harm—from injury, maiming, and death. The most overlooked, however, is emotional protection. Many people believe that verbal assault is not abuse. Yet when adults, emotionally assaulted as children, were asked, they said that the words hurt them the most. They invariably exclaim, "The physical wounds will heal, but the emotional scars last forever." or "At least with a black eye you know you've been hit." When people witness or live through emotional abuse, they learn not to trust. This defense mechanism must be unlearned before healing occurs.

What Your Children Witnessed

When your children witnessed your abuse, whether they were struck or not, they, too, were battered. Their senses of safety were shattered by the assaults they witnessed upon you. Therefore, the goal should be to get healthy enough to develop your protective instincts again. Somehow along the way that natural instinct was lost. Perhaps, you were not nurtured as a child, or conceivably your batterer beat the instincts out of you.

To overcome your odds, learn the skills necessary to safeguard your children. Mothers often ask whether they have the right to confront people who are being unjust to their children. The answer is, absolutely, *yes.* You have the *right* and the entitlement to be the decision maker in your children's lives, no matter what anyone else thinks. You know what is right for your children and it's your responsibility to do something about it.

Control: It's a Trust Issue

Building a Bond of Trust

Your children may detach from you for whatever reasons, but as the imminent threat from your batterer is no longer present, the bonds can be rebuilt. To heal effectively, connections must be reestablished. Your first step is to verbalize that they are the priority. This will contribute to rebuilding the trust. Initially, they might be apprehensive, so be patient. Although they may appear hard and calloused, underneath the rough exterior, they are very fragile and needy. To build the bond, use the following list of comments:

- "I will always be there for you."
- "Nobody will ever come between us again."
- "We are in this together."
- "You are the best thing that has ever happened to me."
- "I am so lucky to have you."
- "I am so blessed to know you."
- "You can count on me."

Your children have suffered a tremendous loss, and it may take years to undo the fear, rejection, and abandonment issues created by the abuse. The negative input is so ingrained that their automatic reaction is to scrutinize anything said or done to them. Especially if you have minimized what your batterer has done to you. They may struggle with trusting that you understand the severity of your abuse. Unwittingly, in your quest to protect them, perhaps you made excuses like, "Oh, Mommy fell down the stairs." or "Oh, clumsy me, I ran into the door again."

Battered mothers who use responses such as these unconsciously teach their children not to believe in them. Many victims report that their children never witnessed the abuse. Conversely, when asked, the children invariably say that they had. So stop fooling yourself. Even when they were not present for the physical altercation, they read through the tears and preoccupation. What you said and how they felt conflicted. The non-disclosure sent the message that something was very wrong. They knew instinctively that their mother was not being honest.

To see change, you must be fully aware of your circumstances and be their protector. Otherwise, their role and stance becomes, "My mom can't protect us, so I will!" Your children are not equipped to take care of you. They are supposed to be kids, and you need to be the adult.

Understand that relinquishing of their position, however, will not happen until they can feel safe. This means that you are now the lioness of your den. You must prove that you are in charge and capable. You ultimately want your children to feel secure. Therefore, creating that sense of safety for them directly affects that security.

> A teenage girl admitted that at times she just wanted her mother to hold her. She commented that any attempt to get physically close to her mother was met with great resistance. When confronted, her mother laughed nervously and said that her daughter needed to grow up. I explained that no matter how old we get, there are times when we need our mother's love. At this point, she admitted that she too missed her mother sometimes. Children are limited emotionally. They need an adult's guidance, support, and love to grow. This relationship requires an emotional connectedness to repair the damages and can only be accomplished when the mother's role becomes a nurturing one.
>
> Both she and her daughter practiced touching and loving each other for several weeks. The mother eventually permitted her daughter to rest with her on the couch. Interestingly, the daughter became confused by the gesture and questioned her mother's motivation. Her suspicion hurt her mother's feelings. This teenager longed for this interaction for so long yet challenged the relationship once it was presented to her. They will both have to work on feeling comfortable with loving each other.

Building trust requires creating a bond of strength. In the next section, we will discuss how to take charge of your life and your children's lives. Trust can be accomplished through creating consistencies, making eye contact, and encouraging touch.

Creating Consistencies

Your children would benefit greatly from knowing that they have events, rituals, and times that are concrete. They desire good times they can anticipate. You could rent movies on Fridays, have pizza on Wednesdays, or go to the park on Saturdays. This gives them something they can rely on. These rituals permit them to gradually learn how to count on their environment and on you.

Next, try to establish consistent emotional patterns like hugging, winking at, or kissing your kids for no apparent reason. Initial discomfort will occur, but with consistency the feelings will subside. Living in violence taught them that their emotional and physical treatment was conditional (which usually meant mistreated). There wasn't much positive interaction. Now, as you introduce this new dynamic which provides consistency and *unconditional* love, you can change how they feel. Once they recognize your sincerity, they can start trusting and loving you for it.

Making Eye Contact

Emotional connection and building trust are best accomplished through eye contact. This may be anxious for your children but they need to make the bond. Without this connection, they can develop problems such as reactive attachment disorder, which could potentially lead to more serious trouble later. When children are permitted to avoid eye contact for too long, pathologies could develop. Many adults unwittingly view children's distance and disconnectedness as a sign that they want to be left alone. But in actuality, these children are fearful. For example, one young boy was so disconnected that his teachers let him sit in a corner by himself, simply so they did not have to deal with him. As time passed, the isolation caused more dislike for the boy. He interpreted their attitude as rejection, which made him feel like an outcast. Eventually, he stopped interacting with everyone. The staff described him as a strange child that was a nuisance. When I began working with him, we discovered that he was incapable of making any eye contact. Any attempt to connect created such discomfort that he would curl up and cry out, "My eyes, my eyes, it hurts, it hurts." The severity of abuse made eye contact unbearable for this young boy. He was so traumatized that he was fearful of anyone who looked at him. As difficult as it was, we had to make him connect. The eyes are the windows to the soul and he needed someone to reach in and pull him out. The problem with most children who have suffered serious abuse is that others fear reaching out to them emotionally. In Chapter 9, you will learn how to campaign for your children so that they have a better chance of succeeding. For now, do what you can to make as much eye contact as possible.

Encouraging Touch

Kids from family violence may struggle with physical touch for many reasons. One reason is that they learned through repeated assaults that touch hurts, and another is that they are guarded emotionally to avoid further rejection. Their concept becomes, "I will not let anyone ever hurt me again." Although they defensively think this way, it does not necessarily mean that is how they feel. Avoidance is a coping mechanism that allows them to dissociate from the pain. Your job will be to reconnect your children with the world. This can be an excruciating process that tests you to your limits. Be prepared for the long journey.

> A mom once complained that her daughter did not permit anyone to touch her. The girl squirmed and fidgeted when anyone displayed affection toward her. Her mother reacted by sending her daughter to her room for being disrespectful. Unfortunately, the problem increasingly worsened. The young girl had learned earlier that loving someone was painful. To prevent being hurt, she deliberately sabotaged her mother's efforts to avoid connecting to anyone. My recommendation was to change the strategy. Rather than permit her daughter to escape the interaction, she could draw her daughter in closer through unobtrusive touch. She could brush her hair lightly or gently rub her shoulders. This approach will create discomfort, but eventually, this young girl will get the message that she cannot withdraw and run away from the world.
>
> The mother indicated, as expected, that her daughter initially struggled to avoid her touch but she stayed consistent. With time her daughter succumbed and relinquished her control. The mother reported a positive change, one that she thought was not possible.

Many children from family violence suffer from detachment disorders. The impact varies in degree, depending upon the length and severity of exposure. But regardless of the extent of the abuse, kids are affected in one form or another. When emotional detachment has occurred, physical and emotional contact are avoided at any price. For example, Katlin's body stiffened tightly and became rock hard when touched. He fought anytime I approached him. Physical interaction with him was not a good experience, but a necessary challenge that had to be met. To combat this problem, I implemented a new technique, which I have coined "Love time." Love time is something that helps an unattached child reconnect. The objective is to motivate a child to *want* touch or to recognize that not touching holds a far greater consequence. Katlin's love time required him to sit through five minutes of affection each day or be subjected to ten additional minutes for resisting. Needless to say, he tolerated the former. Gradually, he submitted himself to the affection and even looked forward to it at times. One day, Katlin's head vulnerably rested upon my shoulder. I knew in that instant that I had finally reached him. Prior to this momentous day, I agonized over his future because he controlled his emotions to the extent that he never cried or acknowledged his pain. Children who do not feel cannot empathize with others. The repercussion for this apathy is that the cycle of violence repeats itself, because they cannot comprehend what pain feels like.

As the nonviolent parent you must make the connection for them. They are guarded and defensive. They reject others before others can reject them. They cope by pushing people away and shutting down emotionally. Now is the time to reintroduce attachment to them. Children depend on their parents to see their pain. They cannot disclose their vulnerabilities because their hurt runs too deep. They won't succumb without a fight because trusting others is just too scary. But the reality is that true healing cannot take place without trust.

Peer Pressure

There are so many external influences that impact children. A gamut of obstacles, including their peers, can make coping difficult. To help them manage more effectively, discuss their feelings regarding their cohorts. Find ways to change how your children react to their peers. The sad reality is that many kids from family violence become targets for other abuses. They unconsciously wear their emotions on their sleeves. Adults may not always see the signs but kids usually do. Peers are great at picking up when other children suffer from abuse. In this case, not only are your children suffering from the aftermath of abuse at home, they are also getting abuse from outside sources. This further exacerbates the trust issue and drives the need for control even more. Teaching your children how to cope will be imperative. Peer interaction can be devastating otherwise, because these vulnerable children are sought out then tormented. Taunted children genuinely believe that they are the only ones experiencing this reprehensible violation. They cannot trust anyone to protect and care for them. Because of the great shame, disclosure is often not an option for them. They believe that they have nowhere to turn.

School and other activities with peer involvement become unpleasant experiences. These children often feel unsafe because someone might learn their secret and expose them. To compensate, they may cling to family members and generate separation anxiety. As odd as it sounds, victims, both adults and children, develop a symbiosis to protect one another against outsiders. Their reality is that nobody is there for them. As a result, they may resort to destroying any opportunities to participate in activities, which makes them susceptible. The dynamics of the violence taught them to be suspicious.

Starting over with your new rules combined with the demands from outsiders might confuse your children. Although your family no longer lives in violence, they are still playing by the old rules. Motivating them to venture out into the "big bad world" might be challenging. Some examples might be getting them ready for school or other activities—they will claim illness, complain that they are too tired, or just be unmotivated to get ready for their day. School, although a reprieve from the memories, is not always a fun place to be. Peers tease and call them ugly, fat, and stupid. The pressure to perform and fit in can be incredibly overwhelming. All they will want to do is run away. If the anxiety gets too great, motivating them to want to venture out will be difficult. They will retort, "I hate that stupid place" or "Everyone hates me, I don't want to go back." Your children will not want to relinquish the control they have built for themselves, so encourage them as much as possible to let go.

Children could have adverse negative reactions to abuse, which vary in appearance. Some may display victim tendencies, whereas others may exhibit abusive behaviors. For example, one of Katlin's classmates had experienced family violence. His reactions to the abuse were to cower down, cry, and withdraw. But Katlin, who had also experienced family violence, was aggressive, physical, and defiant. Needless to say, the two found one another, and it wasn't pretty. The mother reacted strongly to Katlin's interaction with her son. She wanted to keep them apart. But my position was that the two needed to learn how to get along. Children from family violence always find one another. My philosophy was that it would be better to teach them how to cope rather than run away from each other. This mother agreed and we began working on more appropriate behaviors and attitudes. We showed them how to constructively get their needs met, set boundaries, and communicate more effectively with one another. Their relationship improved. It also helped the other mother empower herself and see that she could help her son not be victimized by others.

To help your children depersonalize others' behavior, try to relate to them emotionally. Use your own experiences as a child to create a level of trust. For example, you could say, "You know, once someone beat me up when I was a little kid, and boy did it make me mad. I bet that bothers you, too. But those kind of kids aren't really happy, and so we need to figure out how to deal with them." Kids personalize the attacks. They believe that others pick on them because there is something wrong with them. The reality, however, is that children who bully pick on others because the receiver's reactions are so strong. Bullies say, "Hey, let's pick on Jake because we can make him mad." or "Let's go tease Sally so we can watch her cry." What children do not understand is that reacting to the peer pressure takes away their control even further. The very thing they are trying so desperately to maintain is taken from them in an instant.

Perception of Other Adults

Children from family violence are so misunderstood. Outsiders view their behavior as aberrant and intolerable. Children sense being disliked and unwanted. The biases are dreadfully apparent to them. Consequently, their reactions to those discriminations catapult and magnify their behavior even further. They cannot differentiate between negative attitudes at school and the abuse at home. Kids believe in what others say, so if that input is negative, their behavior will match that expectation. We will discuss this issue more in depth in Chapter 9.

Your children need help understanding the truth about themselves and discerning between what is real and what is not. If you are not getting through to them, rely on others to help out. Whoever said, "It takes a village" knew what they were talking about. Warn the adults, however, that your children may not be receptive initially. There will be apprehension and suspicion. This is a natural reaction because of the lack of trust. I am sure they are thinking, "Okay, why should I believe that you want to help me when all I am is a screwup." They genuinely want to believe the positive feedback, but they are just too scared. With time, consistency, and credibility, most kids will come around.

Control Freaks

In school, children from family violence try to control their environment by challenging others. They don't want anyone telling them what to do. The resistance, however, only ensures a trip to the principal's office for defying the teacher. They think that by fighting back they are winning; yet they repeatedly place themselves in a losing situation. They upset those around them to the point that they are branded as troublemakers. The outside labels create assumptions that automatically blame the children. Sometimes, unjustly, these kids are blamed, which further exacerbates the problems. To counteract the hostility, they fight back more to regain control, only to find themselves more deeply entrenched in this cycle. The sad part is that they rarely win and they eventually feel like the world is against them. Each event builds on the last. Unless they learn to trust the people trying to control their lives, they will never experience peace. They will walk around defensively with their fists clenched, ready to fight. Teaching them how to relinquish some of their power will allow them to relax and let go of the desperate need for control. Judging who to trust and who not to trust will require some guidance.

Kids must hear out loud how to trust credible people, especially you, without feeling that their safety will be jeopardized. Verbalizing is particularly important because children are often incapable of identifying what they really feel. When they can put words to emotions, then they can begin to let others in. When they know that you know their secret feelings, they can relax. Without trust, however, these kids gradually become defiant and question everything down to the smallest detail to maintain and manage their lives. For example, you may tell your child to wash her face and she may immediately retort, "I don't have to." or "I'm not dirty." To counter her challenge say, "You need to trust that my decisions are made because I love you, not because I want to punish you. Please go wash your face." Initially, recognizing what they are feeling may be difficult, but as you grow with your kids, you will understand exactly what is going through their little heads. Now it's time to take that knowledge and help your kids learn to cope with their distrust.

Placing the Blame

Children need to realize that the battering was not their fault. They have been forced to accept the blame for their maltreatment and their batterer's unhappiness. They must recognize the relationship for what it was—one-sided and abusive. Children are great at taking responsibility for their parent's actions. Unfortunately, they internalize that behavior and their senses of worth and value become a direct result of the interpretation of their parent's attitudes. Children need to develop confidence and have a good sense of self-worth. To do this, they have to understand that they did not cause the abuse and that their violator has to take responsibility for what he does. Anger is a choice, and children cannot control their parent's responses. As you know, there was nothing anyone could ever do to please your batterer. Abusers are doom-and-gloom pessimists who would complain that their ice cream was too cold and it would somehow be someone else's fault.

On the other side of the coin, your children may blame you for the abuse. They have heard repeatedly that you could have avoided a beating *if you had only* said "good morning" a little more nicely, or made sure the house was clean when their father got home from a long, hard day at work. Now that you are separated from your batterer, he will cause havoc by blaming you for your family's problems. He may use emotional extortion to generate fear so your kids are forced to side with him. They comply to control their safety. It is imperative that you understand this dynamic because your batterer will do whatever it takes to keep your life in turmoil. Listen very carefully: If your children act like they do not love you, do not believe it! Your batterer taught them to mistrust you. They will unconsciously push you away. If you buy into the façade that your children don't love you, your relationship will suffer.

One woman who lost custody of the children to her batterer was only given weekend visitation. Her children told her regularly that they hated her and hated being with her. She listened to their hurtful words and considered relinquishing her visitation. I encouraged her to be a stronger parent. She needed to tell them that she loved them, that the weekends were her time and that she would never give that up no matter how mad they were. To the mother's amazement, her daughters both hugged her and said, "We love you, too, Mommy." This woman found out later that her ex-husband would beat the children if they didn't pray at night to be thankful for not having to live with their mother. They were physically and emotionally terrorized. Eventually, this mother was able to regain custody of her children, but what would have happened if she had given up? How would her children feel about themselves if she had walked out of their lives? Thanks to her strength, however, they were able to rebuild their trust and place the blame where it really belonged.

Giving Kids Some Control

Letting kids have a say and some control often helps reduce the need for full control. Negotiating and providing choices can make all the difference in the world. Empowering them with voices allows them to know that they are being heard and that their opinions count. Therefore, allowing your children to *think* that they have the control helps a great deal. For example, when Katlin was younger, I wanted him to eat spinach. I knew he would fight me on this issue, so I would give him a choice, "Do you want spinach, or do you want salad?" His response was, "Salad." I would assent, tear up the fresh spinach, put it in a bowl, and place dressing on it. He found comfort in making his own choice, but the bottom line was, he ate spinach. Consequently, we both won.

Food can be a major control issue for abused children because it is the one thing they can have power over. But for most parents, not eating is a source of contention because they worry about their children's health. Therefore, their children's need for control in this area makes parents crazy. Somehow children have to have some say in this matter.

Let's look at another way to give children more control regarding food issues. Allow them to choose two food items per week that they dislike, and then tolerate their refusal to eat them. Say, for instance, your children do not like tomatoes and green beans. Let those be the items that they are permitted to refuse for the week. Make sure that they understand that these are their choices and that they cannot switch midweek. This is to help them internalize that they made the choice and now they have to live with it. Next, serve these two items often, with an additional vegetable available, like peas. They can look at the items of disgust and feel in control. Then you can serve them the peas and have your requirement for nutrition met. If they say they don't like peas, remind them that peas were not on their list, but that they could make that choice next week.

Giving your kids some control over their lives makes them feel better about themselves. Negotiation works well to motivate this process. For example, if you want your kids to go to bed by nine o'clock, negotiate by telling them they can go to bed at eight or nine. Tell them it is their choice.

Set boundaries that feel comfortable for you, and then begin bargaining at a lower amount. For example, you can negotiate time spent out with friends, amount of junk food consumed, or any other quantifiable issue. You need to verbalize your expectations while still giving them options.

The following are a few examples that you can use to show your kids that they have some control, yet you are still very much in charge:

- "You can clean your room in fifteen minutes or you can do it now—your choice."
- "We can have hamburgers or meatloaf for dinner—your call."
- "The towels need to be picked up now, or you can have extra clean up time—you decide."

"Your choice . . . Your call . . . You decide." Can you see how the control is placed on them? Giving them the decision-making power helps them internalize their consequences better. A warning should be made, however, that if they choose not to do what you asked and they accept their consequence, then you must live with their decision. You could perhaps caveat your request by telling them that their task must be completed at a designated later time. As your children learn that they are truly in charge of some aspects of their lives, they can ease up on maintaining full control. They have to learn that giving partial control to others will not produce total chaos. This is an important lesson because no matter what a person does in life, there are times when others have control to some extent. It could be a teacher, a spouse, or a boss. The sooner your children "get" this, the better off they will be. They must feel comfortable with relinquishing part of their control to someone they deem trustworthy. Currently, your children probably feel that it has to be all or nothing. They need to realize that there does not have to be an extreme. Moderation is the key.

The Cause and Effects of Mistrust

Emotional deprivation creates mistrust, which leads to a life fueled by a sense of urgency. The result is that some children generate poor impulse control. For my nephew and many kids like him, the devastating consequences cause severe problems. No matter how good their lives might seem, they are coming from a deficit-based standpoint. They can only see what they don't have. The need for more is always there. They starve emotionally, and desperately depend on external sources to meet their internal needs. You can buy them a hat, but they want two more. You can take them to the park for an hour, and they want to stay for three. Their needs become insatiable. This has been one of our toughest challenges, and one that Katlin and I have not overcome at this point. Children might hoard food; they might worry that they will be left out; and they may be disappointed when others have more than them. These deprivations cause trust issues. Unfortunately, the effects leave them feeling cheated and they view the world as cruelly unfair.

Not knowing whether an environment will be fair causes other control problems for these children as well. They struggle with issues like taking turns, not being first, and respecting boundaries. They are often viewed as selfish and mean, when in fact, they are just trying to survive in an unfair world. Knowing this should make it easier to understand their frantic need to be in charge. It is to guarantee that they get a turn and not because they don't want others to have one. They truly believe that they have to take it while they can or else the opportunity vanishes. They have learned that their needs won't be met unless they take what they need themselves. They live in a dog-eat-dog world. Their future is uncertain, so right now is all that counts. It's now or never. This belief creates a sense of desperation that others misjudge. The anxiety generated by the unknown is a key component for kids plagued with distrust. They have learned how to interpret and anticipate their environment by maintaining strict control. The cause and effect from this introduces a new dynamic. They panic when they cannot predict what happens next. They no longer understand what to do and the fear creates anxiety for them.

Depending upon the severity of the abuse that your children suffered, you may have to deal with similar issues. Be prepared. The best way to handle these episodes is to constantly reassure them that they are safe, and that it is okay to not be in total control. If you decide to venture out with your kids to help them feel safe with the unknown, make your trips fun and review the rules for new places several times during your travels. The more exposure you can give them to new experiences the faster they will improve. This won't be any type of picnic, but you will be building your children's ability to let go of the control.

Getting Kids to Trust Themselves

There are negative people in the world with opinions that simply are not healthy for your children. Therefore, you must create a balance, wherein your kids can trust themselves yet still comply with adult demands. This can be accomplished by explaining that sometimes in life, they may have to "take it" from the people around them; but that doesn't mean that they have to "take it in." What this implies is that they might have to suck it up and do what they are told, but they do not have to personalize or accept what others say as true. So, if a teacher calls your child names, such as "loser," he doesn't have to buy into it. Children were conditioned early to understand that adults are always right, so you may need to help recondition them. I heard a little girl at a festival declare to her grandmother that she could not see the puppets on the stage. Her grandmother in utter disgust proceeded to slam the young child in a front-row seat and spout off, "You are such a pain in the ass!" I was mortified. What lesson did this child learn on that day? What will her self-image be in ten years if the message she received that day continues? How will she be able to cope with those hurtful words if the input is not counteracted?

When children experience family violence, the words are everlasting. If children "take it in," the abusive words can haunt them forever. The pathetic part is that abusers usually do not even recall spewing those hateful words, nor do they care how they impacted their children. Has this attitude contributed to your children's distrust toward others? If so, how do you change these wounded feelings? Start by surrounding them with positive people who can provide nurturing and unconditional love. Eventually, with support, they can learn to trust themselves.

Magic—It's a Powerful Safety Net

Young children believe in fairy dust, magic wands, and genies who make wishes come true. Their imaginations can be great tools to overcome fear. Magic makes the impossible possible and has the power to change reality. You can use your children's imaginations to symbolize the prospects of safer lives. Children want to have faith in make-believe because then all things are possible. When Katlin was six years old, he suffered from severe night terrors. He jolted awake screaming too many nights to count. These dreams were too frightening for him to fall asleep again. Consequently, we both had many sleepless nights. After several weeks, I concluded that sleep deprivation wasn't working well for me, so I used magic as a means of changing our situation. I took a crystal earring that was bursting with colors, glued it onto an index card, and placed it over his doorframe. I then proceeded to explain that the crystal had magical powers that would never allow the bad dreams to come back. From that point on the nightmares stopped.

When he was nine years old, our house was being painted. The painter waived the index card and inquired, "Hey lady, what do you want me to do with this?" I turned to Katlin, who was now old enough to understand the limitations of an earring glued to a piece of paper, and asked, "What do you think?" He thought for a moment and said, "Let's keep it, just in case." Even with his maturity, he wanted to believe in the magic because that one small symbol made it possible for him to relax and feel safe. The power of magic can be a wonderful tool. Use what you can to take away their fears.

Your Control

This chapter has primarily focused on how to help your children learn to let go of the control and learn how to trust. Now we should discuss how the abuse has impacted you. It is important to educate yourself so that you can make informed choices about your life that make sense and are healthy for you. You never want to repeat this vicious cycle again. At some point you might want to start a new relationship with someone, a relationship with healthy boundaries that will require trust. But in order to find a healthy partner, you must be a healthy person.

Apply what you have learned about your kids' trust issues to get started. The only disadvantage you might have (that your kids didn't) is a parental figure to support you. You might have to rely upon yourself and be your own parent. That means taking care of your needs because there isn't anyone else to do it for you. Even when you have parents, they may not be emotionally available. It would be unrealistic to expect them to be there for you. Their unavailability may be where you learned to mistrust in the first place. Learning how to care for yourself will seem foreign because your focus has always been on others. But it really is your turn to be taken care of. That begins with learning who you are and what you deserve. The likelihood is that your life was spent trying to appease your batterer. But in the process, you lost your identity. You spent countless hours trying to make things right. Yet, you were never able to control your abuser's emotions. Consequently, you were so busy meeting his needs that somehow you got lost in the process. Now it is time to take control and start trusting yourself.

Trusting Yourself

Trusting others requires learning how to trust yourself enough to make good judgments. This means looking within yourself and recognizing that you are no longer going to permit others to control you emotionally. You have to realize and truly believe that you are in charge of who you think you are. You get to decide whose input you accept and whose you do not. Then you choose whom you let into your life and whom you do not. But first, you must get past the fear. Trusting seems like a double-edged sword: darned if you do, darned if you don't.

You might feel suspicious of a new partner or friend's motives and be afraid to let him or her in emotionally, yet simultaneously yearn for the company. I have had victims say that they would never trust a man that takes them to fancy restaurants, or does nice things for them, because they realized that their batterers tricked them with romance. It is critical to understand that not all men are bad and that you can trust others without being hurt, so long as you trust yourself to make the right choices.

It would be incredibly lonely to exclude and be suspicious of nice people who genuinely like you. Your batterer had a motive for his kindness but that is not the case for everyone. Just listen to your gut; it will tell you when something is not right. Don't be afraid of kind gestures, they can make you feel good.

Many victims stay away from relationships after they have left a volatile one. People may believe that they do so because they don't trust anyone; but the reality is that they don't trust themselves to be a good judge of character. You might be confused as to how you could have allowed yourself to be so mistreated. You might start making excuses and rid yourself of anyone who tries to penetrate your barriers. Keeping yourself too safe is a lonely way to live.

Trusting will be hard, but as you choose healthy people for your life, you can do it. We all need to have support, and as scary as it sounds, we have to eventually let others in. Initially, though, it is okay to be alert and mindful. The old habits die hard, and caution must be taken so you do not repeat your mistakes. Take your time reentering relationships, but do not sever relationships with all men. It might behoove you to practice setting boundaries with male co-workers, brothers, neighbors, and platonic friends. As you gain confidence to get what you need from them, you can move forward with the real thing.

When you become healthy, you will serve as an outstanding role model for your children. Life from this point forward gets to be the way you want it to be. If you are still struggling with your batterer, just remember that attitude is a choice. Take away his power; gain control over your life, and trust again.

CHAPTER 8

Monkey in the Middle

Experiencing family violence and divorce as children is like being tied
on a medieval rack, then drawn and quartered. The only difference is no
one hears their screams.

—*Christina M. Dalpiaz*

Children caught in the crossfire of divorce and family violence suffer
greatly from being trapped in the middle of an emotional tug of war.
Their situation seems grave because no matter what they do or how
they feel, they can never win the approval of both parents. If they
love one, the other feels betrayed, and vice versa. These children are
often forced to volley between parents, making them the monkey in
the middle. They are expected to take sides, which invariably disappoints someone. They are in a no-win situation, which leaves them
feeling guilty and inadequate. In this chapter, we will discuss how to
understand their predicament, and what you can do to help them
cope more effectively.

The first order of business is to understand that you are contend-
ing with an unscrupulous deviant. This places you at a significant
disadvantage. Competing with your abuser's demented mindset can
be nerve wracking. His mission is to destroy you emotionally,
financially, and physically even if that means using the children.
Your batterer's behavior is incomprehensible, and can leave you
off-kilter.

You might question how a parent could exploit his kids like this. The reason is clear: He only cares about his needs and they are the trump card. His actions are not directed necessarily toward them, but toward you. His intention is to hurt and punish you for running away. When all other methods to control you fail, the children become the secret weapon. His quest to maintain control borders on lunacy.

Batterers develop distorted thinking patterns that are so twisted that comprehending their train of thought is virtually impossible. Their actions are unconscionable to the average person, which leaves victims unprepared for the attacks. One example that comes to mind is a victim who shared that her ex-husband stapled their family pet, still alive, to their house for her to discover. The victim then fears that she and her children are next. Examples such as these show the difficulty of anticipating what a batterer's next move may be.

You can no longer stand idle and wait. You need to be ready for anything and everything. You must become an offensive rather than a defensive opponent. The man you once loved is now the enemy, and you must forget the past, and concentrate on the present. You have to take charge of your life for the sake of your children. This means you will have to be on your toes, and ready to respond at all times to his deception.

One way to combat your batterer's manipulation, lies, and trickery is to never assume that he is coming from the same emotional place as you are. For example, do not think that he cares about the children just because you do. The only interest he has, at heart, is his own. You cannot underestimate his deviant thought processes. The levels he might go to are far reaching. In his mind, your children are no different than the property that he owns. The kids are used as pawns in his twisted games.

Coping with the Deception

As you probably already know, a batterer will say and do anything to get even with his estranged partner. He may break, burn, and destroy precious mementos, or he might hurt or kill your pets just to cause you pain. What appears ridiculously absurd to the average person becomes an integral part of a battered woman's life. The children are usually included in this relentless plot to destroy the victim. Understand that any attempts to control what your batterer says to your kids will only frustrate you, not to mention that the attention gives him what he is so desperately seeking. Instead of playing into his deceptive practices, teach your children how to cope with the psychological warfare that he is inflicting upon them. To accomplish this task, help your kids stop internalizing what is being said to them by explaining your batterer's limitations, and letting them know that his behavior has nothing to do with them. Use the following examples as starters:

> "Your dad had a really hard life, and he never learned how to love anyone. If he could love anyone, it would surely be you."
>
> "Your father doesn't understand how to talk to kids because his parents weren't very nice to him. Someday when he is older he might realize how painful his words were."
>
> "As much as you want your dad to be at your game, he just doesn't understand how to support you."
>
> "Your dad is not mad at you, he's mad at me. Don't personalize his words."
>
> "You can love your dad, and not like what he does."

Children often take responsibility for the problems in their parents' relationship. Their abuser has instilled in them that they are the roots to all the marital troubles. The batterer blames everyone, and anyone, but himself for his behavior. Kids generally want to keep peace in the family, and will do their best to make sure they can. They think they can actually control their parents' moods. They will desperately work to achieve peace, but the batterer won't let that happen. When the children finally do everything right, then the batterer blames the other parent for his behaviors. Now, the kids are placed in the middle, and forced to "fix" their nonviolent parent. At this point, the batterer has succeeded in using the children to regain control over his victim. He uses manipulation and lying to confuse the kids, and upset their safe new world. The following deceptive statements are commonly used to get children to side with the batterer:

- "I only wanted to love you, but your mom wouldn't let me."
- "Your mom broke up our family even after I said I would change."
- "Do you want your last memory of me to be that your mom put me in jail?"

- "You never needed me anyway; your mom turned you against me."
- "Because of your mom, you aren't allowed to see grandma."
- "I can't give your mom child support because I have to pay for lawyer bills."
- "Your mom makes up stories because she wants you to hate me."
- "I said I was sorry, but she holds grudges forever."

You can see how children get the impression that their non-abusive parent wants them to hate their other parent. The abuser has convinced the children that the victim has torn up their family. After all, he said he was sorry, and he promised that the abuse would never happen again. If the lengths your batterer has gone to do not already astound you, they soon will. Unfortunately, the possibilities are endless.

In one such case, a batterer told his children that their mother only wanted them for the child support, but he was surprised with his victim's next move. This financially secure mother took away his power by distributing the money equally to the children, and making them responsible for buying their own clothes and school supplies. After all, that was where the money was going anyway. She was able to demonstrate that she wasn't interested in the money. This worked for her, but, unfortunately, many women fleeing family violence do not have the luxury she had. If you are limited financially, you may have to talk to your kids about adult issues such as rent and utilities, so they understand what basic living expenses are. Although this seems so unfair, this may be the reality. It may be necessary to write out a budget, and ask them where they feel their support check should be applied. As unjust as it is, you must deflate the lies. The price your children pay for understanding the truth is their loss of innocence. Your batterer has not left you with many other options. They are forced to grow up sooner by going through the school of "hard knocks." Now, the goal should be to get them through these lessons as unscathed as possible. You will have to learn counter-moves to discount his warped mentality.

Another way to counteract the deception may be to tell the children that the new clothes you just purchased for them came from their dad. Swallow your pride, and do what's right, because in the end, you will be the winner. If you present him in a good light, the children will be forced to see that he is in the wrong.

Being the "bigger" person can help discount your batterer's input. As they grow older, they will be able to discern the truth. The revelation usually occurs around the age of twelve or thirteen. Until then, however, you must work relentlessly to keep your kids out of the middle of the conflict. You must somehow discount your batterer's words without putting him down. For instance, you could say, "It is okay that your dad is mad at me. He has a right to be upset. This fight is between him and me. It's okay for you to love both of us. It's not necessary for you to take sides." As absurd and unfair as this defensive move sounds, this is your life as a battered woman.

Right now, your abuser feels that he is calling the shots, and he will do whatever it takes to gain compliance. This is difficult and frustrating as a parent who is trying to establish normalcy. Try not to resist his behavior, but rather learn how to deal with it. You cannot control what he says, but you can control what you do and how you respond to his games. When you react negatively toward your batterer, your children may question whether or not he is telling the truth. You must prove that you are not the problem by being consistent, honest, and steadfast. This requires you to keep your composure. If your batterer is calm, cool, and collected and you are hysterical, upset, and out of control, which parent do you think they will believe? As difficult as it might be not to react, do not show your kids how his behavior impacts you. The dynamics of family violence makes the hope for complete peace improbable, but countering the trickery can help take your children out of the middle.

Being a Loyal Subject

Loyalty plays a significant role in how children respond to abuse. They understand that the negative input doesn't feel right, but they still love their parents, regardless. Help them separate the two feelings, and somehow make sense of them. As I mentioned earlier, separating what your batterer does from who he is will probably be your best bet. Your kids need to be able to stop defending their position as their father's children. They may even make the correlation that, because you hate their dad, and they are a part of him, that you hate them also. This creates another dimension that you may have to contend with. Whether the association is real or not, they will believe that you have resentment toward them. It would be best to avoid phrases like, "You act just like your father," or "I know you didn't get that attitude from me." These types of comments only serve to make your children feel more trapped in the middle. The turmoil created by family violence makes the loyalty issue a big deal. Do what you can to relieve the pressure. Remember, this was not their choice to be brought into this relationship. They need you to make things smoother.

A common response from children of divorce is "I wish my parents could just get along." This is a dream almost every child desires, but this is particularly true for children from family violence. The emotions can be so intense that children actually feel like they are imploding. They view parents' fighting much differently than the average child because the rage associated with the argument has the potential to be life threatening. They have to be extremely careful how they respond, because the batterer's distorted thinking can be catapulted into rage beyond comprehension. For example, one young boy confided to his abusive father that his mom was being "unfair." Later that evening, his father called, and threatened to kill his mother for treating "his" son so poorly. The boy recognized from that one situation that getting frustrated with anyone is not an option. The price he paid was high. What he learned was that emotions should be stuffed and left unexpressed. To this day, that young man avoids conflict. He realized that a simple teenage reaction could have ended with grave consequences. How will he cope with conflict in the future? Will he be willing to assert himself when someone is being unfair, or has he learned that his needs are not so important compared to the consequences?

The emotional conflict that results from witnessing other family members being abused can be so overwhelming for children. They are torn between the love they feel for their abusive parent and the knowledge that what that parent has done is wrong. One young boy confided in me, "My daddy always treated me good, but he was really mean to my mommy and my sister." This boy feels torn because he has a connection with his father, yet he still understands that what his father did was wrong. He feels guilty for loving his dad, yet he is drawn to him. He struggles with how he feels because he still recognizes wrong from right. The mixed message relayed to him is that love doesn't always feel good.

The Love of a Child

Children by nature are caring and loving. They fantasize that if they could get their parents back together, the dissension would stop. They may believe that their father would feel better if he just could be with his family again. They hope that their batterer won't be mad all the time if mommy just gives him one more chance. Children are often peacekeepers, and want the very best for everyone. Their naïvety creates a perspective that is much different than those of the adults around them. We have all heard the phrase, "Out of the mouths of babes." Children see the solution as a simple one, "Why can't everyone just get along?"

A way to help your kids feel that they are not trapped in the middle is to set boundaries that limit their exposure to the fighting. You cannot control your batterer's anger, but you can find ways at times to postpone the inevitable until your kids are not around. For example, you could restrict your telephone conversations with him to when the children are not present. Use Caller ID® to monitor your calls, and simply do not pick up the telephone. If he persists in his attempt to reach you, disconnect the phone. If that does not feel comfortable, take your kids out to avoid the confrontation. If you choose to answer the phone, tell him that you cannot talk right now, and that you will call him when the children are not present. Your batterer will stoop as low as he needs to regain the control, even if that means using the children. He will use them as an excuse to call and torment you. If you participate in his game, before you know it, the topic will go from school projects to name-calling.

As a victim breaking free, you have rights. With a restraining order, he is legally restricted from calling and telling you what he thinks of you. When the conversation reaches the point where you feel berated, you have the option to hang up. The mistake most victims make is that they tolerate the abusive dialogue because they feel they have no choice. They continue to stay on the line, and listen to the crap being thrown at them. They argue with their batterers, or try to defend themselves from the accusations. No matter how great your debating skills are, you will not convince him that you are not what he says you are. Debating with him gets you nowhere. Any attempts to do so will only frustrate you further. When he can pull you into his distorted world and upset you, he wins. This manipulation usually includes the children, because they overhear the fights.

To be fair to them, do not buy into his ploy. If your batterer has the right to call his children, but is not permitted to talk to you, get another phone line just for the kids. This way you simply do not answer the line because the call is not for you.

Some victims still believe that they are responsible for the abuse they suffered. The fact is that no matter what you did or how hard you tried, he was mad. Remember some of the ridiculous reasons why he hit or emotionally abused you. It's time to take away his power. Depending on the severity of your batterer's abuse, and his reaction to your new boundaries, you may have to seek refuge until he calms down. Safety must be first, but you have to work toward taking back your life.

You Are the Monkey in the Middle

One of your batterer's ploys could be to create utter chaos in your new household by keeping the balance tipped. This is accomplished through generating dissension between the children, which intensifies the turmoil in your life. The emotional conflict within your children can trigger fights amongst themselves. Their agitation toward their circumstances might cause them to physically strike out against one another. They have learned well from their batterer how to target one another. This conflict makes life around you seem utterly unbearable. You are constantly stepping in to break up fights and are often forced to choose sides. And, no matter how hard you try, you disappoint someone. The batterer's skillful actions now make you the monkey in the middle.

Parenting requires developing methods to counter this sibling rivalry. Although children from "normal" families have rivalry, kids from violent homes have greater dynamics. The batterer may favor one child over the other, or one child may feel protective of the victim while the other is trying to appease the abuser. Consequently, the rivalry mounts. Finding ways to motivate your children to want to get along will promote healthier interactions between them. Your goal is to achieve a certain degree of harmony, and theirs is to trust you to get them through this. Their acting out indicates that they are struggling and unable to cope with what they are feeling. Teaching your children how to get along with each other is a talent developed through nurturing. It is difficult to be caught in the middle of your kids' constant bickering, but for safety purposes, you may be forced to referee at times.

Pitting Parents Against One Another

As children get older they might see the advantage of pitting their parents against one another. Say, for instance, you are adamantly against the children staying out past 10 P.M. Because your batterer despises you, he deliberately gives them the freedom to stay out as late as they want. His motive is based purely on his contempt for you. He disregards safety issues simply to get even with you. Because kids are opportunists, they see their father's carefree attitude as an advantage, especially when they feel that you are too strict. They can rationalize that what they want is reasonable, and that you are mean and unfair.

One teenager complained to his father that his mom forbid him to play videogames. He described her as a wimp that does not understand that games are just fun. The father proceeded to buy him the most violent games imaginable just to infuriate the boy's mother. Unfortunately, children cannot see the value in limitations until they are much older. They see the separate households as a means of meeting all their needs.

Children sometimes participate with their batterer's way of life to appease and validate him. This, however, causes pain and anguish for you. Once they return home, time is needed to get their attitudes and your harmony back to normalcy. As I have mentioned throughout this book, do not personalize their behavior. They are not deliberately trying to hurt you; they are only trying to exist in a world filled with violence. Their coping is commonly referred to as survival skills. As a victim, you know all too well what that means. Be patient, and focus on getting your kids regrouped.

Deprogramming After Visitation

When your children return home after their visitation with your batterer, emotions might be raw and unchecked. What you do and how you respond makes all the difference in the world. Your interaction with your children directly following their return is the most critical period for your family. That time sets the stage for the hours, days, and weeks that follow. If that time starts off wrong, recovering will be difficult. Each interaction and reaction, whether negative or positive, builds on the next. Help them bounce back as quickly as possible.

The visits with their father can be an incredibly anxious time for them, and for you as well. If their initial return home is stressful, the following days can be taxing for you. Obviously, their emotional meltdowns make being the best parent you can be very difficult. Justifiably, you may react inappropriately to their anguish during these anxious times. The interaction mimics an emotional boxing match, and you are in the center ring. The propensity is to lash out at them because their behaviors assimilate your batterer's. This is an incredible feat to overcome. You should know, in advance, that you might not always be successful. You will grieve when you see your children reverting to old patterns. Now more than ever, you need to be supportive and patient.

To overcome these obstacles, generate a plan that puts your children in a healthier emotional place. Participate in enjoyable rituals where they do not have to defend their father. This time is the most critical for nurturing. So hug, kiss, read, and cuddle with your children whenever possible. Avoid asking how their weekend went, because they know how you feel, and they will not want to admit if they had a good time. Allow the information to come to you when they are ready to present it.

Additionally, reviewing household rules after each visit reminds them that your family participates in making nonviolent choices. In essence, you are deprogramming them from the violent input they have been conditioned to understand. Deprogramming must occur, or dissension will linger amongst the family.

The following story is an example of how batterers can place victims in a position where they feel trapped in the middle. In this example, deprogramming the children after the visits becomes crucial.

One mother shared that her batterer sent jewelry and flowers home with the children for her on Valentine's Day. There was a restraining order in place, and gifts of any sort were a violation. Unfortunately, her daughter saw this as a peace offering, and became agitated with her mother when she refused to accept them. In her mind's eye, she saw her dad's gesture as one of good faith, and her mother's rejection was unreasonable. At this point the victim began to question her own feelings and doubted herself.

Prior to this event, regularly scheduled deprogramming visits occurred to help this girl cope with returning home and leaving her father. On this particular night, she appeared annoyed and agitated. She had been elated that her father had bought expensive gifts for her mother. To this young girl, the gifts meant a small reprieve from the antagonist behavior she had to usually endure. She admitted that it felt good to see her dad "happy." However, on the other, she didn't understand how her mother could be so cold and heartless. She equated her mother's rejection as intentional provocation. Refusing the gifts meant that life returned to the status quo, and emotional violence would resume once more. The batterer was successful in creating dissension, and forcing the child to choose sides. His deception made her mother the bad guy.

Giving gifts and manipulating through remorse are commonly used ploys to confuse victims. As we discussed earlier in Chapter 1, family violence is cyclical. The emotions go round and round, and upside down. In the previous example, the batterer's gestures generate doubt and create the illusion that the victim is overreactive, emotional, or even crazy. The children become confused with the cycle of violence, because they live in the present, and what they see feels good. What the batterer did in the past is irrelevant. They want their mother to see what they see, so they can go back to the familiarities of their old lives with their friends, neighbors, and their own rooms. Kids can usually forgive and forget the bad stuff when enough time has passed. Poor judgments are made during this period, which helps perpetuate the cycle. In the previous example, the girl believed her father and insisted, "Daddy is sorry, he just wants to make it up to you. Why can't you just forgive him?" Buying into the supposed remorse is the worst thing this mother could do. As discussed in Chapter 3, what this mother can do is empathize and validate her child's hurt feelings by using the RAVE technique. The goal is to encourage dialogue that explains healthy and appropriate behaviors. The nonviolent parent should try to respond matter-of-factly so the child doesn't have to defend her father.

The Guilt of Separation

Children caught in the middle of family violence and divorce normally feel guilt for leaving the other parent behind. They might even be led to believe that they caused the problem. The strong connection between kids and their abuser make them feel responsible. Your children need help accepting the separation and *leaving daddy*. Purchasing a journal for them to write the day's events in and give to their father can provide some comfort. Then they can share the information with the estranged parent when the opportunity arises. Journaling gives them the opportunity to connect to their abusive parent in a safe environment. It also can relieve the children's guilt because they have something tangible to present to their dad that *proves* they love him. Another way to ease the discomfort is to make a scrapbook, which includes test papers, artwork, and achievement awards. The idea is to get your children to feel better about the changes you have made in their lives. Yet, on some level, the batterer can still be included.

No matter how much you dislike your ex-partner or how much you believe him undeserving of your children's love, your batterer is bound to them by blood. There is nothing you can do to break that biological chain. The best way to help your kids cope with the separation is to provide an environment that validates their loss, rather than penalizes them for having those thoughts. The guilt they feel is too great to compare to any animosity you may feel toward your ex-partner. Don't contribute to their guilt.

Batterers often use trickery with children to instill guilt and pity. They count on their children's feelings to make their next move. The batterer can appear as loving and fun to create the illusion that life with dad would be wonderful. Leaving their father after the visit then generates emotional conflict. One abusive father would call his estranged wife and taunt her before each scheduled visitation. The mother immediately became depressed and sad. When the father would show up for the visitation exchange he presented himself as happy and animated. What their daughter witnessed was that dad appeared to be the better parent. The girl drew pictures of what she thought her two households looked like. The picture with her father depicted them driving away laughing and joking, whereas the picture with her mother showed an unhappy and miserable family. I asked her how she felt about everyone being sad. She said, "I'm sad because my mom's sad." She then drew a picture of her family when her mom and dad were fighting. She placed herself in the middle between them. This young girl was caught in the crossfire. To avoid being the monkey in the middle, her parents need to have minimal contact until the victim can heal from the abuse she suffered. Otherwise, the dynamics of violence will continue to plague this child.

Avoid Playing Monkey in the Middle

The following example illustrates the length a batterer will go to keep his victim trapped in the middle. A distraught ex-husband constantly left messages on his victim's answering machine to frighten her, even though a restraining order had stated no contact. He explained to the courts that he kept losing the babysitter's phone number, and that his purpose was only talk to his children. The ex-wife was instructed at that time to record the following message, "If this is such and such, here is the sitter's number; please do not leave a message." This infuriated the batterer because she could now cite him for harassment if he chose to violate the restraining order. She found a way to fight back and not be responsible for passing messages to the children. Use the following strategies to help you and your children get out of the middle:

Set boundaries—Tell your abuser that you are limiting your conversation to the children only. Do not allow him to lure you into his web. If he does not respect the boundaries that you set, simply tell him to call back when he is ready to stick to the rules. The most effective means of accomplishing this is to have your attorney put the boundaries in writing.

Stop explaining yourself—Discontinue justifying your actions. So long as you are willing to explain yourself, your batterer will continue to draw you in. The more interaction you have with him, the more stuck in the middle you are. You no longer have to answer to your batterer in any way. Keep your conversation limited to the kids. For all other information that he is requesting, refer him to your lawyer.

Prevent exploitation—Mask your weaknesses. Your batterer will exploit and use them to poison your children against you, or worse, he will use them in court to gain full custody. Assess your flaws, and determine how to avoid the attacks that are certain to come. If you have any habits that can be construed as unhealthy, your batterer will use them against you. Say, for example, you like to have a drink with dinner. He might say that your drinking was the major reason for the breakup. He would misuse that information to "prove" that you are a bad mother. Play it safe and put those habits by the wayside until your children can discern the truth. Your batterer will stoop as low as he can to get to your kids, thereby getting to you. The secrets you shared with him will be used against you with your children. For example he might tell them that you smoked pot, slept around, or stole when you were younger to tarnish your children's perception of you.

Give up the concept of fair fighting—Stop projecting. Although you want peace between you and your batterer, the fact is that he is not going to fight fairly. In his mind's eye, you are a runaway slave, and should be punished for your transgressions. The best you can do is to avoid problems as much as possible by not reacting to his unscrupulous games. You have to always keep in mind that he is playing by a different set of rules than you are. Although your hope is that he will change, the statistics suggest that only a small percentage ever recognize or acknowledge that they even have a problem. I personally believe that anyone can change, but they must acknowledge and educate themselves first.

Anticipate setups—Be alert. Your batterer can create situations where he sets you up, and makes your life a living nightmare. He could use manipulations and ploys to hurt you and the kids. One example comes to mind in which a batterer promised his son he would take him to a ball game. He then told his ex-wife that he would meet her at a certain drop off point. He didn't show. Instead, he went somewhere else, then told his son that she purposely went to the wrong place, so he couldn't go to the game. Guess who got to take the blame?

Some batterers provoke their victims. One woman lost custody of her children because her husband towered over her and taunted, "Hit me, hit me." In her frustration she pushed him away from her. He then proceeded to call 911. She was arrested, and the judge retorted, "If you are violent with your husband, you are probably violent with your children, too. Therefore, you do not deserve those children!"

The Need for a Father's Love

In this country, many children are failing in life because their positive male role model is missing. Research shows that children do better socially and academically when a man is present that loves them.[1] Unfortunately, batterers are often emotionally unavailable for their children, and do not contribute to their children's well-being. They, in fact, compound their children's problems. Victims believe that their children need their father, no matter how abusive he is. This is absolutely absurd. Any parent who consciously abuses a family member does not deserve the privilege of children. Anyone can produce children, but it takes commitment, love, and patience to be a parent. Many victims make the mistake of believing that their batterer loves their children as much as they do. This belief lends false hope to their children. Don't confuse them by saying something that just is not true. Loving parents would not purposely expose their children to violence and danger. Give up the fantasy for your kids' sake.

If your batterer is emotionally and physically abusive toward the children, don't force them to have a relationship with him, especially when the children feel uncomfortable with him. Many victims, in an attempt to make the children feel better, assure them that their father loves them. The intention is good, but the outcome is not. The nonviolent parent does not want her children to feel the pain of rejection, so she will "smooth over" the bad feelings. The reality is that kids know when they are not loved, and convincing them otherwise only serves to confuse them more. Children repeatedly get disappointed and hurt when they are let down. The mixed message sent to them is that they have to try harder to get their father's love. And no matter how great their attempt, their abuser still does not acknowledge them. It reinforces the hurt feelings that already exist. When children are told that their father loves them, it only confuses them when he disappoints them. Real love requires action.

Getting Hit in the Crossfire

Children witnessing abuse are caught in the crossfire. They are dodging as fast as they can to miss the emotional bullets. They are successful with dodging at times, but unfortunately, at others, they should have zigged instead of zagged. Children barraged by conflict find themselves in a foxhole cowering for their lives. This is a very dangerous time for children, and you need to take it very seriously. Batterers who lose total control might resort to killing their kids to get even with their victims. You can read almost daily an instance of someone annihilating his family because the victim refused to return. This is the ultimate price to pay. He might let his victims live after he killed the children because he wants her to suffer the mental anguish for her "misdeed."

The most dangerous time for victims and their children is during the exchange of the court-ordered visitation. Amazingly, society refuses to recognize that risk, and the victims are left fearing for their loved one's lives. We all need to take a closer look at how the violence impacts and threatens children. For so long we have believed that domestic violence was an issue between a husband and wife. Today, however, many child advocates are changing the focus because they recognize how the destructive patterns affect children's lives. This is not domestic violence; it is family violence, and everyone suffers. Because violence is learned, we need to start earlier, and prevent the violent behavior from being integrated into their childhood.

Owning the Problem

Children trapped in the middle of violence often take ownership for the problems their family is experiencing. An important goal will be to make your children return the problem to its rightful owner. Now, it is time to make them understand that they simply do not have the power to fix their parents. Instead of owning their parents' problems, they need to work on redirecting their lives and being responsible for their own personal happiness. The bottom line is that no one else is to blame for another's unhappiness. Children deserve a happy and violence-free childhood. If we can encourage them to reach within themselves, and to understand that they are not responsible for their parents, we can work toward preventing them from being monkeys in the middle.

CHAPTER 9

Labels: Breaking the Molds

Victimization shatters necessary assumptions about a safe world.
—*Kendall Johnson, Ph.D.*

Children who act out in school or other social settings may do so because they cannot cope with the violence at home. These kids are virtually imploding, with no one recognizing the behavior for what it is, a cry for help. Instead, society labels these children, making it nearly impossible for them to succeed. Our society, in general, tends to perpetuate the stereotypes that these kids are "problem children."

This chapter provides insight on what needs to be done to help society react differently to what children of family violence are really experiencing. Only recently has the focus on family violence been directed toward children. Consequently, because children were not considered part of the dynamics there is little documentation regarding its affect on them. There are a small number of scholars and professionals now diligently working to educate the public whose efforts should be commended. Therefore, in order to prevent overgeneralization and exclude those people hard at work, my reference to *society* will mean the social group that is not properly educated, adequately trained, or amply astute to the nature of children and family violence.

A common response for many adults dealing with "difficult" children is to medically diagnose their problems. As a result, they rely upon the professional world (i.e., doctors and therapists) to give them the answers. Unfortunately, some professionals could have an agenda which is not always in your children's best interest. Do your homework, know the professionals' goals, anticipate that your children may potentially be used as research projects for the medical community's gain, and be ready to challenge anyone working with your kids. The pressure to maintain a prestigious position forces professionals to do research, which usually requires them to have subjects to study. To ensure that professionals are working in your children's best interest, always get a second opinion before accepting any disorders that affix a permanent label on them.

Close attention should be given to the newest disease of the day, bi-polar disorder, formerly known as manic/depression. I have learned some disturbing facts regarding this new shift. Insurance companies have placed a moratorium on the previously popular disorder Attention Deficit Disorder/Attention Deficit Hyperactivity Disorder (ADD/ADHD), and are no longer supporting major studies for this disorder. Therefore, researchers have moved on to bi-polar disorder as their new project. Consequently, your children's potential to be misdiagnosed with the disease *du jour* is high. Unfortunately, the supposed treatment turns the focus away from the real issues, and exacerbates your children's problem even further (all for the "better" cause).

One mother reported that her 11-month-old baby was given the bi-polar disorder diagnosis. Although I am not a doctor, this seems incredibly absurd. How can a doctor with the slightest amount of conscious draw this conclusion? Bi-polar disorder is a real disease with severe consequences, and misdiagnosing children in droves makes a mockery of its devastating impact on people. As your children's advocate, do your homework and ask a lot of questions before *any diagnosis* is accepted as fact.

For example, one study indicated that 25 percent of sexually abused children were misdiagnosed with ADD/ADHD, when in fact they were suffering from post-traumatic stress disorder (PTSD).[1] A key question professionals frequently ask is, "Do your children have difficulty concentrating?" The obvious answer is yes, because they are suffering from trauma. They were living in a war zone where everyday was stressful and dangerous. These considerations are rarely acknowledged or diagnosed as PTSD, because accurate family histories are not collected.

How can we expect a child to possibly sit still or concentrate when he has been up all night worrying about his mom's black eye and swollen lip? A recent study found that 85 percent of its subjects who had witnessed domestic violence had moderate to severe symptoms of PTSD. It also indicated that witnessing domestic violence was the most toxic form of exposure to violence for children.[2] If we took a long hard look at the world of family violence, and the children in it, we could conclude that some physicians are unnecessarily treating many of these kids. Many ADD/ADHD symptoms are similar to PTSD. Unfortunately, when the professionals are looking in the wrong direction, the prognosis and treatments are inaccurate. It's like doing surgery on the right eye when the left one has the problem.

In the *Diagnostic and Statistical Manual,* the psychological bible, it states that kids with ADD/ADHD will have difficulty remaining seated, or will fidget. They are easily distracted, and have difficulty waiting their turn. They have difficulty following and listening to instructions. They lose things and engage in activities that are dangerous for them.[3] Do these symptoms sound familiar? Some of them should. Living in violence creates an anxiety-based reaction that makes staying on task difficult. Yet, not many adults recognize the correlation between violence and anxiety. When kids cannot concentrate because they are reliving the abuse at home, they struggle with accomplishing anything.

It reminds me of an article where a grandmother who was interviewed commented, "Ever since his mother died, and his father went to prison, he's been acting out, and the Ritalin just isn't working." It doesn't take a genius to understand what is really going on here. This boy feels stressed out, anxious, scared, and abandoned. He is not hyperactive; he is hyper-vigilant due to his circumstances.

To better understand your children, put yourself in their shoes. Have you ever been in a stressful situation where you tried to focus on a specific task, and failed miserably? If you experienced abuse, were you ever distracted at work after a beating, or a major fight with your spouse? The answer is probably yes. Now imagine what it must be like for young children who either witnessed that same abuse or were also beaten. Kids have not been given the coping skills required to handle the wide range of emotions that they are bombarded with. Yet we expect them to go to school, sit still, and concentrate on their studies. They don't care about the theory of relativity; they just want to survive. Living with violence has the potential to impede their emotional, social, and academic growth. How adults react to them will determine how well they succeed.

Finding the Root of the Problem

In most cases, we need to dig deep to find the answers to our children's problems. But it doesn't take a rocket scientist to understand that living in violence causes severe stress and fear. The environment is usually the problem, yet rarely do we factor that into the equation when assessing children's bad behavior. One boy professed that since he left his dad, he was finally able to fall asleep at night. He disclosed that when he lived in the violence, he tried to stay awake as long as he could to make sure his dad did not hurt his mom. Then he remarked, "My mom never knew why it was so hard to wake me up in the morning." This boy literally stood guard every night until his little eyes would not let him. Imagine how restless his sleep must have been. Could you focus or perform under these conditions? The sleep deprivation, more than likely, caused him to be less attentive and more agitated at school. Unfortunately, the school staff does not understand the real issue. Not understanding the root of the problem is when labeling takes place.

Asking the Right Questions and Giving the Right Answers

Professionals do not always ask the right questions, so you must provide a thorough background so your children can be served appropriately. Minimizing or covering up the abuse only prolongs the problems and makes matters worse. Acknowledging your situation is the first step to managing your children's lives. Your kids need you to be honest with yourself, and those who are trying to help you. As humiliating as it feels, you must look beyond yourself for your children's sake. They are being judged, and their sense of self is being developed by those prejudices. This can no longer be about you if you want your children to survive emotionally. The professionals need your help to make the correct assessment and to get your kids back on track.

Labels: Breaking the Molds

When you explain what your children are going through, others can generate plans that will make your kids more successful. This process has to start with self-disclosure. You should realize however, that some people may use the information against your children, but the reality is that they will probably be labeled anyway. At least with self-disclosure you have a 50/50 shot of getting some support. Without it, others will draw conclusions based on their perspective, and invariably, they will be wrong.

Parents desperately search for explanations for their children's bad behavior, but they are looking in the wrong place. Most see this as the children's issue when, in fact, the adults' behavior is the real problem. With this misinformation, parents frantically rely upon doctors to medically diagnose their kids, and give them a quick fix. Being a parent is difficult enough, but dealing with traumatized children can be unbearable. Still, medication is not usually the answer. In my humble opinion, most drugs are intended to sedate the problems, not to eliminate them. These problems are generally compounded by the misdiagnosis, which resulted from non-disclosure.

Your job will also be to ask your children the right questions so that you can get a clearer picture of what is happening in their lives. You need to find out what is bothering them so they can change their self-image. Ask them whether they feel that someone has mistreated them, or made them feel bad. Make sure that you are paying attention to body language and mood shifts. One of the mistakes I made was not always listening to Katlin when he said his teachers were being mean to him. Because his behavior could be so inappropriate, I automatically assumed he was the problem. I would learn later that there were many times when teachers had been cruel and hurtful. The self-image created from those experiences still haunts him. I encourage all of you to view your children's problems through their eyes, and not your own. You will be amazed at what you see. Although you never want to give your children an excuse for their bad behavior, you can certainly understand that there is a reason for it. Asking the right questions helps resolve the problems more quickly.

A question you might ask yourself is whether there is a correlation between your children's bad behavior and their exposure to their batterer. Upon examination, a link between visitations with the abuser and subsequent behavioral problems might be evident.

If you notice a decline in their behavior and attitude after visitations, a pattern may be emerging. One mother reported that her daughter became hostile toward her teachers and other children immediately following visitations with her abusive father. She pushed a student into a fence, and she bloodied her teacher's nose. After several days of being away from her batterer, she was able to calm down. Unfortunately, hard feelings develop when the behavior is that extreme. Normally, this child was very sweet and kind, but each time she reacted to the triggers caused by the visitation, the adults around her could only see the bad behavior. They described her as unpredictable and moody. They were unaware of the scheduled visitations. All they knew was that they walked on eggshells around her, and waited for the next explosion. What is the social message being sent to this young girl when others become leery of her? Because the problems must be defined before they can be resolved, do your kids a favor: ask the right questions, and give the right answers.

Social Problems

Children exposed to family violence often struggle socially because they fear others will learn their secrets. Although they think they are doing a good job of stuffing their emotions, usually the opposite is true. They are wearing their feelings in bright colors out on their sleeves. Other kids see this as an opportunity to pick on them. Children can be mean, and in-tune to how others are feeling. They understand too clearly who is vulnerable to attack, and they use that information to find their targets. Assess your children's personalities, and determine how to teach them to cope socially. For example, if your child is shy and withdrawn, he may be teased relentlessly. This further adds to his social isolation, and his feelings of inadequacy. Teach shy children assertive behaviors like making eye contact and changing their body stance. If your child is aggressive, and verbal toward others, her peers may pick on her just to watch her flail. Teach aggressive children how to disregard the taunting. Without some help, the children's reactions are guaranteed to perpetuate the labeling. Once teachers and peers have marked them, the branding is difficult to undo.

Some teachers target reactive children simply because they assume that the troubled children are the problem. For instance, I observed a child watching a video during class when two others students proceeded to kick his chair. He tried to move away from them, but they shifted toward him. Eventually, the teacher humiliated the boy by asking him if he needed to sit in the front of the classroom. At this point, I spoke up for him and corrected the situation. But, had I not been there, he would have been considered the problem. What message would have been sent to him? How can a child cope when it is his word against two others? Who is going to protect him from these perceptions? Ultimately, without support, this boy will get the message that he is worthless. How can he rise above what the adults and his peers think about him? Parenting in the aftermath of family violence may require you to assist the school with understanding your children better. As you know, there are good qualities in every child. The adults just have to be creative enough to find them.

The Pendulum Swings

Labels can be generated as a result of parents overcompensating, and reacting defensively to other adults who are correcting their children. Parents understand their kids' pain, and want to protect them at all cost. Consequently, they may regard any punishment as too harsh. They feel that their children don't deserve to hurt or suffer anymore. They cannot understand why no one else can see that. The problem with overcompensating is that your children do not get the balance they need to understand how to react appropriately. When the pendulum swings too far in the other direction, you teach your children that they can be victims of their circumstances. As long as they can use their situations as excuses, they never have to take responsibility for their lives. They also get the message that there is no such thing as boundaries. What you teach them, unwittingly, is that they can use their past as a reason to fail, or get attention for it.

What your children really need, then, are distinct boundaries that guide them toward a successful future. This is not to say that adults should not be held accountable for how they treat your children. It only means that your children need to understand that everyone plays a part in the interaction and each has responsibility for their own behavior. How your children choose to participate determines how successful they become. As much as it hurts to watch your children suffer, sometimes that is just what they need. Adults learned through their failures and consequences, and children must do the same. To be most effective, weigh out each issue, and base your decisions on logic, rather than emotion. No one listens to distraught people. If you want what's best for your children, approach the outside world from a perspective that suggests that you are credible and capable. Otherwise, you will be written off, much like your children have been. So, balancing your emotions appropriately is the answer.

Impulse Control

Children from family violence often have difficulty with impulse control issues. They essentially act and speak before they think. Although children, in general, don't always think, kids from family violence display impulsivities that are exasperating for adults. For the record, impulse control is a physiological problem, and not just kids making bad choices. Research has shown that trauma may contribute to and provoke behavioral problems. Your job will be to educate the system on how to deal with these issues and what works best for your children. It is important, however, to get the educators to buy into the concept of impulse control. I explained to a principal once that Katlin had impulse control problems, and his response was, "I don't believe in that impulse crap; if he wanted to control himself, he could." Needless to say, we had a rough time because they didn't *want* to understand how hard Katlin struggled with his past. Unfortunately, I have found this attitude to be the rule rather than the exception in most of the schools we attended. The hardest part of raising Katlin was dealing with the adults who found it easier to label him than to support him. Although I always held Katlin accountable for his actions, I found that some adults refused to accept any responsibility for the breakdown in interaction.

In any relationship, whether intimate or casual, everyone contributes to the outcome. This includes teachers, coaches, counselors, daycare workers, and other adults. Don't assume that because your children are displaying bad behavior that this is entirely their fault. Although they need to learn how to deal with difficult people, others must realize that traumatized children cannot always keep it together. Children must heal from their pain before they can manage their lives effectively. That means the adults must understand the dynamics of their lives, and work from a different perspective.

Here is an example of a time that was good for us. Katlin had a teacher who had taught in the inner-city schools for twenty years.

She worked with the roughest, most challenging kids on the planet. When she met Katlin, her perception of him was that he was a piece of cake. She was a tough teacher, but a loving one. He adored her. She worked and guided him in a more positive direction. As a result, he shined. The principal had even congratulated him for not being in his office and not earning any suspensions. Unfortunately, before the school year was over, the teacher was transferred. The new teacher could not stand Katlin. Consequently, Katlin was labeled difficult, and out of control. The difference was that one teacher chose to view Katlin from a perspective that suggested that he could make it, while the other found him to be a pain in the rear. Children only live up to the expectation they are given. If your children have teachers who are rigid and inflexible, they are going to have a hard time emotionally.

Teachers are usually the second most important adult in children's lives, and they are often the first positive person for children enduring family violence. Teachers need to recognize how critical their role is to child development. They also need to understand the incredible responsibility they have toward helping these kids succeed. Teachers can be overwhelmed by the demands placed upon them, and can often treat children inappropriately.

I know this firsthand from dealing with many teachers who just couldn't understand the intense pain Katlin had. He was kicked out of one school in the first grade. The principal refused to work with us. I was willing to volunteer in the classroom to help monitor his behavior, but she didn't want to bother. When the principal asked him to leave the school, she remarked, "Perhaps you should put him in a public school where he can duke it out, our children are just too patsy for him." Can you believe an advocate for children's education would use such callous remarks? I retorted, "The last thing this kid needs is to be reinforced that violence is the answer." To make matters worse, this principal contacted other Christian schools that we had applied to, and strongly recommended that they not allow him in. She went to great lengths to have him discarded like a piece of trash. I would find out over the years that there are a lot of teachers and administrators that are willing to throw these kids away with no regard to what their actions will do to their future. Initially, I thought maybe our problems in school were because Katlin was a fighter, or maybe we just were really unfortunate to find such uncaring adults; but my experience with other families of violence showed me that this attitude was prevalent, and these kids were paying the ultimate price. In many cases, I don't think that the teachers were mean on purpose. They just felt helpless because they didn't know what to do. Teachers are not trained properly to deal with the difficulties of abuse. This is where you come in. You have to educate them. Adults need to learn how to motivate children to learn rather than teaching them from a book. What reason does a child have to learn when all he can think about is his safety? Children need to feel secure before they can behave themselves. Hopefully, this book can show you how to achieve that objective.

Misunderstanding Children

Children from family violence who act out are frequently misunderstood. They are regarded as angry, insensitive, and apathetic. The reality is that they are scared, lonely, and ashamed. The following is an example of how adults misinterpret and mislabel children from family violence.

A boy is beaten, and also witnesses an assault on his mother at home; he goes to school unable to cope with the violence, and he acts out. Next, he is suspended. After repeated episodes, he spirals down quickly. He falls into an emotional abyss, and feels there is no way out. He relinquishes himself to the label he has been given and continues to lash out. How would you help save him from self-destruction?

You could start by discounting what the world is telling him. Teach him that it is his choice what to believe in. Self-perception is generated by what an individual chooses to take in and embrace. Accepting negative input from others seems to be easier than challenging it. But, that acceptance does not serve children well and, consequently, they misunderstand themselves. Nobody benefits from self-hatred. An intensive amount of positive feedback will be required to undo the damage, but the time and energy are well worth it.

Children with Low Self-Esteem

Some children with low self-esteem do not believe they have the right to speak up against others. Their batterer taught them that their needs were unimportant. Consequently, they may resort to manipulation to get their needs met. But, because children are naturally

162

honest, the trickery does not feel good to them. In turn, getting what they need makes them feel guilty because they know that what they did was wrong. The combination of manipulation and guilt begin to form their senses of esteem and value. Your challenge will be to teach them that they deserve to get their needs met without using exploitation to get it and that they are worth it.

One way to demonstrate esteem and value is to take a large dollar bill like a ten or twenty, and throw it on the table. Then ask your children, if you gave it to them, if they would pick it up. The obvious answer would be yes. Next, take the bill, crumple it, throw it back on the table, and ask if they would still take it. I am sure the answer would still be yes. Then, take the bill; throw it on the floor, and step on it. Now, ask them the question again. To date, not one child has ever said no to the money. The reason is clear: the money is still worth its value. Children are very much the same. They are born with a value, and no matter how much they are crumpled, or stepped on, they are still worth the value they started with. I would encourage you to use this comparison with your children. Because they are very concrete thinkers, they will understand the message you are sending them.

Esteem is such a vital part of how children behave. When their esteem is good, so is their motivation and excitement for life. With a high esteem they can excel, and mostly make good choices. But, without it, they can develop despair and hopelessness. When there is nothing to strive for, they lose their desire to try.

If your children already have a low self-esteem, don't give up. Remember, children believe what others say about them. As the key figure in their lives, you have more pull than you think. The objective is to override the message of worthlessness and replace it with something grand.

"Crazy About Me" Attitude

Successful adults who were abused as children invariably explain that the reason they turned out well was because someone in their lives loved, honored, and believed in them. I was fortunate enough to have several people in my childhood that were "crazy about me." I attribute my success today to these people. Two people, in particular, were my foster parents. After my parents' separation, this couple took care of my sister and me. On one stormy day, I watched the falling rain through the window. The day seemed to fit my sad mood. I really missed my mother, but I was not comfortable sharing those feelings with anyone. My foster mother sat beside me, put her arms around me, and pointed to a puddle. She then said, "See the drops of rain in the puddle? Those are really ballerinas dancing, and they are dancing for you. What a beautiful sight, the puddle is their stage." We sat together for a while in our little fantasy world, and never said another word. Although the pain of missing my mother was great, I found comfort in this very special woman. She allowed me to feel bad without criticizing or forcing me to share what I was thinking. Yet she soothed me, and discounted what I was feeling: unloved. There were many moments like this one during my stay there. What she and her husband did turned my life around. They planted a seed that said, "You are a worthwhile person, and you deserve to love yourself." They gave me permission to love, and to believe that I was worthy.

This message is exactly what your children need to hear. Therefore, recruit people who can present the "crazy about me" attitude to them. The more adults you can find to discount the hurtful words inflicted upon them, the better. Because of the gender issue, using positive men is extremely important. Boys, for example, need input from other men because they are searching for someone to identify with. They are learning how to be men, and that development is best accomplished through role modeling. As a mother, you can only do so much in that department. So try to surround them with healthy, positive men. Girls benefit greatly from having positive men in their lives also. The interaction shows them how men are really supposed to treat women. When you can demonstrate how real men should act, it can help break the cycle of violence for your children. Often adults do not think kids are paying attention, but they are. The people you introduce to them will impact them either positively or negatively. Life is a stage, and your kids are in the audience. Ask yourself what they have learned about interacting with others.

Promoting Healthier Self-Images

Children who have low self-images usually do not care about punishment. Their world is not a happy one, so punitive correction is just par for the course. They view adults outside their violent family as inferior and less frightening. Therefore, threatening children with low self-images usually does not work. Schools are more limited than an abuser to what disciplinary actions that they can take against children with poor behavior and some kids count on that. They use the system to unleash their frustration. They rationalize by saying, "My father beats me, what are you gonna do, take away my recess?" The terror they have endured makes other authority figures look like the Pillsbury Dough Boy. They use combative and argumentative behaviors in school to exert their sense of control. The educational system serves as a scapegoat for these kids' aggression because it is a safe place for them to emote. For at least part of their day, they feel less helpless. Imagine how it must feel to so desperately need that sense of power. They are willing to challenge anyone outside the family system to get it.

Your children will be healing for years to come. Continue to take the initiative to educate yourself on abuse, and have the drive to learn more. It would be in your children's best interests if you were to take control and guide their destiny. You must become their advocate. Children will change their behavior when adults change their reaction.

Warning Signs

Your children may be displaying some of the following warning signs. Use this list as a guide to understand your kids better. The behaviors (left column) and reactions (right column) are a direct result of being exposed to family violence. Addressing these signs will make it easier to help your children.

Absent/truant	Annoyed
Anxious behavior (e.g., nail biting, hair twisting)	Behavior disturbance
	Crying for no apparent
Blames self for the abuse	reason
Bullying	Doesn't seem to care
Change in behavior	Drug abuse
Defiant	Excessive need to be first
Drop in grades	Extreme reaction to
Eating problems	change of routine
Excessive passive behavior	Fight or flight response
Hoards food and items	Frequent nightmares
Lacks motivation	Guarded or defensive
No boundaries	Guilt, shame, humiliation

Painful, intrusive memories

Preoccupied

Reactive

Roller coaster emotions

Runs away or threatens to

School difficulties

Sexual acting out

Sleeps in class

Suspicious

Unusual temper outbursts

Vandalism

Withdrawn/isolated

Irritability

Mistrusting

No eye contact

Personality alterations

Physical complaints

Regressing to behavior of
an earlier age

Severe startle responses

Unusual change in weight

Worried about the future

Your children could have one or all of these symptoms. Use this list as a baseline for dealing with your kids' emotions. Provide your results to the adults who are working with them. When adults can see that there are clear reasons for the children's behavior, perhaps they could take a different approach with them, one that is more understanding and nurturing.

To address these warning signs, you may need outside help. Turn toward a counselor, minister, or a good friend for assistance. Make sure, however, that the person or persons you choose are healthy and know what they are doing. Parenting is difficult to do alone, yet caution must be taken to discriminate and choose your help carefully. Otherwise, you could be compounding the issues.

Educating Others

The impact family violence has on child development has many predicable outcomes. Children suffer from fear, shock, recurrent anxiety, and distrust. Although you can change their environment and make it safe, they are still plagued by the past. Consequently, they can appear to have recovered from the abuse, yet a triggering event causes them to digress. The adults around them will become weary. And although giving up is much easier than working with these kids, it is not the right thing to do. Your challenge will be to convince others that your children are worth saving, and that you want the adults to have the wherewithal to help them succeed.

Labels: Breaking the Molds

Success in the Classroom

Children's success in the classroom requires scrutinizing ineffective practices that simply do not meet their special needs. Some teachers automatically assume that children who misbehave should be removed from the group, or placed in the back of the classroom. This is an emotional death sentence for them. These kids already feel like social outcasts, and using this method of punishment only reinforces their lack of self-worth. They become resentful and apathetic. If your kids are going to be successful, they must be able to stay on task, which means being part of the group. They should be placed in the front row, where they can be gently reminded to behave. The teacher can establish a signal or visual cue that keeps them on track without humiliating or embarrassing them. The idea is to get them to win. But a different perspective is necessary to accomplish this goal. Teachers need to stop teaching and start motivating children to learn. When they are motivated, they succeed.

Because teachers are taught to teach in mass, you may have to guide them in regards to your children. Explain that isolating them does not serve to promote better behavior. It only makes their behavior more difficult. Your job is to ensure that the people interacting with your kids do the right thing. That may mean attending school board meetings, parent involvement groups, or daily contact with the school staff. Whatever it takes, find a way to ensure that all parties involved are working together to make your children successful.

Emotional Implosion

Children surviving family violence have more than likely stuffed their emotions for years. They are literally bursting from the inside out. Their emotions are building to a point where turning back is too hard, and holding it all in is no longer possible. A physiological response actually occurs as a result and they "lose it." The repressed emotions once released cause stress hormones to soar, which wreak havoc on the body. These secreted hormones stay in the body for hours.[4] Consequently, when multiple episodes of conflict occur, they produce a state of utter physical turmoil. The stuffed emotions place children in a position where they cannot take anymore. Unfortunately, they usually unleash the pent-up emotion on an unsuspecting person. Now, the emotional implosion is an external explosion and the children are labeled, and written-off like bad checks. Kids need to learn how to cope and express themselves more effectively. But, the onus needs to be placed upon the adults to make the changes. The children are barely coping with their emotions, let alone trying to generate solutions to their problems. And they need the adults to lead them.

Tolerance and Compassion

Adults who are not familiar with the dynamics of family violence unwittingly contribute to children's fears, anxieties, and insecurities. The expectations are often too high for these kids, and when they cannot perform, they tend to react negatively. Naturally, the adults can get annoyed and label the children as disruptive, defiant, or learning disabled. The adults push too hard, and want them to "Just deal with it." The confrontation usually creates more conflict, which results in a virtual meltdown for the kids. Who gets blamed? The children. Rarely do adults attribute their behavior to a situation involving children. For example, in one school, a young man had teachers, except for one, who said he was cooperative, hard-working, and smart. The one teacher professed the complete opposite. He stated that the boy was lazy, uncaring, and difficult. Looking at the differences in opinions, one could only conclude that that teacher was the one with the attitude. Unfortunately, the teacher is also the one with the power. Consequently, the boy's report card reflected that he had a problem. Your children really do need to learn how to cope with adversity; yet, they also must take ownership of their participation in the conflict. There is a fine balance.

Evaluate each situation carefully, and stop automatically assuming that your children are always the problem. Another boy who was constantly reprimanded in music class needed an evaluation. I was asked to assess why he was having so much trouble. The teacher was unaware of my presence when she entered the room. She had a pack of pink disciplinary slips in her hand and bellowed out while smacking them in the palm of her hand, "I've got a pack of pink slips, and I am not afraid to use them!" This boy, when placed in an anxious situation, experienced a physiological response where his ears turn red. I observed this child's eyes follow her around the room, as his ears grew redder and brighter. Needless to say, I understood and could determine who had the problem. But again, the school didn't see it that way because the boy reacted to her aggressive manner with a defiant approach.

Although children must learn conformity and do what is right, they also need understanding and support. Do not allow your children to go through this process alone. Be ready to participate and fight for them when it is necessary. You may be all they have.

Dealing More Effectively with Non-Coping Children

Children coping outside your home may need your guidance to make it through their days. You might have to go to school everyday with them to understand the dynamics they are facing. You can learn a lot from shadowing your kids and watching how others treat them and how they respond to others. When their perception is that no one likes them, then they behave in such a manner that perpetuates their problems. You must show them how to correct that behavior.

Changes in behavior may be as simple as telling your children how to act or what to say around others. Kids from family violence often lack the social graces to interact with people. This deficiency is the reason why some kids struggle. Social expectations are overwhelming, which makes them act inappropriately, and the world sees them as obnoxious.

Another harsh reality for them is that their teachers do not love nor tolerate them as much as you do. They push their teachers' buttons to a point where the adults have been sensitized. The result is that they are considered major thorns in their teachers' sides. When this happens, the educators may become ineffective and impatient. Out of sheer frustration, and lack of control, they could resort to comments that are inappropriate and hurtful. If this happens, you might have to teach your children that they cannot always fight back.

Lets face it, we have all worked with, or for, jerks; but we knew we couldn't react to them. This is the lesson your kids must also learn. The sooner they understand, the better. As unfair as it seems, the reality is that your children will encounter some teachers that voice their opinions and criticize unjustly. During these times, they might have to learn how to not internalize the hurtful words. The problem in the past has been that they were forced to comply, and they personalized the criticism. Each emotional assault contributed to their decline in self-worth. Your job will be to help them learn how to depersonalize others' attitudes so that the problems are not compounded further. Otherwise, not only are your children's egos shattered, society now sees them as trouble. The following is an example of how you can teach your children how to cope with others.

> A young boy was getting into trouble for fighting on the bus. He professed, "Well they called me names, and they made me mad." As an exercise to help him not personalize others' behavior, he practiced saying silently to himself, "I don't have to believe that!" Part of the exercise included role-playing. I called him names, and told him to repeat the phrase. After several minutes of name-calling, he began to smile. He realized that the words could not hurt him if he did not accept them. His mother reported later that he was no longer in trouble on the bus. She also stated that one day his cousin was calling him a name, and he retorted out loud, "I don't have to believe that!" She was amazed, and pleased with how he was able to cope more effectively with others.

Your task will be to help your non-coping children develop skills that will allow them to be successful. You know them better than anyone else, so tap into their spirits, and encourage your children to really know and love themselves.

Tagged, You're It

Once your children have been labeled or tagged, they are heading for a point of no return. No matter what they do, they will be viewed as the problem. Others assume and give full responsibility to the tagged children. As a result, others minimize their own actions and participation by placing blame on the new scapegoat. The following is an example of what happens when kids get tagged.

> An incident occurred at school where a young man was trying to correct his test paper to improve his score. He corrected the paper four times, but each time the teacher impatiently returned the paper, and showed her disgust for his mistakes. He thought he was doing his best, yet her reaction disturbed him. He had been tagged, and no longer had the benefit of the doubt for giving his all. He finally lost control, and exploded. His victimized mother was still

traumatized and unable to protect him from the situation. He admitted that he could not depend on her to rectify the problem, and that he felt alone.

What this boy needs are skills that help him cope better with his frustration. The fact that he was able to return four times before exploding was amazing, and shows that he truly wants to succeed. He needs help implementing his options. The best way to accomplish success, though, is for his mother to physically and emotionally be there for him. It is also vital that his mother convince the teacher that a different approach should be used to move him in a more positive direction.

Parenting a child from family violence is very real and personal for me. Katlin has struggled in school his entire life. We have had some outstanding teachers, and we have had ones that have made our life a living hell. The problem with many school systems is they think they are always right, and that children should be seen and not heard. Adults must recognize that their reactions are equally important to their interactions with children. That is why they call them relationships. It takes two. To show you the difference, I will use Katlin's eighth grade class as an example. At the beginning of the year, he and one of his male teachers were not getting along. Once a meeting was held, at which I shared Katlin's past, the teacher immediately turned the situation around. He was compassionate and understanding. His attitude toward Katlin shifted, and a new outlook was born. He reported months later that Katlin was a good student, and that all the problems had stopped. Yet, another teacher that consistently struggled with him made life difficult for Katlin. As a result of her prejudicial actions, he was on his way to expulsion. The difference here was that one adult recognized that he contributed partially to the problem, whereas the other one did not. In fact, she intentionally provoked him, and punished him unfairly.

We must take a stronger look at the impact adult behavior has on children, and what we can do to promote healthier interactions. I would like to believe that most teachers do not intentionally set out to hurt children, but there is definitely a level of ignorance in regard to how their attitude contributes to the breakdown in behavior.

As parents, we must also take part of the responsibility for our children's failures. There were so many times when I blamed Katlin for his struggles in school. I was emotionally exhausted from endlessly dealing with his episodes. I suffered from hypo-activity disorder, and was simply burnt out. At times, I screamed hysterically, and made him feel bad. Then I would learn that the problem wasn't his at all, but his teacher's. It is easy to assume that your children are to blame because everyone around has reinforced that. But the last thing they need is someone telling them that they are bad; they already have that message. We have to support, understand, and love them. Then somehow, we have to get them to love themselves.

Les Brown, a motivational speaker, talks about children and the message they get from adults. As a child, he was placed in special education classes because he upset an adult with his behavior. The message he received was that he was stupid. For years he lived up to the label he was given until one day a teacher told him that he didn't have to be what others said. That comment was a pivotal moment in his life because it allowed him to change how he felt about himself. The irony is that he changed his self-perception because another adult told him he could. He concluded that a person "feels worthy by permission."[5] This is exactly what children need from us. They need someone to change the message they have gotten to one that instills hope, encouragement, and promise for a brighter and happier childhood.

Boundary Breakers

One of the biggest problems for children from family violence is the concept of personal space or boundaries. Their batterer violated their space, and never afforded them the opportunity to feel safe or respected. They struggle with the concept of boundary breakers because it was never taught to them. What you must strive for now is introducing them to a set of new rules. They need to know what society expects from them, and how their behavior impacts the perception of others. As we discussed in Chapter 6, behavior is a skill that must be practiced. Use the following boundary breakers as your goals to practice:

- No means no
- Stop means stop
- Don't means don't

Play a game using these statements as your goals. Actually, tell them that you are going to intermittently use them throughout the day and that they must be alert and catch the phrases. Each time they respond correctly to them, they can earn stickers. Establish a value or reward for earning five, ten, and fifteen stickers. For example, five stickers could equal a movie rental; ten could equal a pizza; fifteen could equal a trip to the zoo. Once they have accumulated a certain amount, allow them to cash in on their prize. This is a proactive method of behavior modification, and it's fun. You will have to think of ways to introduce these boundary breakers into your conversation, but practicing the new behavior is the best way to make the changes.

Children are not consciously rude and disrespectful. They just need your help recognizing that healthy boundaries make everyone happy. When children can practice and be triumphant with the new boundaries, they will feel much better about who they are. Consequently, they will behave their way to success.

Re-labeling and Breaking the Mold

It is so important to support your children and break the mold they were cast into. Provide information and suggestions to adults so that they can re-label your kids. In the past, services for battered children were few, and by the time their needs were identified, it was often too late. They were left to their own demise, and they made bad choices based on their self-perception. Juvenile detention centers are now filled with kids who were misunderstood and mislabeled. Don't let this happen to your children. Be their advocate, and never give up. Ten adults might struggle with them, but one might not. Embrace that adult, and work toward breaking the mold. Research your options and use the resources that are available to make this process better.

CHAPTER 10

To Be or Not to Be a Victim

No one can make you feel inferior without your permission.
                                        —*Eleanor Roosevelt*

As has been mentioned throughout this book, no one deserves to be beaten, physically or emotionally. When abuse repeatedly occurs and patterns emerge, however, a serious look must be taken to determine how we participate in our circumstances. The signs are there. We just have to recognize them and act accordingly. Life, and how we manage it, is a choice.

I have had the distinct pleasure of watching many families turn their lives around. Unfortunately, there were some that did not. As simplistic as this sounds, the only difference between those families that succeeded and those that failed was their choices. If you want to avoid future oppression, then consider your options and consciously make decisions to participate differently.

It is important to define the word *victim* somewhat differently so that you can fully appreciate my intent. For purposes of this chapter, the word *victim* is defined as a state of victimization caused by the *interpretation* of a violating act. Commonly, during an event such as this, an individual is referred to as a victim. Although this is true at the time, it is more important that one does not remain in the state of victimization, meaning that how a person interprets the event can create a mindset that says the person is required to embrace the event either by holding onto it or by moving forward. The former is a type of self-punishment which holds severe emotional consequences.

Therefore, you have two options, you can dwell on the past and become its prisoner, or you can let it go and free yourself. To get there from here and "fix" your life, you have to overcome your circumstances by openly acknowledging how you respond to the dysfunction. Next, you must stop behaving in a manner that keeps you in the victim role.

There is an age-old story, in which an old donkey falls into a deep well. The farmer hears the donkey braying and discovers his predicament. After some thought, the farmer decides that the donkey is too old to bother rescuing. He calls upon his neighbors to help him fill the well with dirt and cover the animal alive. As the shovels of soil hit the donkey's back, he realizes his demise. He must quickly think of a solution in order to survive. As the dirt hits him, he shakes it off and packs it into the ground. Diligently, the donkey persists, shaking and stomping, shaking and stomping. Eventually, he lifts himself from the well and runs to safety. This story represents tenacity. He could have accepted his fate; but instead, he chose to rise above his circumstances.

We all choose how we live, and the state of victimization is only an option if we allow it to be. Viewing abuse as something we experienced rather than something that victimized us will lend us better results. Although any tragedy greatly impacts us, we do not have to succumb to it. Lets say, for example, that you survived a plane crash. Your outlook would forever be altered, but it is not your whole being. I hope this chapter helps you realize that surviving your battering experience can make you strong, confident, and better than ever. So long as you do not surrender to the label of victim, you will not be one. Instead, you will shine above all others because you know that getting out of the relationship was the most courageous thing you have ever done.

Repacking Your Baggage

Everyone has emotional baggage. Deciding how much we are willing to carry or repack determines our load. If you still consider yourself a victim, you are carrying too much. To be more effective, reassess what you have; keep the lessons you have learned, but let go of the pain. For now, put some of your baggage away and pull it out now and then when it's appropriate. Feeling sorry for yourself, occasionally, is okay. Those days can be referred to as PLMs (Poor Little Me). Having a PLM is normal, but being in the "pity pot" is not. It serves no positive purpose to stay miserable. If the feelings persist, you are probably getting an emotional payoff from your pain. If this is the case, examine why you would want to feel bad, and then do something about it. Give yourself permission to grieve sometimes, but then pick yourself up and move forward.

Most of us have experienced something traumatic during our lifetime. But we cannot let a few bad experiences ruin our opportunities for a good life. We cannot change what happened to us. Therefore, embracing those memories only serves to weigh us down. My advice is to lighten the load and make the journey through life less arduous. It is time to repack your bags and have a fun trip.

Also be mindful not to carry other people's baggage. You have enough of your own without overloading yourself even further. Say, for example, that you have carried your parent's baggage into your relationship with your children, meaning that now you are parenting your children like you were parented. At this point, you might want to reconsider your load. Parenting styles are generally passed from one generation to the next. There is sometimes no rhyme nor reason for how we treat our children, except that our parents did it to us. If you did not have an ideal childhood, you will need to be careful not to repeat the same mistakes your parents made. Your job will be to recognize why your parenting styles are what they are.

Say for example, that your mother frequently dated men and was not emotionally available. You would not want to overcompensate by never dating. Your children's experiences are different than yours. The men were not responsible for your mother's choices, she was. The reality is that she would have probably found another way to avoid parenting you if she really wanted to. On the flip side of this scenario, you could be repeating your parental baggage unwittingly by rationalizing that you can handle it. One victim complained that her mother jumped from relationship to relationship; yet when confronted with her three failed marriages, and four live-in boyfriends, she remarked, "Well, I am different because I am always there for my kids." I would venture to guess that her mother believed the same thing. Therefore, adults who experience deprivation as children may either overcompensate with kindness or repeat the abuse. In each case, the end result is not favorable. Remember that your baggage is just that—yours. Don't give it to your children to carry like your parents may have done to you.

Childhood Trauma and Its Interpretations

As you become an adult, carrying past baggage holds emotional implications. Commonly, projection occurs due to the traumas you endured and it misguides your behavior. Say, for instance, that you feel sorry for your partner because his parents were cruel to him. You sympathize with him because your childhood experiences were similar. You want to help him through his pain because you understand what the abuse meant to you. This is a form of cognitive distortion (crooked thinking) that allows you to justify and minimize your abuser's behavior. You thought that if you loved him enough, those bad feelings would go away. After all, you would have been grateful if someone had done that for you. But, this is not the case for him. To recover from abuse, you must recognize that your batterer is not you, because he does not think or feel like you. As long as you are willing to buy into the fallacy that you are responsible for his happiness, you will be a victim.

The most effective strategy here is to separate your childhood history from his. See your batterer for what he is: pathological and self-absorbed. To heal from your childhood trauma, own your pain and stop giving it to your batterer.

Over-Functioning

Many people who experience family violence, including children, learn over-functioning to maintain control of their environment. They work harder than most to compensate for their circumstances. As a result, they perform feats the average person cannot. They do it all: they cook, clean, work, chauffeur, fix things, take care of everyone's needs, and rarely complain. The problem with over-functioning is that it creates martyrs. The amount of energy required to get through the day makes it impossible for them to focus on their issues. Over-functioning makes healing from the past difficult because the painful events are not addressed. Problems cannot be fixed unless they can be focused upon and that requires emotional availability.

If you over-function, make the decision to slow down and reflect on your mistakes. Otherwise, you are destined for burnout. Your children will ultimately pay the price, because they will have a depressed, unhappy, and unfulfilled parent. The love they once felt for you will be replaced with pity, disgust, and resentment. Although what you experienced was incredibly painful, you must question whether staying busy to avoid your life is really worth it. You can either pay now or later.

De-Selfing

De-selfing is a term I learned from the audiotape *The Dance of Anger,* by Harriet Lerner. The word implies a stripping of one's self so that no value or worth are evident. Once you have been de-selfed, you become non-existent: invisible. You no longer have a voice, an independent thought, or an opinion to call your own. You have learned to accept your batterer's reality. Your ability to think, make decisions, or contribute becomes lost. Your life is no longer yours.

Understanding how the de-selfing process works will move you beyond victimization. You can overcome the defeats in your life by recognizing and appreciating your true value. Reversing the de-selfing process requires a closer look at who you are and what you are really worth. Accomplishing this, however, can upset some people, because for years they used you to meet their needs without regard to how you felt. When you become less available, some may abandon you in your hour of need. Those who do are not really your friends. Wayne Dyer once said, "If you can't say no in a relationship, you have to say no to the relationship." De-selfed individuals usually cannot say no, because they feel undeserving. You must move from de- to re-selfing to be successful. Practice the following statements to help you through this process:

"That really doesn't work for me."

"No, that's not in my best interest."

"That doesn't meet my needs."

These statements assist with balancing the scale so that you get what you want and what you need, too. Practicing these retorts is incredibly uncomfortable at first; but as you apply them, others will learn how to treat you. If, by chance, no one in your life nurtures you, start now and find a new support system. If individuals are sucking the life out of you, get rid of them and replace them with others who care. For those of you who are more fortunate, assess how these people contribute to your life, and then nurture those relationships. Re-selfing is necessary, so that you can feel good. To get a baseline for your new journey toward self-discovery, write down some of your attributes. If you struggle with re-selfing, use the following questions to help you embrace your qualities:

- Are you mean to people on purpose?
- Do you go out of your way to help others?
- Are you considerate of how others feel?
- Do you deceive or use people to get your way?
- Do you hurt others so that you can feel better about yourself?
- Do you possess integrity?
- Overall, would you consider yourself as a kind person?
- Are you honest?

The point here is to embrace and personalize your value. Your life will only have quality when you believe that you are worthy and deserving. Start today and ask yourself, *"Should I feel good about who I am?"* If the answer is yes, you are moving toward re-selfing. If the answer is no, keep looking for your value, it is there.

Personality Types

A therapist once told me that every individual possesses three personality types: an adult, a parent, and a child. Individuals utilize specific personality types according to particular times and interactions with others. The predominant personality usually is dependent upon how we have adjusted to our environments. As we mature we tend to become reliant upon one of these personality types more than the others. Review the personality types and ask yourself where you fall in the spectrum.

Adult Personality

The adult personality normally indicates that you trust your environment and that you are confident that you can take care of yourself. You respond to others in a mature, adult fashion that makes you equal to those around you. Conversing about mature issues in an appropriate manner suggests that you are using your adult personality. Usually, the adult personality is assertive, self-assured, and has a keen sense of purpose. People with this trait do not rely upon others to tell them who they are or what they should be. Normally, the use of the adult personality serves to make mature decisions and solve problems more effectively.

Parent Personality

The parent personality usually means that you are interacting in a manner that makes you an authority figure. When you are in a situation where you are talking with your children or interacting with incompetent people, you would probably use your parent personality to deal with them. Your tendency would be to take care of others and make decisions for them because you know what's best.

When you rely upon your parent personality, you normally maintain control so you can determine your own fate. You take care of business and use a proactive approach when dealing with your life. For example, adult children of alcoholics often develop their parent personality more than others because they are forced to care for their dysfunctional parents. Although the parent personality can serve you well, it can set you up to be an enabler for others.

Child Personality

Finally, the child personality is dominant when victimization has occurred as a child. This personality is fearful and distrustful of others. A sense of self was never established, which makes a person feel insignificant. As a result, the child personality may present itself more often than the others. This personality normally develops and fixates as a result of emotional and physical abuse.

Typically, when the child personality becomes more prevalent, individuals have no sense of control over their lives. They are often incapable of taking care of themselves. They feel small, helpless and regard the world as an unsafe place. Unfortunately, what results from this type of exposure is that many adults desperately seek approval from others and rarely look within for internal validation.

When to Call upon the Different Personalities

We all utilize each of the three personalities at some point. We just have to decide when it is appropriate to do so. There are always situations where one or more of the personalities are accessed to interact with the world. Learning when and when not to use them is paramount. For example, you might need to use your adult personality when negotiating contracts for your company, but then you may need to access your parent personality with a bungling employee.

Developing your adult or parent personality also helps protect the scared little girl (child) within. Proving to yourself that you are no longer that small child can expand your competency. Once you create a sense of safety, you can be a more confident and better parent for your children. Periodically accessing your child personality makes relating on your children's emotional level easier. You can interact by pretending, telling stories and coloring.

Now ask yourself which personality is most predominant and best describes you. Next, determine whether that personality type is serving you effectively in your day-to-day interaction with the world. If it is, then you are on track. If it is not, move toward the type that would better meet your needs.

Becoming Non-believers

Non-believers stop accepting the hurtful words inflicted upon them by others, and start believing in themselves. Self-discovery is an effective means of discounting erroneous input. For example, my ex-husband once remarked that I was too stupid to drive a standard shift. His criticism served to paralyze me during our marriage and haunted me for some time after. Later, I felt compelled to disprove him by purchasing a four-speed standard shift. That day, I went on a quest to learn what to do. I jerked and stalled that car countless times. By the end of the day, I was a semi-expert. Today, I drive a six-speed standard shift. And although I don't usually dwell on the past, there are times, as I shift into sixth gear, when I think, "Ha, ha, mister, I am too smart enough to drive a standard." I could have easily fallen prey to his criticism and limited myself, but I needed to prove that what he said was absolutely, positively wrong.

As you grow confident, the verbal abuse you experienced will seem like it is worlds away. Once you recognize the truth, you can free yourself from those disturbing memories. Put your experiences into perspective: a woman's lifespan is approximately eighty years. As you look back on your life, do you want the person that abused you forty years ago to control your life until the end? It is time to join the other non-believers so your life has the quality it deserves.

Transference of Control

At some point, you must transfer the control back to you. As this transference occurs, you will be freed from his grip.

> During a lecture, a woman shared that the police had killed her husband twenty years ago during a family violence dispute. She said she has cried everyday since then. My response was, "Your batterer is dead; he cannot feel anything, yet he's still beating you. When do you stop being a victim?" After class, another woman approached me and lamented that she was doing something similar. Her husband had been gone for ten years, yet his clothes were still in her closet. She got physically ill every time she saw them. She explained that she didn't have time to get rid of them. My reply was, "A college student and twenty dollars would get rid of those clothes. What is the real reason you keep them?" She then vowed to be rid of his things before the weekend was out.

What these women did was keep the status quo. They permitted their batterers to continue victimizing them. To move forward, recognize your motivations for staying in the victim role. Once you understand, the picture will be clearer and the transference of control can occur.

Self-reliance

I learned the term self-reliant while watching Miss Shirley Temple portray a young girl trudging through her tragic life. Although she always overcame her circumstances in every episode, one in particular stood out to me. She boldly proclaimed to an adult, "I am very self-reliant!" As a child, I wasn't really sure what that meant, but it definitely sounded powerful. She announced her independence with such vigor and confidence that I just knew being self-reliant was a good thing. Although she was a fictitious character, her message was strong, "Stop waiting for someone else to take care of you." This valuable lesson is one we all need. In the big picture, at some point, we will be alone and forced to fend for ourselves, so we need to know what to do.

This reminds me of a wonderful story about an elderly woman. She had taken her car in for repair. There wasn't anyone to help her get the car home so she drove her other car to the shop. She proceeded to alternate driving each car a certain distance. She would get out of one car and walk to the next. As she took turns driving each car, she eventually made it home. What an impressive determination this woman had. She could have let her circumstances get the best of her and profess herself as helpless. But how would that have gotten the job done? Rather than complain and remain a victim, she chose to be independent and self-reliant. She chose to take care of herself when no one else would.

Do you have obstacles like this? Are there memories that debilitate you? If so, look deep within yourself and decide how you want to live. I once heard that if there is something wrong in your life, change it or shut up. Those words seem simplistic and abrasive, but they are true. All you really need to be is self-reliant. The rest will follow. Ask yourself what you can do to be a stronger more confident person. As you grow and learn, you will be amazed at what you can accomplish.

Building Your Strengths and Challenging Your Weaknesses

We all have strengths and weaknesses as a result of our life choices. The fact that you are reading this book shows that the desire to understand them is there. What you need to do now is learn how to accentuate your strengths and minimize your weaknesses.

Strengths

To focus on your strengths, you must be willing to see your value. Many people stuck in the victim role hate themselves and believe that somehow they deserved to be mistreated. This self-loathing serves no purpose but to be beaten down further. Embracing this negative perception clouds judgment and does not leave room for growth. Therefore, it is a must to recognize your strengths before you can begin your new positive journey.

Recipients of abuse usually possess incredible attributes. Most are caring, giving, and loving. Many actually work in the healthcare field. The irony is that nurturing people end up being victimized because they believe they can fix everyone's problems by creating more for themselves. They see this as a challenge and as their lot in life. There is a price to pay, however, for this mentality. There may be something to that old phrase, "Nice guys finish last." Although being selfish is not the answer, neither is being selfless. You need to recognize that you deserve more than you are getting. That means concentrating on your contributions. If loving yourself feels difficult initially, at least recognize the good you have done. Start keeping a journal of your strong points. Use the following questions to help you:

- Do you do kind things for your friends, families or neighbors?
- Are you sensitive to other people's time and commitments?
- Do you have strong morals?
- Are you loving and affectionate toward others?
- Do others admire your accomplishments even when you don't?

If you feel good about your answers, you have the qualities it will take to move away from victimhood; you just have to appreciate them. If you did not feel good about your answers, start making goals to change them.

Weaknesses

Challenging your weaknesses will be a tough job. You have to tackle them head on. Weaknesses generate fears that are often irrational. This thought process has no real basis other than to paralyze you. Review the following questions and see whether your fear is stopping you:

- Are you afraid to say no because you want to be accepted?
- Do you ever voice your opinion when you oppose others?
- Are you too dependent on others to make decisions for yourself?
- Do you have a sense of purpose?
- Do you use others as an excuse for your failures?

Do not get too discouraged with your answers. This is your opportunity to change them. Life is all about improvement. Ben Franklin said it best, "When you are finished changing . . . you're finished." Do not get caught up in the regret or guilt of your past behavior. Start now and improve your life. Follow the old adage, "This is the first day of the rest of your life." Make it count!

The Double-Edged Sword

Some characteristics can be construed as both strengths and weaknesses depending upon your experiences. For example, opportunists take advantage of kind-hearted people. They can spot a good soul from a mile away and they move right in for the kill. Then, the violated person proclaims that she has "learned her lesson," and will never be nice to anyone ever again. Avoid this attitude; it only makes you bitter and the other guy wins. Being distrustful makes you a victim. Just because your batterer was unappreciative does not mean others should be penalized. Besides, if you stop being kind-hearted, you stop being you. Having a good spirit counts for something. You can make a difference with your compassion, so long as that energy is given to someone who deserves and appreciates it.

Another strength that can cross the line into weakness is tolerance. Although tolerance is an incredible attribute, it can be used against you. When someone crosses the line, breaks boundaries, and is *forgiven*, it can be seen as a victory and a sign of superiority over you. A time comes when you have to say, "This behavior is unacceptable and will not be tolerated." A line in the sand must be drawn and anyone who crosses it must be challenged. Otherwise, you will be repeatedly victimized. Saying no is okay. You cannot please everybody all the time. And since you are a part of the human race, your opinion has to count.

Strengths and Weaknesses Are a Matter of Opinion

The next area that requires attention is deciding what your strengths and weaknesses are. Although your batterer never recognized your gifts of strength, that doesn't mean they did not exist. It only means you chose the wrong person to give your gifts to. You have simply been taken for granted by the person you loved. The time has come to reevaluate your character and see your strengths for what they really are. Stop looking toward external sources to determine your true nature and start internalizing your strengths.

Batterers' *modus operandi* is to spend half of their time searching for their partners' interests (strengths), and then utilizing the remaining time berating and patronizing their discoveries. Their insecurities run so deep that they find it necessary to strip away any strengths their partners may have. They desperately need to be the only presence in their victims' lives. Say, for example, that you have always been regarded as an outstanding corporate manager. Then your batterer says something like, "God! It's hard to imagine that you can run a company; you can't even figure out how to balance our checkbook. Your company must be desperate for help." These types of insults, over a period of time, break you down: little by little, piece by piece. Initially, the comments just really hurt; but gradually, they create doubt about your capabilities. Take the time to evaluate these criticisms and determine whether they are accurate or not.

Another time strengths and weaknesses can get confusing is when a person regards any help as a sign of weakness. Realistically, everyone needs support at some point. As the staff at Families First always says, "Asking for help is a sign of strength."[1] A horrific violation such as what you have experienced warrants support. Know that you can depend on others without being dependent upon them. Your presumption might be that needing someone got you into this mess and thus not needing them will get you out. The truth is that your batterer's support was conditional. Real love is not. Reach out to the friends and family that *really* love you. With help you can start redefining your strength.

Rebuilding Your Children's Strength

You are not the only one learning how not to be a victim. Your children have also profoundly suffered. Now, after the devastation, rebuilding their strengths is a must. Their batterer's messages were made perfectly clear, "You are pathetic, worthless, and unloved." Now, you must show them otherwise. That means giving them the attention and love that they were previously robbed of. Your kids may be displaying outbursts that are simply cries for help.

Some parents believe that their children are overreacting to seek attention. Understandably, the adults counter their children's dramatization with, "Oh get up! You're not hurt." Although this may in fact be true, they might need reassurance while rebuilding their strengths. Just telling them that they are okay does not make it so. Instead of making them brush-off the pain, gently pick them up and love them. Do not make them grow up too fast. They have already experienced more than most people should in a lifetime. If possible, avoid making statements such as the following:

> "She can do it herself; she is acting that way to get attention."
>
> "He knows better than that; he just wants you to feel sorry for him."
>
> "She's not scared; she's just being lazy."

All children seek attention, but especially ones surviving the devastation of family violence. Their behavior is not a deliberate attempt to suck you dry, nor is it their sole purpose to annoy you. Mostly, younger children do not cognitively plan psychological warfare on their parents. They learn that later through dysfunctional role modeling. Children have limitations which need to be appropriately assessed.

Fulfilling their need for attention guides and makes them strong. Self-confidence and self-love are the greatest gifts you can give to your children. The effects last a lifetime. Your dedication will not only serve your children, but it will contribute to generations to come. Your children's strengths will grow by leaps and bounds when they stop being victims. The drawback may be, however, that their newfound power can be too liberating. They may use it to put others down in the process. They might relentlessly compare their achievements to others' inabilities, which is unhealthy. Do not be too disappointed if this happens, because sometimes there must be a revolution before a balance can be found. This new sense of self has empowered them. Now, they need help managing it appropriately. The balance is teaching them that a good self-esteem is possible without making others feel bad. Help them rebuild their strengths and be confident.

Recognizing Triggers

To move your family away from victimhood, recognize the triggers that created their reactions. Basically, certain associations elicit particular responses. Once they have been identified, you can begin the process of de-programming everyone.

Triggers create havoc. For example, a homeless family was repeatedly abused in their father's blue van. They made an association between the pain and the color of the vehicle. Now, years later, when the children see a blue van they recoil into the fetal position and tremble. The established emotional connection has paralyzed them. They need assurance that the blue van is not what hurt them.

To cope more effectively, children need to react differently to their triggers. You can reduce their triggers by introducing them in a safe environment. Undoing triggers can be equated with teaching children to walk. You do it in baby steps and one at a time. Eventually, they can stop being victims. You can refer to Chapter 1 for parenting tools to desensitize your children's triggers.

Don't "Should" on Yourself or Your Kids!

Many people live restricted lives because they have learned how to *should:* "I should do this, you should do that." I call these people *should-ers.* They put themselves and others in a position where they are emotionally paralyzed by unrealistic restrictions. They are incapable of moving forward, because they believe they cannot do what they want to. Note whether any of the following sound familiar:

- "You should love your father because he is your dad."
- "I should have tried harder to make this work, then we wouldn't be in this mess."
- "You should stop crying before you make yourself sick."

Can you see how *should-ing* positions your family for defeat? When you *should* on yourself, you regret your behavior in the past; you generate doubt about your options in the present; and you deter your choices for the future.

Should-er versus Shoulder

When you look at the word *should-er,* doesn't it really spell shoulder? When we unwittingly *should* on our kids, we are actually trying to be a shoulder. But in our haste, we make the fundamental mistake of *should-ing.* No one gains anything from being *should-ed* on. It only sets up defenses and makes internalizing and doing the right thing difficult. For example, if your child lashes out at a teacher and storms off, don't immediately assume that he is wrong for doing so. Don't lecture him by saying, "You should not have yelled at your teacher!" Instead, discuss how to avoid the conflict next time. I am sure he already understands that he did the wrong thing, but *shoulding* on him only makes him resistant to changing his behavior. Besides, maybe the teacher reprimanded him inappropriately, and your son just did not know how to handle being cornered and attacked.

In your quest to be a good parent, try harder to be a better shoulder. Listen to your children and stop judging them. If you just take the time to understand them, you can stop *should-ing* and start training them for a successful future.

Society's Perception of Victimization

Society's perception of battered women often perpetuates the stigma that keeps them in the abusive relationship. Although information and research are now available that describe its impact, many still believe that family violence is a private matter. They ignorantly suppose that if a woman really wanted to leave, she could. Some even rationalize that she stays because she is materialistic (i.e. she wants the car, the house and the money); or they think she is lazy (i.e., she doesn't want to work).

One day, I was describing a battered women's circumstances to a police officer who retorted, "We don't help with that kind of stuff; these women just need to stop thinking they should maintain their past economic status. They could live on less; they just don't want to." This comment mortified me, to say the least. My observation, in most cases, has been that victims live a modest to substandard life once they leave their batterers. They only want enough to feed and care for their children. This peace officer's job was supposedly to serve and protect. He boldly said to me, "It's not my job to sit and watch her take her husband's belongings." This blatantly disrespectful and uncaring attitude further perpetuates the social stigma and isolates these families more. Society needs a reality check. We have come a long way in the quest to help battered families, but we still have so much more to do.

Unfortunately, society still sees you as part of the problem. Consequently, you cannot wait for someone else to rescue you.

You are in charge of your life now, and it is up to you to make the necessary changes. The good news is that many more resources are available than ever before. Getting help can still be difficult, but if you are persistent you can find it. Join a support group and learn how to break out of victimhood. Then share what you have learned with others so they can have a better understanding of the dynamics of family violence. Perhaps your experience, like mine, will lead the way for changing the social stigma for other battered families.

Being in the Good Space

To stop feeling like a victim, you must be in a good space emotionally. This means taking an honest look at your life and determining where you stand psychologically. Mental attitude contributes to every aspect of your life, including your physical health. The constant exposure to abuse may mean that you are suffering not only emotionally, but physically as well. Bad relationships can produce moderate to severe symptoms of depression. Evaluate the following symptoms to determine whether you are in a good space or suffering from depression:

- Do you have feelings of hopelessness and helplessness?
- Are you perpetually tired or uninterested in activities that should be fun?
- Do you have an overwhelming sense of sadness that you really cannot explain?
- Do you over- or under-eat?

If you answered yes to most of these questions, you may be suffering from depression. This is a very real and physical illness that can impede your progress. Seek treatment by your family physician or a counselor. Finding a good space gives you a sense of purpose and makes you feel differently about your life. Look within yourself and ask, "Why am I here?" Everyone has a positive purpose, yours may just have gotten lost in the shuffle. Mine is to motivate others to feel better. My work reinforces that I have the control I need to accept my past. Being in a good space will help you see your life differently.

Breaking the Patterns

Breaking the patterns means letting go of the past and what it meant to you. To feel like you did the right thing by leaving, you have to recognize why you are mourning the loss of this relationship in the first place. Ask yourself some basic questions like:

- How did your batterer contribute or add value to your life?
- Love is a verb, not just a word. What actions did he take to prove his love?
- Does he want to meet your needs?
- Did he encourage your children in a positive manner?

Victims who never ask these questions get stuck in destructive patterns, and their children are watching. What are they learning from the abusive relationship? How has role modeling taught them to relate to others? When men do not have to contribute, children interpret the male's role as an uncaring and non-participatory one. Conversely, they may conclude that women should not expect support from their significant other and that the female's role is to do everything and receive nothing. Is this what you want your children to learn? If you cannot break these patterns for your sake, then do it for theirs. They need to be shown what to do, who to be, and how to act. Help them understand how families are supposed to work.

To see just how unfair your relationship has been, take a deck of cards and lay down one card for each nice thing you did for your partner. Now, put them in one pile. Next, deal out a card for each nice thing your partner did for you then place them in another stack. The first pile is your partner's and represents what you did for him and the second pile is yours and represents what he did for you. Count the number of cards in each pile. Who holds most or all of the cards? I am guessing that he is, which doesn't seem quite fair. To change your victim status, you need more cards in your hand than you currently have. It is difficult to win in life's game when your partner holds all the cards. Stack the deck and deal yourself a new hand.

False Hope

If you don't want to be a victim, stop having false hope. See this relationship for what it is: over. He promised he would change and he didn't, so see that. What you are grieving for is the loss of a relationship, not your batterer. The love you once felt has now been replaced with pain and anger. Instead of asking, "Why, oh why, did he do this to me?" tell yourself, "Why ask why?" Asking why you were battered is futile. There is no good answer except that you just were. Stop giving your batterer a reason for his actions. There is nothing that a person could possibly do that warrants being abused. Nothing! It's time to quit personalizing his behavior. He would have battered anyone; you were just unfortunate enough to be the one he got to first.

Batterers can only change if or when they acknowledge that they have a problem. Everyone makes mistakes and an opportunity to rectify their actions is fair and worth forgiving. But apologizing means that the behavior *never* happens again. So, if he is genuinely sorry, it's okay to forgive him once; but if it happens again, it's a habit. I was fortunate enough to have a mother who pounded it into my head, "First time he hits you, shame on him; second time he hits you, then shame on you." That one piece of advice got me out of my relationship. If your batterer has hit you more than twice, all your rationalizing is false hope. I remember visiting a woman at the hospital who had been stabbed, choked, and beaten. The words still resonate in my mind: "My husband's picking me up tomorrow." When do you give up and say that enough is enough? When does hoping become ridiculously absurd? To test yourself, count how many times you believed the battering would stop. If the number is higher than two, give yourself permission to let go. The chances are great that he is never going to change. You can accept that now or you can waste a few more years living with false hope. It's your choice.

Commanding Respect

Commanding respect should not be confused with demanding respect. Demanding normally means that you are unreasonable, harsh, and difficult to ignore. Commanding respect, on the other hand, is a more palatable and less aggressive approach that works more effectively. When you command respect, your confidence shows that you can hold your own and that your requests are appropriate. It is time to recognize your full potential. When you believe in yourself and behave as such, you can command respect. Getting past the sense of worthlessness that was assigned to you will be challenging but liberating. This is not going to be easy. Anytime you make drastic changes, the process can be painful, yet bittersweet. The best advice I can give is to bite the bullet. It will be well worth it! I once heard that everything turns out in the end, if it hasn't turned out, it's not the end. Try to keep this in mind as you work your way to a new and better you.

When you begin to practice commanding respect, others will be taken aback because in the past, you had not required anything in return from them. They saw you as a doormat, a non-person without needs. Gradually and sometimes unwittingly, they dehumanize you and make you invisible. They regard your only purpose as one to serve them. As you think and act differently, you will temporarily generate mass confusion. Initially, others will not know how to respond and some people will walk away from you. But that's all right; the ones who leave were just using you for what they could get.

Projecting the Look

To begin your journey toward a more self-assured you, your physical presence may require an adjustment. Projecting confidence means standing straight, shoulders square, with your head held high and using direct eye contact. The awkwardness will subside with time, but for now you have to *fake it 'til you make it*. Being comfortable with your external posture will promote your internal stance. You need to feel confident and competent on the inside. How you project your own self-image determines how others see you. If you are self-critical, others will follow your lead. But if you feel self-assured and strong, others will see you that way. You must demonstrate that you know who you are and what you are worth. Then establish appropriate boundaries and make your opinions known.

You have been in a passive role for far too long with someone who has been aggressive and unfair. Now would be an excellent time to change your role to an assertive one. An example, after my divorce, was when my co-workers decided that others took advantage of me. To help me become more confident, they enrolled me in an assertiveness training course. Since then, there's no stopping me. I recognized my worth, and I always voice my opinion when I need to. Years later, the joke is, "We created a monster!" That course gave me the confidence to command respect. I recognized that I deserve to be heard because I am somebody. And you are too!

Glamorizing the Batterer

Children from family violence are so ashamed of their situation that they often glamorize their batterers to compensate for the ugly secrets they keep. Typically, kids from average families go through a process where they think their parents are stupid and embarrassing. Abused children, however, might speak highly of their parents to create the image of a stable life. They portray their families in a good light so they don't feel judged or embarrassed. Admitting that their parent make mistakes would interfere with their illusion of a "normal" home. Only when children know that they can love their batterers without liking what they do, can they let go of their fantasy world.

Empowering Learned Helplessness

Individuals violated by others can potentially suffer from learned helplessness. Their behavior is a result of being repeatedly victimized and feeling defenseless. Without treatment, some children remain victims and some decide to victimize others to avoid feeling helpless. The latter develops a dog-eat-dog or kill or be killed attitude to survive. This behavior can start at a very young age and be carried into adulthood. When you see children who bully others you can bet they suffer from learned helplessness. They have created a rough exterior so that nobody messes with them. They intimidate and tease other children relentlessly to prove that no one is ever going to hurt them again. They minimize their behavior by saying, "Oh, I was just kidding, can't they take a joke?" The problem with this attitude is that the recipient doesn't think it's so funny. This type of behavior violates boundaries and shows a total lack of regard for others. Their taunting serves to make them feel powerful and in control.

Take a look at your batterer and decide whether he fits this description. Is he mean and cruel when he is "teasing" other family members? Does the teasing get out of hand? How do your children respond to the violation? Do they become aggressors or victims? This mindset is a common denominator for aggressive children. They provoke fights with their siblings and other children as a form of interaction. Adults minimize by saying, "They're just being kids." This is absolutely wrong; this behavior is abusive, plain and simple. They are developing patterns that will last a lifetime unless you help change them.

Learned helplessness includes obsession, which is often mistaken for love. Victims rationalize their batterers' fervent behavior as, "Oh, he cares about me, that's why he calls me every half hour." The truth is that batterers feel helpless and insecure, which drives them to know their victims' every move. They attempt to curb these unstable feelings by controlling their partners. Obsession is dangerous because the batterers' thought process is so distorted that they can rationalize just about any behavior.

Recognize what these destructive behavior patterns have done to your family. Observe your children's behavior and determine whether they are also suffering from learned helplessness. One parent complained, "My son is displaying similar behaviors as his father. He is loud and disruptive to get attention. His friends can't stand him anymore and he's being shunned." The problems this boy faces are rejection and isolation. He has not learned how to get his needs met appropriately. With each unsuccessful attempt, he can potentially feel more helpless. The more helpless he feels, the greater chance he has to become more insecure. As his insecurities grow, so will his need to control. What this young man does not understand is that he deserves to be heard and cared for. His mother needs new skills to help him seek positive attention. Learned helplessness has life-altering consequences. You have to provide an environment that permits your children to grow strong and confident.

Attitude Is Everything

Attitude is key to changing your life. As we near the end of this book, you have to decide what you want from your life. So often we become reactive to those around us and we continue on a path of self-destruction. We are all motivated by the things we choose to do; how we choose to think and what we choose to be. Assess what you get from this abusive relationship. What is your motivation for participating in this dysfunction? And do your children deserve to be there?

Role model to your kids how to create a better attitude. Teach them how to control their destiny without giving their power away. This brings to mind a young man that was doing poorly in math. He blamed his performance on his dislike for his teacher's assistant. Blaming her for his failure allowed him to maintain his victim role.

He could not foresee the impact she would have on his life thirty years from now. Although his failing would not reflect upon her life, her behavior would have permanent consequences for his. She will retire with a white picket fence and a pension, while he washes dishes because he is a high-school dropout. I asked this young man who the winner would be in the end if he continued to fail, and he said, "The teacher." Help your children react wisely and have the right attitude so their future is successful.

Warning Signs and Red Flags

There are so many signs if you just have your eyes open. When you look carefully at the tactics batterers use, you can see that you've been had. Wake up; otherwise you will be replaying your victim role over and over again. Use the following questions to determine whether you and your children are in this victim role. Do you or your children:

- Take responsibility for other people's happiness?
- Wonder what you could have done differently to make him want to change?
- Ever say, "if only I . . ."?
- Believe your batterer's unwarranted criticism?
- Feel compelled to make this relationship work?
- Personalize or internalize the abuse?

As your family heals, issues such as these may arise. You can cope with them as they appear. But in the meantime, be aware of the signs and break the victimization patterns as they arise. Each person has a choice to emotionally walk away. If you can recognize the warning signs and red flags sooner, breaking free will be easier.

Protective Factors

Protective factors are a form of measurement that identifies how adults defend children against harm. Some of today's families lack the appropriate skills necessary to recognize the danger their children face. In earlier times, we had communities and extended families that helped raise and protect our children. With the redefining of families and the disintegration of community support, we are forced to look solely upon ourselves to ensure that we create an environment that is protective of our children. Therefore, we must provide extra safety measures for them to gain a sense of security.

An article in *National Geographic* several years ago best described the lengths one parent took to protect her children. The article showed the aftermath of a forest fire in Yellowstone National Park, where a forest ranger discovered a bird literally petrified on the ground near the base of a tree. The ranger discovered that three tiny chicks were alive beneath their dead mother's wings. The loving mother understood the impending danger her babies were in if they remained in their nest. She couldn't get her offspring out of the forest, so she carried them to the base of the tree and covered them with her wings. She refused to abandon her babies. Knowing the blaze would scorch her small body, she remained steadfast anyway with no reservations. Because of her willingness to protect her children, they were given the opportunity to live.

Parenting requires sacrificing our needs and sometimes our safety. Our job is to protect our children from the elements. They depend upon us to know what to do. Some parents lack the natural instinct to keep their children safe. Many have lost their ability to recognize danger. The world is no longer a safe place to be, and we must hone in on our sensors and recognize the incredible responsibility we have to our children.

Children from family violence are exposed to potential danger on a daily basis; yet often victims report that their kids were not involved. If this happens to be your rationale, I would strongly encourage you to reconsider your reasoning. You may genuinely believe that you protected them from the conflict, but you did not. Kids are perceptive and know what goes on around them. Although they may not have seen the actual assault, they still felt the aftermath. They saw the tears, the sadness, and the bruises. Stop kidding yourself and start taking steps to protect your children. They deserve to have a healthy and violence-free childhood. You can no longer be a victim; you must be a victor! You must take care of them. Although you are scared, protect them with all you have.

Reattaching to Life

Family violence can cause some people to dissociate and detach from themselves and others to cope with their trauma. Their fears make them avoid relationships or situations where they could be left vulnerable. This is commonly referred to as the *walking wounded*. They respond by shutting down to avoid the emotional pain associated with the abuse. They segregate themselves and refuse to relate to others.

If you have allowed yourself to become victimized by your circumstances, you might isolate yourself and stop interacting effectively with those around you. As frightening as it feels, you must reattach to people. As social creatures, we need others for support. But to reconnect successfully with healthy people, you must be more positive. It's time to embrace your life rather than run from it. Life has no guarantees, and now is all that matters. If you waste time feeling sorry for yourself, you have spent your time unwisely. Don't allow the circumstances of your life to strip away the joy and promise that awaits you. Make your connections to others and live your life to the fullest.

Being Single and Being Okay

Although relationships are important, being alone for short periods of time is not only okay; it is necessary. There are differences between being alone and being lonely. And it is better to be alone than to wish you were alone. Moving forward holds uncertainties and you might unwittingly fall back on what feels comfortable. Your guilt, fear, and loneliness might steer you back to the familiar. You may even entertain thoughts of reconciliation because being alone is just too frightening. Remember, your conditioning taught you to feel worthless and to believe that no one else would want you. What you might not understand is that change for your batterer is unlikely and old patterns will reemerge once you go back.

Do not feel stupid for yearning for your partner. Most victims go through this emotional process an average of seven times before they find the strength to leave. No one can tell you when to leave, but know that you cannot stop being a victim until you sever these ties. Your decision might be easier if you remember that there are others involved, like your children, sisters, brothers, parents, and friends who love you.

The choice to stay in your battering relationship is yours, but understand clearly that the clock is ticking and know that staying has severe consequences for you and your children. The cost for staying too long can be great. It can take years to undo the damage wreaked upon them by just one person.

Redefining Your Experiences

It takes courage and tenacity to move out of the victim role and into one that defines you differently. Because your role developed over time, a position of helplessness may leave you feeling like you have no other options. But nobody can take away who you are unless you permit it. As scary as it may be, you must redefine your experiences in order to change your outlook. As a child, I was abused in every way imaginable. My childhood experiences were ones that no one should ever see. I could have used these times as an excuse to give up and blame the world. I chose, however, not to do so. At some point, I learned that I had something special to give. I believed that God had a purpose for me, but it was not to be a victim. I was determined to alter my outlook and take charge of my destiny.

Stop seeing what happened to you as an end all. Do not surrender to your experiences. Take your tragedies and turn them around. Many people become incredibly successful despite their obstacles because they made the choice to live differently.

How do you want to define your life? Are you going give away your power, or take it back? It is time to take your experience and make a difference. For me, I gain satisfaction from helping other children survive and thrive from their experiences.

Now, it is up to you to decide what kind of life you want for your family. Realize that just because you lived in violence does not mean it has to be a permanent part of your life. Everyone has the opportunity to heal from abuse. Don't limit your children's options, nor your own, by assuming that you are all damaged for life. Instead, redefine your experiences and see them as a tool for rebuilding your future.

CHAPTER 11

Success Is Your Final Answer

You are guaranteed to miss 100 percent of the shots that you don't take.

—*Wayne Gretzky*

In your quest to achieve success, you may need to revamp and overhaul your entire life. You can no longer use the tools you learned living with your batterer. Although you were physically and emotionally abused, the time has come to be a winner. You are on your way to being *unbeatable*. This final chapter's purpose is to show you how to regain the life you once had or the life you always wanted. The question for you, now, will obviously be: "How do I get there from here?"

To begin your journey, a better frame of mind, body, and spirit will be necessary to conquer what lies ahead of you. Therefore, self-nurturing is paramount. Living in violence never afforded you the opportunity to consider your needs, but now is different. No one in your family benefits from your self-neglect. Ignoring your wants permitted your batterer to treat you disrespectfully. At the time, challenging the "small" stuff did not feel worth it. But collectively, over time, it made a difference in how you were treated. Consider your needs like an emotional bank account. When you constantly give away your assets and never replenish them, your account becomes overdrawn and depleted. Eventually, the result is emotional bankruptcy. To truly be successful, temporarily, the focus must be on you. The old saying, "When mama's happy, everyone's happy" really does apply. Caring for your children and yourself is possible when you distribute your time differently. Balance is really the key.

Make today a new day. Begin your mornings by loving and knowing that you matter. To accomplish this task, set a goal each day to do something nice for yourself. As you learn how to embrace and appreciate how deserving you are, you can move toward periods of joy, and someday, happiness. You have a lot of bad feelings to undo, so be patient. Do not expect to be an overnight success. But always keep in mind that to achieve happiness you must understand what makes you feel good. Most people know, all too well, what makes them feel badly, but rarely do they understand what makes them happy.

The trick to overcoming bad feelings is to make short-term goals that help you start searching for happiness. Some examples might be (saying to yourself then following through), "Making my favorite breakfast would make me happy" or "Reading a book every evening for a month would make me feel good." Make your goals achievable and realistic. Take baby steps and make small changes, then embrace those moments that you have given to yourself. You will be amazed at how the little things count.

Internal Drive

Our internal drive predicts our level of motivation to succeed. To accomplish anything, we need to have the desire to do so. That desire is determined by our ability to let go of the past and focus on the present and future. It is not enough to just want a better life and hope that something good happens. We have to make it happen. The mindset needs to be that failure is just an opportunity to start over. Life is one big lesson, and everyone learns through making mistakes. If we do not fail, we do not grow.

The misconception most people suppose is that they do not have time to be successful. But literally, everyone is allotted the same amount of time. I bet Oprah never complained that she didn't have enough time to be successful. Instead, she found her passion, and she worked to make her life happen. Now, you must learn what successful people have learned: Try to work smarter rather than harder, and work harder when it's necessary. Passion and desire really are the driving forces that make people winners. Therefore, you really have to know what you want, and then you have to strive to achieve it.

Internal drive comes from learning what excites you. Right now, you probably think that nothing really stimulates you. And that's okay. Don't be discouraged; learning to embrace life again will take time and practice. You need to start rearranging your thoughts and actions to get motivated from the inside out. This requires a plan—one that is organized and well-thought out. To begin, create a daily schedule to map out your future. Plan something fun. For instance, say you loved art, but you stopped painting years ago because your batterer considered it a waste of time and money. Give yourself permission to take an art class at the local community college or paint a picture at home. The energy you get from this small joy will motivate you further. You will be internally driven to want to do more. Your attitude and behavior become cyclical: The more you love, the more you do, the more you love to do.

During an interview, people over a hundred years old were asked what the key to longevity and quality of life was for them. The common responses were, "Always give back to the community, it makes you feel good," and, "Do what you want to do first and what you have to do second because you always get done what you have to do. But if you do what you have to do first, there's no time left to do what you want to do." This is a great testament for enjoying life. It creates passion and purpose to stay internally driven.

Passion and a Purpose

Passion is the fuel that ignites your life. With it, all things are possible. Take a serious look at how you are living and find the missing pieces. There was once a time when you dreamed, had goals, and desired things. Your batterer shelved many of those for you; but now, it is time to take them out of the closet, dust them off, and display them with pride and dignity. For me, I was an artist: I sketched portraits. It took years before I was willing to pick up a pencil again, but my talent was still there. It had laid dormant waiting for an opportunity to make its presence. Find your dreams and make them come true. You only have one life to lead, and you are the only one standing in the way of your success. When you generate your passion and purpose, you represent energy and serve as a great role model for your kids. What better gift to give to your children is there than that?

Finding Your Children's Motivators

Within every child, there was once a passion or desire that he or she possessed. Throughout time, the abuse beat it out of them, literally. Now, your kids need to reconnect and delve into their aspirations. So often families of violence are simply getting by, and they feel limited. They might believe that there isn't much to look forward to. Originally, the concept of family life was intended to be somewhat fun. So expose your children to as many new opportunities as possible. Teach them how to hope and dream again.

Finding motivators for your children requires that they grow emotionally with you. One way to accomplish this is to permit them to contribute to the family. Let them teach you something for a change. Allow them to make decisions and add value to the relationship. Your job is to prepare them for the world, which requires them to be competent and capable. And their job is to eventually leave home and start a successful life.

Teach them that with rights come responsibilities. Learn to negotiate with your children and give them some control over their lives. As they learn to be more self-reliant and confident, they will develop motivation, passion, and desire. When they achieve their goals, success will be their final answer.

Behavior Patterns

We have discussed behavior patterns sporadically throughout this book. Understanding how you behave and interact with others determines how successful you will be. To help you get a better insight on your behavior, review the following four methods and ask yourself where you fall on the spectrum.

Passive

Passive people generally become scapegoats for all the problems in the world. They take the responsibility for everyone's unhappiness. They rarely consider their own needs as important, and they do not speak up for themselves when others have wronged them. These individuals generally regard their passivity as being kind, when in essence they are being used. This behavior pattern obviously does not serve its recipient well. Behaving passively usually makes an individual feel worthless and invisible.

Passive/Aggressive

Passive/aggressive people believe that they cannot get their needs met unless they are sneaky about it. They use manipulation, lies, and trickery to get what they want. Essentially, they want to get their needs met, but fear rejection. They resort to passive/ aggressive behavior, rather than a direct approach. Although this is probably a step up from being completely passive, this behavior is not healthy, and should be avoided when possible. This behavior pattern makes others feel used and betrayed because they feel manipulated through guilt. Those who practice passive/aggressive behavior really don't feel worthy enough to get their needs met the right way.

Aggressive

Aggressive people have no regard for how others feel. Their sole interest is in meeting their needs, even at the expense of others. They use intimidation to achieve their goals, and their demands are often unreasonable. They do not care who gets hurt so long as they get their way. Although aggressive people often win, they also eventually find themselves alone. They generally do not have good-standing friends, and people avoid them as much as possible. Their needs might be momentarily met, but the cost, socially, is so great. Aggressive behavior only meets immediate needs and doesn't produce quality results for the long term. Aggressive people usually are disconnected and apathetic. They thrive on external and instant gratification because they have no sense of internal worth.

Assertive

Assertive people work toward getting their needs met without hurting others. Their concept is one of win/win. They believe in reciprocity, they are respectful toward others, and believe they deserve respect in return. They give to others, and ask others to give to them. They truly believe that you get what you give. They can voice their opinions without attacking or accusing others. Their needs are met and they feel good about the outcome. Assertive behavior is the healthiest and most successful way to handle interaction with others. It makes people feel confident and good about how to get what they need.

Your Conclusion

Now that you have a clearer picture of the different behavioral styles, assess whether or not you like who you are. If you are satisfied, great! If not, figure out what you have to do to make healthier choices and change your life.

Success—Defining and Designing

What does success mean to you? How do you measure when you have achieved it? These are the questions you must ask yourself. Recently, a woman told me that when she first left her batterer and bought her own place, her son asked, "Aren't you afraid Mom?" With tears in her eyes she explained, "I can't be scared right now because if I am, I will never make it." She then explained to me, "At that point in my life, I realized that what I had left behind was far scarier than what I was to face in my future."

This woman's courage and strength allowed her to overcome her fears. She had to start caring about how she felt and what her family needed. If this is your predicament, start having a "what about me" attitude to become successful. You must take care of your needs and know that you deserve nurturing before you can do what is right for your children. To break the cycle of violence, you need to feel worthy. You must now help your family, and perhaps even yourself, to see you as an individual.

Success is really all about having a great attitude—one that looks at life as good. Show enthusiasm toward your children's work and accomplishments, or be proud of yourself for what you have been able to achieve. If you genuinely appear excited, your children will get energized and follow your lead. After all, attitudes are contagious.

Your family needs to learn that their behavior is an attitude which contributes to the direction their lives take. So often the only difference between successful people and those who are not is their frame of mind. With a positive attitude comes the ability to behave differently. The course of your life will change drastically simply by changing your attitude. When you set your mind to define and design success, there is no stopping you. There may be some detours, perhaps, but you can reach your final destination with a great attitude.

"I Can" Attitude

To become successful, possess the "I can" attitude. Be willing to do whatever it takes to be a winner. Stop looking for excuses and start doing what you need to. Your children are counting on you to be strong and take them away from the violence. In the past, you were trapped in a restrictive and unyielding relationship. You have never had the opportunity before now to stand tall and do what was right. The "I can" attitude allows you to take back your power, because now you know that all things are possible. Change is not a question of whether you can achieve your goals; it's a matter of when. Remember the story about the "Little Train That Could?" We read this story to our children and asked them to believe in themselves. Now, is the time to role model and show them how it's done.

Strategies for Change

Overcoming obstacles in life requires you to extend from your fear and face the world. Being fearful does not stop the world from revolving around you. Life still happens, whether you are afraid or not. Don't let your circumstances control your destiny. Being paralyzed by fear is like being locked behind a closed door, and you have the only key. Unlock the door, change your strategies, and explore your new world.

Your abuser has had control for far too long. In the past, saying and doing the "wrong" thing guaranteed abuse. You tried to avoid making "mistakes," but you were never successful. He hurt you regardless. The bottom line is that you did not cause the abuse. He mistreated you because he was cruel and unfair. Therefore, you must change your strategies.

If you genuinely fear your batterer, he has probably reached a dangerous point. Your life is in jeopardy no matter what you do. Intuitively, you probably fled because you recognized the eminent danger. You recognized that you could no longer avoid his scorn or how he chose to respond to you. Because of his mental state, you might want to take additional safety precautions before standing up to him. But know that leaving was the only answer.

To begin your new successful life, forget trying to convince your abuser of anything; it's futile and frustrating. Anytime he can draw you into a dialogue, he wins. Your job will be to set the boundaries, because he does not know how or care to limit himself. Use some of the following statements to combat his attempts to manipulate:

- "My life is no longer up for discussion; I would appreciate sticking to business."
- "Please stick to talking about the kids; otherwise, I need to hang up now."
- "Any questions regarding our divorce should be handled through my attorney. I need to go now."
- "Name-calling and screaming are not appropriate; call back when you're calm."
- "I don't feel comfortable with this conversation; I am hanging up now."

Standing up to your batterer is going to be really scary, especially if he can no longer be reasoned with. Try your best to make sure that you have safety nets in place before implementing any of the previously listed boundaries. Generate a safety plan that has you thinking one step ahead of your aggressor. Some examples are:

- Leave your home after a telephone confrontation so that he doesn't know where you are.
- Leave a spare set of keys hidden with a friend or neighbor.
- Take different routes to work; don't be predictable.
- Flex your work schedule if possible, or transfer to a new location.
- Change daycare programs, or alert them to any trouble.

- Have emergency contacts and plans for what to do in a time of crisis.
- Prepare a suitcase with spare clothing and keep it with a friend.
- Maintain additional copies of important documents outside the home.
- Invest in a cellular phone.
- Have Caller ID.

Although defending yourself to these extremes seems unfair, it is the harsh reality. You can either lament over the unfairness, or you can do something about it. The former really doesn't make things better. Anytime you leave an abusive relationship, danger is probable. You can lie down and give up, or you can work toward breaking free from him. Giving up, however, keeps you in danger regardless. I remember a story of a woman who tied her children to a tree every night so her husband wouldn't beat them. As horrific as this sounds, she thought it was the only way to keep her family safe. This woman stayed because she thought she could control her batterer's anger. Unfortunately, she misjudged the intensity of his rage until it was too late. She allowed herself to do the unconscionable to her children. One day, her husband decided he wanted to be mad anyway, and he killed her. She thought she could appease him by meeting his demands. The fact was, however, his needs could never be satiated.

As the recipient of the abuse, know that no matter how hard you try to pacify your batterer, he will find something wrong with you. Is this what you envisioned for your life or did you expect something better? As frightful as this is, escaping gives you at least a 50/50 chance of survival. Without it, you live in a minefield and wait for the final explosion.

One woman shared that her mother was a battered wife who was stricken with throat cancer. The husband regularly insisted that his wife start his bath then bathe him. The daughter came to her mother's rescue one night and said, "I'll start your bath, Dad!" Her father proceeded to empty the tub and then demanded of his ailing wife, "Get your ass in there right now and start my bath!" The treatment went on until the end of her life. On her deathbed, her husband was screaming at her; she looked at her daughter with her last fading breath and said, "Could you please just make him shut up?" Her batterer taunted and abused her "until death do they part." This is how she lived and died. It didn't matter how kind or giving she was. Her batterer made her suffer. To assure this doesn't happen to you, find the courage today to stay out of your abusive relationship before it's too late.

Knowing the Truth

Your batterer's perception has distorted your thought process and there may initially be times when you still buy into his crooked thinking. Keep in the forefront of your mind that his input was all you were given for years. You need to be reprogrammed, but your batterer will interfere by doing whatever he can to confuse you. For instance, he may recruit other family members or friends with the same dysfunctional attitude to "prove" his case and make you believe that you are the "crazy one." A personal example for me was when my mother-in-law lectured me and said that I needed to try harder and give her son a chance to change. My reply was, "I'm not waiting until he puts a gun to my head like you did." She tried to convince me that I was the problem. Fortunately, I believed enough in myself, and I knew that my batterer's behavior was wrong. It may be difficult to see through the manipulation, but you must look past the insanity and see the truth. In order to be successful, you need to recognize your batterer's twisted thought processes for what they are: another means of controlling you. Earlier in this book, we discussed credibility and the power it has. Just because someone says something negative to you doesn't mean you have to believe it. Always remember this, "What you think . . . you are."

Society often doesn't see the truth and places the responsibility for the abuse onto the person being battered. I once had a lawyer say, "It takes two to tango." I retorted indignantly, "Yeah, but if he's stepping on her feet, it's a little hard to dance." Unfortunately, this mindset is still the rule rather than the exception, which puts you in a difficult position. The world thinks you are the problem. People buy into the perpetrator's ploys. The reason others maintain this viewpoint is because your batterer plays mind games and provokes hysteria in you. Your charismatic partner portrays you as a crazy lunatic, and the world believes it. You have lost your credibility. This is a time when having a cool and level head is paramount.

Surviving Divorce and Custody Issues

Your challenge with your abuser will be a battle of the minds. If you have not been through court yet, your torment is just beginning. Start preparing yourself for the fight. Consider taking parenting classes to show the system that you want what is best for your children. Any vices that he can use against you like alcohol or habitual dating should be avoided. Also, attending a class or support group that teaches you how to conquer the problem would be beneficial. You must be mentally prepared for whatever comes next. Your batterer's mind is deviant and his imagination limitless; so do not underestimate his potential. As mentioned in Chapter 1, the battering does not stop simply because you have left the relationship. You have to accept that leaving is not going to be effortless. To be successful, you must be ready for anything. Your batterer will do whatever it takes to regain control over you because grooming another person will take too long. He needs someone to control. Now, you have to decide if you're his girl.

In your quest to heal, you might consider medical treatment for your anxiety and stress. This is admirable, but be cautious about medications or psychological labels. Your batterer will use it against you in court to make you look like an unstable parent. My suggestion is to keep a low profile and do the following:

- Receive treatment discretely, he doesn't need the extra ammunition; you are already dodging enough bullets.
- Document everything with times, dates, photographs, and witnesses, if possible.
- Ask professionals working with you to provide progress reports, which indicate improvement.
- Get as many letters of support as possible from credible people.
- Involve family-violence professionals who can shed light on your circumstances.

You need these strategies to win because your batterer can lie far more eloquently than you can tell the truth. Knowing the truth is imperative, but it's not enough. You have to educate others and build a network of people to champion for you. You cannot beat your batterer alone. Therefore, you must send out the reinforcements. The more people who know the truth, the less your batterer has to fight against you with. Stay strong—you can win.

Strategic versus Tactical—Winning the War but Not the Battle

For all intents and purposes, you are in a war with a hostile enemy. You were a prisoner of war and you have just escaped. Your captor wants to get you back. The best way to win is to start thinking on a grander scale. Until this point, you have limited yourself to achieving immediate short-term goals, like not getting hit or berated. This is commonly known in the military world as tactical maneuvers. Although you can be successful from time to time, tactical victories are only winning small battles. They keep you limited, and you are always forced to think on your feet. Dealing with your batterer on a tactical level is like racing against the clock. The trouble with this type of maneuvering is that you will suffer from battle fatigue. You have to start thinking more strategically. In other words, you have to look at the big picture more than the situational here and now. You must take away your batterer's ability to fight against you. A carefully devised plan of action is needed to achieve your objective, one which frees you from the fear of violence. Your strategies must go beyond the immediate crisis. Basically, you have to head your batterer off at the pass and secure your position. You have lived with his twisted mind enough that if you think carefully, you may be able to predict his next move. Solicit and inform others so that a collective mental strategy is developed that makes you the conqueror.

Mental Strategies

Lao Tzu once said, "Muddy water, let stand, becomes clear." There is a great deal of truth in this. If you want to be successful, you must be clear so that you make optimal choices. At this point, you might need to take a step back and wait. Think your strategies through and wait for the right moment to make your decisions. When choices are made in haste, you undermine your own efforts. With the calm comes the right answer. You are playing a mental chess game, and you need to anticipate your batterer's next five moves. Look at as many different scenarios or angles as possible and determine the outcome of each. Prepare yourself for the war against you and strategize. You have to keep it together for your children's sake.

Taking Charge of Your Life for the Sake of Your Kids

Taking charge of your life also means regaining your position as a parent. Your children have suffered greatly and they will need you now more than ever. They might display aberrant behaviors that test you daily. You will need to be strong, assertive, and loving. Although staying focused can be difficult, it is necessary. You must maintain rules and consistency to minimize the chaos. The key to your children's success will depend, in part, on your willingness to go the extra mile.

Many who experience family violence reach high levels of stress and need support to develop more effective coping skills. Your parenting may not be at its best right now because you have become reactive to your children's behavior. The constant tension has sensitized you. The result of practicing poor parenting is the rippling effect it has on your children. Can you look back and see what you did to your kids that may not have been so good? Now that you are in a safer space emotionally, you have to take charge so old patterns never rise again.

Resilience

Children need encouragement to fulfill their hopes and dreams. Therefore, parents must work toward developing short-term goals, which helps them achieve a positive future. Often parents who are struggling emotionally unconsciously overlook their children. They justify their neglect by saying, "Oh, she is a great student, she doesn't need my help." They are so caught up in their own pain that they don't recognize that their children are also faltering. The most common complaint children share with me is that they do not feel that their parents will help them because they are too busy. Parents, unwittingly, ignore their children's genuine needs and compound their problems further. If you fall into this category, you are sending them a destructive message. They need your help building their resiliency. Remember that you are the parent, not the other way around. They cannot cope alone; they need you to show them how to be strong and confident. Teach them courage, morals, and values that strengthen their endurance. To build emotionally and physically resilient children, you must help them understand their full potential. Without support, however, their lives can be permanently transformed.

New research suggests that exposure to violence impacts brain development and the immune system.[1] Not only are children affected emotionally, the violence is physically altering necessary brain functions that impact them forever. This exposure may rewire or destroy neurological processes, which will impede their ability to build resiliency. Professional help may be required for your children if any signs of physical impairments are apparent.

Under "normal" and safe conditions, however, resiliency can usually be built on effort. Therefore, promote an environment where your children can be gently encouraged to recover more quickly from their setbacks. Require them to push themselves a little further each time they struggle. Your job will be to brilliantly persuade them to *want* to improve. Somehow your children have internalized the message that they are incompetent, and they may feel too inadequate to proceed on their own. They need your strength to bounce back and to be able to conquer their fears. Be careful not to label them as lazy, because the fact is, they just lack resiliency.

Tenacity

Tenacity is a key element to success. In layperson's terms, it means to accomplish your goals at a gradual and steady pace, like a slow moving train. No matter how difficult, you never stop; you just chug along. Eventually, you get to where you are going. With every success there will be many more failures, but that's how you win. You must stick firmly to any decisions or plans that you make, without doubting yourself. Make a decision about your choices and stay committed to it. Think about someone who inspires you. How do you think they got to where they are today? My guess is that they never gave up. They kept going regardless of the obstacles. Everyone has the potential to succeed. Now you have to decide whether you want to be one of the winners. If so, then success is your final answer.

Quality: Life and Time

The word *success* infers that a desired level of quality has been met in your life. Usually it means you embrace, appreciate, and make the best of what you have created. As a parent struggling in the aftermath of family violence, you may feel that a quality life is not possible because you are just trying to survive. You may even see the term "quality time" as a cliché that is for other people who can afford it. I guarantee that quality time with your kids, family, and friends is possible if you just strive for it. But if you do not claim your quality time, you will never have it. Make the best of your life by seizing the day. Give yourself permission to have good, clean fun with those around you. The outcome will be rewarding. Quality is based on attitude and spirit and not on the quantity of material objects you possess.

One woman shared that she never knew that she was poor as a child until she turned twenty-eight. She recalled that her mother always showed enthusiasm and excitement over the most insignificant events in their lives. This young woman said that she grew up happy and fulfilled because her mother made each moment with her count. When she grew up, she returned to her home town and discovered that her family had lived in a low-income housing project. Even with that knowledge, she felt complete anyway.

To build a better quality of life for you and your children, promote more personal interaction between your family members. Families in crisis struggle daily with the new adjustments in their lives. The stress involved with those changes may distract families from spending time together. But avoid this trap, because when children do not interact with their families, they find others to supplement their needs. Those relationships may not be in your children's best interests. As chaotic as your life seems, you do not want to regret that you were not available when your children needed you most.

Take time to bond with them. They need you to be paying attention to the good stuff. Designate time each week when your family interacts together for at least one hour. Use some of the following to get you started on your quest for quality time with your kids:

- Frame some of your kids' artwork and hang it proudly in the house
- Teach them to make cookies
- Read together
- Make a production out of their talents (i.e., perform a talent show or a concert)
- Play board games
- Work on a puzzle
- Write stories together

- Go for walks and observe nature
- Close your eyes and go on make-believe journeys to far away places
- Pitch a tent and camp in the living room
- Create adventures

Katlin and I regularly spent quality time snake hunting. Although nine times out of ten we never found a snake, we made it an exciting adventure every time. I was always grateful when we didn't find one of those slithering reptiles, but Katlin's anticipation for finding one was tremendous. If you hate snakes, then hunt for wild flowers, ladybugs, or "rollie pollies" (the bugs that curl up into a ball). Whatever the case may be, strive for the quality time and the excellence your family deserves. Like they say, "You only live once."

Believing in Your Safe New World

Succeeding after family violence means believing that you can finally take care of yourself. You are now competent in your safe, new world and are no longer a victim. You have unlearned the helplessness you once felt. This process started by mastering an external (physical) sense of security, then transferring those feelings into internal ones. Basically, you have realized that no one can ever hurt you again. But, to continue your success, keep yourself in a position where you make good life choices that make you feel safe.

Coping Skills Are Key

Although what you have been through with your batterer should not be minimized, it should not be the focus of your life. As you deal more successfully with the circumstances surrounding your experience, you will see that there is hope. When you have experienced tragedy, you might not always be able to see the light at the end of the tunnel; but when you learn coping skills, you can at least start adjusting your eyes to the dark and making it to the end. Eventually, as you make your way through the darkness, you will find the light. Coping skills are key to surviving family violence. You have to learn from the past, yet let go of the experience at the same time. When you can look at the abuse from a distance and stop personalizing it, you will be more successful. All you can do is look forward and break the cycle.

The following are some coping skills that promote better success:

- Create as many positive thoughts or situations as possible.
- Find an outlet for your anxiety like running, Tai Chi, or painting.
- Recall your past victimization, then change the ending to the experience.
- Remember that the violence was directed at you, not to you.
- Have others support you emotionally.
- Make your dreams come true.
- Don't live in the past; it's like a bad rerun movie.
- Give yourself permission to be happy.
- Don't look too far into the future. It will be too overwhelming; focus on one day or week at a time.
- Develop a good sense of humor, but don't hide behind it.
- Change your attitude from "if I make it" to "when I make it."

Creating Short-term Goals to Meet Long-term Objectives

Your family may initially find it difficult to work toward success. Any attempts to change may feel too overwhelming, but the alternative is living in dysfunction for the rest of your life. Being fearful only impedes your growth and prevents your success. You must have some sort of revelation that shows you the urgency of your situation.

A very successful businesswoman was on a flight when a man who recognized her inquired, "How did you become so successful?" Her reply was, "I found out I had terminal cancer. What I realized was that I had nothing else to fear once I knew I was dying. I decided at that point to live my dream. What I found out was that there weren't any big bad wolves waiting to gobble me up. People wanted to help me and I had nothing to lose." Although her life had urgency because her time was limited, yours probably isn't; or is it? We never know when our time is up. If this were your last day on earth, you might want to ask yourself whether you lived it the way you wanted. You need to take a harder look at your life. If you do not like what you see, make some serious decisions.

Success can be done gradually and in small steps so long as you are moving in a positive direction. This is when assigning short-term goals can help you eventually meet long-term objectives. Remember, you did not get into this predicament in one day, and you cannot get out that fast either. Quitting or avoiding what to do is not an option. Pretending your problems do not exist would be like standing in the road, watching a truck barreling toward you, then closing your eyes, hoping you don't get hit. It is time to open your eyes and do what it takes to get out of harm's way. The thought of succeeding can seem unimaginable and unattainable, but you can do it if you really want to. One survivor described it best, "Making it after abuse is like trying to push your way through a congested Hong Kong traffic jam." There is so much to get through that it feels like you are pushing your way through a crowd. It is normal to feel like you are going backward at times, because there are so many things to conquer. The best way to cope with the gamut of challenges that you face is to master one or two things at a time and allow yourself to embrace those successes before you move forward. Focus on the changes instead of what is left to achieve.

Success is not always about the benefits of winning, but rather, it is about what you have learned from losing. If you have the attitude that you cannot fail, you are setting yourself up for disaster. In David Pelzer's book, *Help Yourself,* he says, "To get a little, you have to be willing to give a lot."[2] That may mean exposing yourself to possible disappointment. The more attempts you make to succeed, the greater your chances of winning. But when you realize that failure is a part of the success process, you can begin your journey to a better future.

Plan Ahead

You must be sensitive to where you are in your life, and then plan the direction that you want to take to get to your final destination. In the military, and now commercially, they have a Global Positioning System (GPS), which is a device that pinpoints your location so you can reach your destination. You cannot make changes without knowing which direction you are heading. It would be like going on vacation and not knowing where you wanted to go. You need to plan ahead and be able to have some alternate routes, just in case there is a detour. It is time for you to map out your life, use your GPS, and stop traveling blindly.

Insight

In order to plan ahead and make the changes necessary for a better life, you have to possess insight. Without the ability to see clearly and intuitively, your chances of repeating the dysfunctional cycle are very real. Therefore, you need education and training to change your current behavioral patterns. You need to make an informative decision based on that knowledge before you can move beyond where you are. With experience should come the wisdom to redirect your life and make the changes necessary to move toward a more positive future.

Healthy Confrontation

In order to create good boundaries and be successful, you must possess healthy confrontational skills. Because confrontation with your batterer did not lend you much success, it might benefit you to practice new confrontational skills on someone less intimidating and more receptive to hearing how you feel. It is time to learn how to get your needs met and stop allowing others to take advantage of you. Although some conformity and compromise are necessary, confronting others at times is in your best interest. When you have valid points and others are not listening, you need to speak up and be heard.

A communication style called parroting can help you learn to confront in a more effective manner. This technique allows you to repeat what others have said to you so that you can ensure that you understood them correctly. So often, we react to others based on our old baggage, and we punish them for our insecurities. To make sure you do not perceive the communication wrongly, parrot what you heard back to others so they have the opportunity to clarify what they meant. This very successful technique helps improve healthy confrontation. What you need to know is that confrontation does not mean conflict. But it does mean responding differently to the people in your life.

New Reactions to Old Responses

Real success comes when you have had a total life switch. That means learning how to react differently to old responses. The old patterns were ineffective and essentially useless. Your methods did not work and they served to keep you entrenched in the cycle of violence. To have success be your final answer, you must make significant changes to your life, and free yourself from the shackles and chains that bind you. A recent study at Duke University suggests that true personal transformation occurs when you possess the following four characteristics:

- An absence of suspicion
- The ability to live in the present
- Not wasting time and energy on circumstances we cannot change
- Faith

All of these concepts may seem hard to imagine because living in violence has undermined all of these qualities. If anything, your batterer reinforced that having these characteristics makes you vulnerable. He has taught you to distrust the world. You cannot get through life very successfully if you have a chip on your shoulder. So, take your life back and build on the characteristics that make you a winner. Take each area and work on it independently. These are not easy issues, but success is possible when you work toward reacting differently to your circumstances. Some solutions are as follows:

- Start trusting small groups of people initially and build your support system as you become comfortable with your choices in friends.
- Focus on today: Yesterday is over, and now is all that matters.
- Stop believing that you had any control over the way you were treated because you didn't.
- Believe in something good, anything that gives you the courage to move forward and have hope.

Because you were trapped in the violence for so long, you may be presently reacting to your environment the way you were conditioned to with your batterer. For example, a mother joked and pushed her son away when he told her that he loved her. She had difficulty accepting his affection because the concept felt foreign to her. Her reaction caused disappointment and rejection for her son. She indicated that he appeared deflated with her response. In the past, this mother had not received affection from her son. He never attempted emotional connectedness before because his father would have labeled him a sissy. In the safety of his new home, he felt compelled to love his mother; but she sent the message that she did not want his love. I recommended that she revisit the conversation with him, admit that she was wrong to minimize his feelings, and share her insecurity with him. This family needed an emotional connection, and with the abuser out of the picture, they could have it.

In the past, your batterer has always blamed you for the problems in your relationship. Therefore, you may automatically respond to others by taking the blame for any misunderstandings or misgivings that occur. Although it is important to self-reflect and take responsibility when you make mistakes, don't own those mistakes if they are not genuinely yours. If someone treats you poorly, they are the one with the problem, not you. You must stop personalizing other people's bad behavior. Being mistreated feels normal because you have been conditioned to believe "that's just the way it is." Now, you must change how you respond to your new environment. You have to see that there was nothing you did to deserve the assaults. Your batterer would have abused someone else had he not found you. The abuse was done at you, not to you. The best way to be successful is to understand this concept. Stop embracing the pain and move toward others who genuinely care about you. Find people who will not create chaos and disarray.

In the past, your reactions were crisis-oriented. You were constantly looking for ways to put out any fires that might spark your batterer. The persistent anxiety created enough havoc that you were unable to think clearly. Creating new responses will help minimize the chaos and clutter in your life, both literally and figuratively. But this means you have to clean up your act: Organize your life and give it some order. You deserve a calm and peaceful existence.

Your children also deserve order. Organization helps them find the control and peace that has been missing for so long. Being orderly reflects how they feel about their lives. Once the external chaos is removed, your family can find internal peace. You can start reacting differently to the world around you and live more successfully. One warning, however, is that too much order would suggest that you are trying too hard to control your environment. Anything in excess is not good. Again, moderation is the key.

Try versus Do

To enhance your life, get rid of the word *try*. That word furnishes you with the excuse to fail. Some examples are, "I tried not to call my ex-husband, but I just couldn't stop myself," or "I tried to get a job, but there wasn't anything out there." If you want to accomplish your goals, you have to do it. Trying is not an option. Give yourself no choice but to succeed.

To be successful and combat your batterer, you have to own your life. Your batterer found ways to control you, but now you have to stop him. He will be relentless in his effort. For instance, when the children go to their father's house for the weekend, he "forgets" to send their clothes back with them. You have to constantly replace items that are necessary for daily living, which keeps you financially strapped and controlled. The solution here is to have your children change their clothes prior to leaving on Friday night so they are fresh, and insist that they wear those clothes home the next day. Your children will not be emotionally scarred from wearing the same clothes two days in a row. And, more importantly, they win because they are able to maintain their wardrobe. You are no longer trying to combat your batterer's ploys; you are doing it by anticipating his mind games.

Another means of taking away his power is to reduce your anxiety by doing something about your situation. Say your children don't get fed properly when they are in your abuser's care. Pack a healthy snack so you know that they are getting some nutrition. If you know that their father habitually takes your children's stuff and "loses" it, stop sending things over there. There is nothing that children absolutely need over a weekend that they cannot live without, unless it is medicine. Even that can be distributed in amounts that are required for the weekend. You may be thinking, "Gosh, I can't deprive my son of his Walkman®, that's not fair. He really loves it." Sometimes life has disappointments. It would be better for your kids to go the weekend without their things rather than to lose them permanently. You must be your children's staunchest ally. They will rely upon you to maintain order in their lives.

Societal Expectations and Their Limitations

The problem most advocates face is helping their clients understand that they are not alone and that they weren't responsible for the abuse. Access to support programs can be difficult for a person who is scared, confused, and in the worse case scenario, running for her life. Fleeing an abusive relationship can be compared to being trapped in enemy territory during war with a hostile nation. The batterer is able to use psychological warfare to confuse his prisoner. This fear can be so great that she is unable to think clearly; then, we as a society expect her to be able to sit down and research her options. She may not know what she needs, or she may be confused about how to verbalize those needs. When she finally does have the courage to call, she might not get the answer she was looking for. She may get discouraged and stop trying.

My sister showed up on my doorstep after leaving her abusive marriage. Because I had been working with battered women for seventeen years, I had every resource number imaginable. Unfortunately, we failed to get any support services. We must have called twenty different agencies. The only one that responded was a housing unit for low-income families, and that came a month later. That is not acceptable!

What does a victim who is not fortunate enough to have a support system do under these conditions? If I, a victims' advocate, cannot get support, then how does an average victim get help when she has been totally beaten-down emotionally, psychologically, financially, and physically? Even when the victim is financially stable, she may not think she has any options because the batterer has isolated her. What most people don't understand about family violence is that the victim can be made to feel that she cannot survive without him. The batterer has told her that no one else would have her, or that she was lucky he wanted her because she's stupid, ugly, and incompetent. It's amazing how those words can reduce a person to a point of incapacitation. There are more resources for victims today than ever before; however, the key is to devote the time, strength, and desire to discover them.

Success Is a Choice

This book has been written to help you understand that there *is* life after family violence. I believe that you can live happily ever after if you make the choice to do so. Every day presents challenges in our lives. When we take the opportunity to meet and embrace them, we are one step closer to happiness. How we respond to life teaches our children what to do. I had a horrific childhood that was marked by fear, rejection, abandonment, and terror. When I fled the abuse at home, my peers literally tortured me. I wasn't safe anywhere. I can give personal testament to the trauma children face and the success you can have if you just choose it. I challenge each and every one of you to strive to be the best that you can be. Remember, your children are watching.

Look around you and take advantage of the wonderful benefits you have been given. It could be good health, a child with a great smile, a vegetable garden, or a library card. What September 11th has proven is that we should take nothing for granted. Albert Einstein once said, "There are two ways to look at your life: One is as though nothing is a miracle. The other is as though everything is a miracle." How do you see your life? Do you believe that you are living your life to its fullest? If not, start today and change your direction and course. If you follow that new direction, I guarantee that success will be the final answer for you and your children.

Notes

Chapter 1

1. K. Daniel O'Leary, Christopher Murphy, Robert T. Ammerman, and Michael Hersen eds. *Assessment of Family Violence: A Clinical and Legal Sourcebook* (New York: John Wiley and Sons, 1999), 41.

2. Margo Wilson and Martin Daly, "Spousal Homicide Risk and Estrangement," *Violence and Victims* 8 (1993): 3–16.

Chapter 4

1. This philosophy is eloquently written in a poem entitled "Children Learn What They Live" by Dorothy Lau Nolte, Ph.D., 1972/1975.

2. Ancient Chinese proverb written twenty-five centuries ago by the Chinese Philosopher, Lao Tzu.

3. January 23, 2002, http://medscapehealth.netscape.com/cx/viewarticle/209207_2.

4. Quote by James Baldwin, Angela Partington, ed. *The Oxford Dictionary of Quotations,* rev. 4th ed. (New York: Oxford University Press, 1996), 48.

Chapter 5

1. Kendall Johnson, *Trauma in the Lives of Children,* 2nd ed. (Alameda, CA: Hunter House, 1989).

Notes

Chapter 6

1. Jay Carter, D.A.B.P.S., Lecture, "Anger Management: Effectively Dealing with Difficult Behaviors."
2. Daniel Goleman, *Emotional Intelligence* (New York: Bantam Books, 1995), 80–83.
3. Stephen Covey, *The Seven Habits of Highly Effective People.* (Throndike, ME: GK Hall, 1989), 287.
4. Jim Fay and Foster Cline, *Didn't I Tell You to Take Out the Trash?* (Colorado: Love and Logic Press, 1996). Audiotape.
5. I heard this on an audiotape many years ago but cannot recall its author.

Chapter 8

1. Douglas Carlton Abrams, "Father Nature: The Making of a Modern Dad," *Psychology Today* (April 2002): 38.

Chapter 9

1. Kendall Johnson, *Trauma in the Lives of Children,* 2nd ed. (Alameda, CA: Hunter House, 1989).
2. Betsy McAlister Groves, "Children Who Witness Violence: The Hidden Victims," *Juvenile and Family Justice Today* 9(2)(2000): 8–11.
3. Judith Rapoport and Deborah Ismond, *DSM-III-R Training Guide for Diagnosis of Childhood Disorders* (New York: Brunner/Mazel, 1990), 97–99.
4. Daniel Goleman, *Working with Emotional Intelligence* (New York: Bantam Books, 1998), 76.
5. Les Brown, *Courage to Live Your Dreams* (New York: Harper, 1995). Audiotape.

Chapter 10

1. Families First is a Denver-based, non-profit organization dedicated to helping families find support and strength.

Chapter 11

1. Ronald Kotulak, *Inside the Brain* (Kansas City, MO: Andrews McMeel Publishing, 1997), 37.
2. Dave Pelzer, *Help Yourself* (New York: Dutton, 2000), 110.

Bibliography

Abrams, Douglas Carlton. "Father Nature: The Making of a Modern Dad."
   Psychology Today, March/April 2002, 38.
Brown, Les. *Courage to Live Your Dreams*. Audiotape. New York: Harper
   Audio, 1995.
Covey, Stephen. *The Seven Habits of Highly Effective People*. Thorndike,
   ME: GK Hall, 1989.
———. *First Things First*. Audiotape. Provo, UT: Covey Leadership
   Center, 1994.
———. *The Seven Habits of Highly Effective Families*. New York: Golden
   Books, 1997.
Goleman, Daniel. *Emotional Intelligence*. New York: Bantam Books, 1995.
———. *Working with Emotional Intelligence*. New York: Bantam Books,
   1998.
Groves, Betsy McAlister. "Children Who Witness Violence: The Hidden
   Victims." *Juvenile and Family Justice* Today 9(2)(2000): 8–11.
Johnson, Kendall. *Trauma in the Lives of Children*, 2nd ed. Alameda, CA:
   Hunter House, 1989.
Kotulak, Ronald. *Inside the Brain*. Kansas City, MO: Andrews McMeel
   Publishing, 1997.
Lerner, Harriet. *The Dance of Anger*. Audiotape. New York:
   Caedmon, 1999.

Bibliography

O'Leary, K. Daniel, Murphy, Christopher, Ammerman, Robert T., and Hersen, Michael (eds.). *Family Violence: A Clinical and Legal Sourcebook,* 2nd ed. New York: John Wiley & Sons, 1999.

Pelzer, Dave. *Help Yourself.* New York: Dutton, 2000.

Rapoport, Judith L., and Ismond, Deborah R. *DSM-III-R Training Guide for Diagnosis of Childhood Disorders.* New York: Brunner/Mazel, 1990.

Scaer, Robert C. *The Body Bears the Burden.* New York: The Hawthorne Medical Press, 2001.

Van der Kolk, Bessel A., and McFarlane, Alexander C. *Trauma Stress.* New York: The Guildfor Press, 1996.

Wilson, Margo, and Daly, Martin. "Spousal Homicide Risk and Estrangement," *Violence and Victims* 8 (1993): 3–16.

Ziglar, Zig. *Raising Positive Kids in a Negative World.* Audiotape. Carrollton, TX: Zig Ziglar Corp., 1988.

Index

Index

Index

About the Author

CHRISTINA M. DALPIAZ is a certified Victims' Advocate and Founder as well as Executive Director of CHANCE (Changing How Adults Nurture Children's Egos), a nonprofit agency based in Denver, Colorado. An international speaker, she was voted Child Advocate of the Year in 1998 by the Autora Family Violence Response Team. Her dedication to helping families is actually a second career. Dalpiaz previously served in the U.S. Naval Reserves and retired as a Lieutenant Commander.